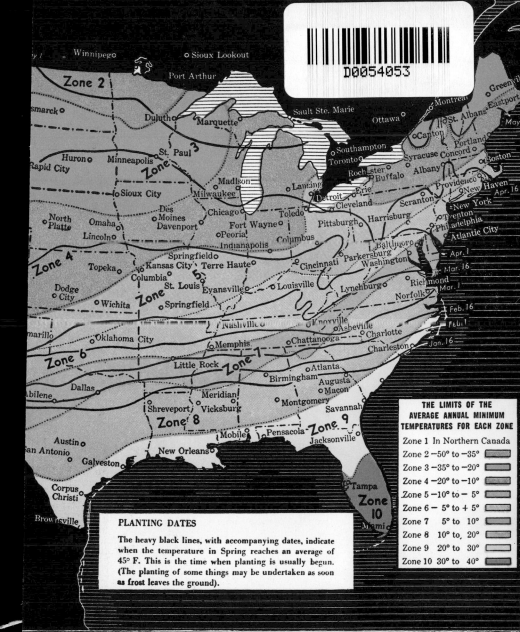

Zone 2

Winnipeg Sioux Lookout

Port Arthur

Bismarck Duluth Marquette Sault Ste. Marie Ottawa Montreal Greenvi... Eastport

Huron St. Paul Zone 3 Southampton Toronto Rochester Buffalo Syracuse Concord St. Albans Portland May...

Rapid City Minneapolis Madison Lansing Detroit Erie Cleveland Albany Boston

Sioux City Milwaukee Providence New Haven Apr. 16

North Platte Omaha Des Moines Chicago Toledo Fort Wayne Pittsburgh Harrisburg Scranton New York Trenton Philadelphia Atlantic City

Lincoln Davenport Peoria Columbus Baltimore Apr. 1

Zone 4 Topeka Springfield Kansas City Terre Haute Indianapolis Cincinnati Parkersburg Washington Mar. 16

Columbia St. Louis Zone 5 Louisville Lynchburg Richmond Mar. 1

Dodge City Wichita Springfield Evansville Norfolk Feb. 16

Nashville Knoxville Asheville Charlotte Feb...

Amarillo Oklahoma City Zone 6 Memphis Zone 7 Chattanooga Charleston Jan. 16

Little Rock Atlanta Birmingham Augusta

Abilene Dallas Meridian Montgomery Macon Savannah

Shreveport Vicksburg Zone 8

Austin Mobile Pensacola Zone 9 Jacksonville

San Antonio New Orleans

Galveston

Corpus Christi Tampa Zone 10

Brownsville Miami

THE LIMITS OF THE AVERAGE ANNUAL MINIMUM TEMPERATURES FOR EACH ZONE

Zone 1 In Northern Canada
Zone 2 $-50°$ to $-35°$
Zone 3 $-35°$ to $-20°$
Zone 4 $-20°$ to $-10°$
Zone 5 $-10°$ to $-5°$
Zone 6 $-5°$ to $+5°$
Zone 7 $5°$ to $10°$
Zone 8 $10°$ to $20°$
Zone 9 $20°$ to $30°$
Zone 10 $30°$ to $40°$

PLANTING DATES

The heavy black lines, with accompanying dates, indicate when the temperature in Spring reaches an average of 45° F. This is the time when planting is usually begun. (The planting of some things may be undertaken as soon as frost leaves the ground).

THE COMPLETE
BOOK OF ANNUALS

BY F. F. ROCKWELL
AND ESTHER C. GRAYSON

The Complete Book of Bulbs

The Complete Book of Flower Arrangement

10,000 Garden Questions Answered (Editors)

Flower Arrangement in Color

Gardening Indoors

BY F. F. ROCKWELL

Around the Year in the Garden

Gardening Under Glass

The Home Garden Handbook Series

THE
COMPLETE
BOOK
OF ANNUALS

by F. F. Rockwell and Esther C. Grayson

HOW TO USE ANNUALS
AND PLANTS GROWN AS ANNUALS
TO BEST EFFECT, OUT-OF-DOORS
AND IN, WITH CULTURAL INFORMATION
AND OTHER POINTERS ON MORE THAN
500 SPECIES AND VARIETIES.
ILLUSTRATED WITH 93 PHOTOGRAPHS
BY THE AUTHORS, 29 IN FULL COLOR.

DRAWINGS BY KATHARINE BURTON

THE AMERICAN GARDEN GUILD AND DOUBLEDAY & COMPANY,
INC., GARDEN CITY, N. Y., 1955

Library of Congress Catalog Card No. 55-6812

*To our long-time friend, DAVID BURPEE,
whose creations in annual flowers brighten
gardens in every nook and corner of the land.*

Foreword

There is no doubt about the fact that annuals, and various other plants which ordinarily are grown as annuals in northern sections of the United States and Canada, have come during recent years to play an ever more important role in American gardens. It is equally true, however, that gardening with annuals is for the most part still largely restricted to a comparatively few species, and that scores of other excellent subjects remain more or less unknown. It is our hope that this book may induce gardeners who have heretofore been content with a very limited number of annuals to extend their plantings and include at least a few of the many excellent but comparatively little used kinds.

For many years we have made it a practice to try a few new annuals—new that is to us—along with the species we regularly grow. Some of these we have found not too exciting; others have proved to be difficult or practically impossible under our own climatic conditions. But on the whole the adventure has been really rewarding, and has given us many new floral acquaintances which we have been glad to keep with us year after year. Who for instance, having ever grown the cheerful little Pansy-faced Torenias, gaily defying the onset of autumn, would again want to be without them? Or what arranger, having once enjoyed the velvet silvery gray sprays of foliage of Sideritis as a blender in compositions of mixed colors, would not wish always to have it available?

In the preparation of this book we have had assistance, in various ways from many friends in the garden world. Among them are Mr. Silas Clark of Wellfleet, Mass., whose garden is shown in the frontispiece, and elsewhere; Mrs. Leon Goldberg, of Nyack, N. Y., for photographs taken in her garden; Mr. Ray Hastings, Executive secretary, since its inception, of the All America Selections Committee; Dr. P. P. Pirone of the New York Botanical Garden;

Professor R. P. Meahl of the Department of Horticulture at Pennsylvania State College; Mr. G. Carl Ball of George J. Ball, Inc.; Mr. Joseph Simpson of W. Atlee Burpee Co.; Mr. Howard Bodger of Bodgers Seeds, Ltd.; Mr. Gilbert Bentley and Mr. Wilfred Berry of Ferry-Morse Seed Co.; Dr. Milton Carlton of Vaughan's Seed Co.; and Mr. D. B. Johnstone of Northrup, King & Co. To all of these we express our appreciation.

F. F. ROCKWELL
ESTHER C. GRAYSON

GrayRock
West Nyack, N. Y.

Contents

PART II: CULTURE

PART III: THE CATALOGUE OF ANNUALS

Color Illustrations

Halftone Illustrations

16   HALFTONE ILLUSTRATIONS

Line Illustrations

PART ONE
— ANNUALS IN THE GARDEN

CHAPTER *1. Annuals*
in the Garden Picture

Too many flower lovers look upon annuals—the plebeian plants that flower for but one season and then are gone—as mere stepchildren in the general garden scheme. There exists a sort of horticultural snobbery among many of those who get beyond the rank-beginner stage that causes them to feel they should consider annuals just a bit déclassé—flowers for the other side of the tracks.

This attitude is most unfortunate, for it deprives many a garden of a great deal of additional beauty which it might possess, and robs the home of an abundance of colorful, cheerful, *and easily made* arrangements that could contribute greatly to its attractiveness.

We had first thought of titling this chapter "In Defense of Annuals." But they need no defense! They are quite capable of standing on their own merits. All they require is that gardeners should learn to know them better and take the slight trouble to learn to use them more effectively. The purpose of this volume is to try to get more gardeners to realize what they are missing when they neglect to utilize annuals to the extent that they might.

As these pages are written it is late autumn. The first frosty nights have nipped a few of the more tender annuals, but even some of these carry on in sheltered spots. Those not quite so sensitive are still little islands of glory in perennial borders where all but chrysanthemums and a few—a very few—of the other late-flowering perennials make a show, and where months ago the spring-flowering bulbs turned to barren beds of browning foliage.

We know that the end is not yet: that after harder frosts come, even after the first snow, the hardier kinds will survive until the very end of the late Indian summer; that the yellow and pale golds of Calendulas, the jewel colors of Verbenas, and the white and deep violet of Sweet Alyssum, hugging gray rocks for a bit of protection, will still provide a balm for our color-hungry eyes and feasts for the golden-winged, nectar-hungry bees.

Double Petunias and Sweet Alyssum trail over a stone wall.

IN THE GARDEN PICTURE

The very great range in habit of growth, in form, size, color, and season of bloom among annuals makes possible their use in the garden in many and widely varied ways. Indeed, one can arrange an all-season flower garden of good design with annuals alone, or even—in the case of Marigolds or Zinnias or Petunias—with a single species. Such gardens have been constructed and have given a very satisfactory account of themselves.

It is, however, as supplements to, or succession plantings after, other plant material that the annuals prove of greatest benefit; and the skill of the gardener as a designer is in large measure demonstrated by his or her success in utilizing them.

By themselves annuals often save the day—or, more accurately, the year—for the new home owner who wishes a first-season flower garden but who, because of a limited time or money budget during those first hectic months, finds it impossible to get a long-range permanent garden plan launched. A few dollars' or even a few dimes' worth of flower seeds will enable him to cover unsightly bare spots with sheets of color and provide weekly bouquets for the interior of his new home.

Even when the use of annuals by themselves is not a necessity they often can be employed to give effects which would be difficult or impossible to get otherwise. For masses of rich color in wide bed or a long border, *over long periods,* no perennials, bulbs, or shrubs can take their place. Many annuals, too, will better withstand extended spells of heat and dry weather and still go on flowering cheerfully than will most perennials, and they are more able to make a recovery after damage by wind or rain.

As supplementary material, in the average perennial border, annuals have perhaps their greatest use. Even an experienced gardener, with every convenience at hand, will be hard put to it in many sections of America to maintain that "continuous bloom" which is the aim of every flower lover—and concerning which apartment-dwelling garden writers so freely scribble. By the employment of carefully selected annuals to fill in time gaps between the peak periods of perennial bloom and to offset those failures which occasionally occur, even the beginning gardener can manage to achieve an almost unbroken succession of flowers, in a very colorful assortment, from April or May to hard killing frost.

Annuals and perennials in a mixed border.

Low-growing annuals used informally to border a grass walk.

To accomplish this most successfully, there should be some definite planning to include the annuals in the planting scheme. Height as well as season of flowering should be taken into consideration. If the supplementary use of annuals with other plant materials is left to chance, to be resorted to only when the need may arise, naturally the results will be more or less hit or miss. It is just such unplanned use of annuals that has given rise to much of the prejudice against employing them as companions for perennials.

As temporary substitutes. But even as substitute material for temporary use, the annuals have their place. The most carefully planned and cared-for garden will sometimes, from one cause or another, develop "holes" which are not only unsightly but leave empty spaces in which weeds find ideal conditions to get a start.

Most annuals can be transplanted readily until they reach the flowering stage, many of them even when in full bloom. In our own garden we always have a supply of them on hand, as thinned-out seedlings in a frame or a seed bed, or in pots, to be used wherever

On the new place, annuals help to clothe the raw edges quickly.

we notice a chance to "stick them in" to advantage. Many a pleasing small-scale effect which visitors exclaim over has had its origin in just such a semi-chance way. If you have done much gardening you have undoubtedly noticed how chance seedlings often appear just where they serve to fit in to good advantage—at the edge of a walk, in crevices between stones, possibly even in a wall. Keep your eyes open for such opportunities, and you can often give nature an assist by providing a few plants—often just an individual one—that will result in a charmingly surprising miniature picture, such as that shown on facing page.

CHAPTER *2. What Is an Annual?*

Beginners are likely to find themselves confused by the simple word "annual" as it is employed in garden literature. Let us, at the outset, try to get this matter clear.

First of all, it may be noted that "annual" is used both as a noun, to denote a particular type or group of plants; and also as an adjective, defining certain characteristics of any plant. The dictionary definitions of these two words are:

> ANNUAL (noun): A plant which *completes* its growth in a single
> year. (The italics are ours.)

> ANNUAL (adjective): Valid for use during one year; lasting only
> one year or one growing season.

When the botanist speaks of an annual he uses the term in the sense denoted by the first of the above definitions. But garden writers and catalogue makers, being less precise with their terminology, quite generally employ the word "annual" as a noun when what they really have in mind is the adjective definition of the word.

The whole situation is further complicated by the fact that a plant which behaves as an annual in one section may, under different climatic conditions, live for two years or even longer; may in fact be, *botanically,* a biennial or a perennial.

In this book, which is concerned with garden practice rather than botany, we have included those plants which, in the North, are ordinarily treated as annuals even though, botanically, they may belong to other groups. The true botanical classification of each is noted, however, whether they be true annuals, biennials, tender perennials, or tender shrubs.

HARDY, HALF-HARDY, AND TENDER ANNUALS

Among the true annuals—which at the moment we have under consideration—there are important differences so far as their culture is concerned. They have been brought to our gardens from many sections of the world, from torrid climates near the equator and frostbitten ones in semi-arctic climes; from high mountains and low meadows; from places where they have nearly a full year to grow and flower, and from others where the growing season is limited to a few weeks. Naturally their life patterns vary widely.

The most important differences, so far as their culture is concerned, have to do with two characteristics; first, what degree of cold they will withstand; and, second, the length of time required from seed sowing to flowering. In general, as might be expected, those requiring the longest period to reach flowering stage are the ones from mild climates. There are, however, startling exceptions to this generalization, even in original species. Furthermore, centuries of development under garden conditions have greatly altered the growth habits of original species. An illustration of this is to be found in Cosmos. Garden varieties of Cosmos, up to as recently as two or three decades ago, required four months or so to flower, but in modern strains bloom in ten to twelve weeks.

Annuals are usually designated as "hardy," "half-hardy," or "tender." While frost-resistance is the primary factor in determining in which of these categories any particular species is placed, nevertheless the length of time to flowering is also a consideration. Some annuals require such a long pre-flowering period that in northern climates they must be started indoors or under glass if they are to bloom sufficiently in advance of frost to make growing them worthwhile. These may be designated as tender, for this reason, rather than for particular sensitiveness to frost. Examples of this type are China-asters and the ruffled, fringed, and double varieties of Petunia.

Hardy

The hardy annuals will withstand several degrees of frost, either in the seedling stage in spring or at the other end of the season. Many of them have seeds sufficiently frost-resistant to be sown in late fall for spring germination. These and others not quite so

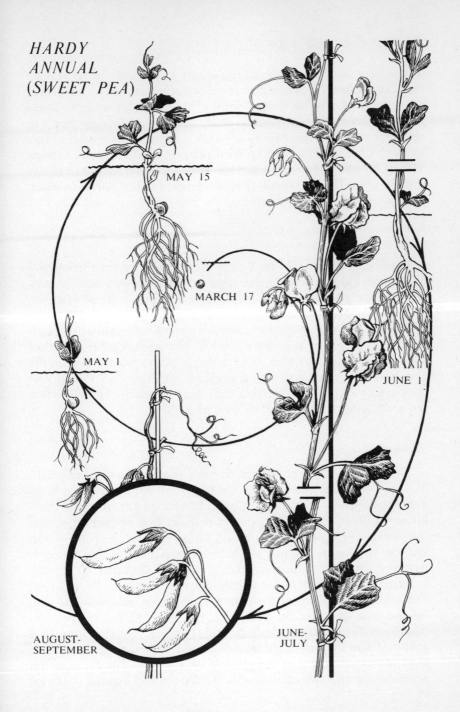

HARDY
ANNUAL
(SWEET PEA)

MAY 15

MARCH 17

MAY 1

JUNE 1

AUGUST-
SEPTEMBER

JUNE-
JULY

robust may be sown as early in the spring as the soil can be worked. Succeeding frosts may somewhat delay germination, but they come up none the worse for wear. Many of them in fact, such as Sweet Peas and Larkspur—germinate better and make stronger plants in cold wet soil than they would if sown a month or six weeks later. In the Northeast and Middle West (approximate latitude of New York, Chicago, Cleveland, and Des Moines), the hardy annuals are usually sown in late March or early April; farther north or south, proportionately later or earlier.

Half-hardy

These may be sown in the open when danger of hard freezing is past, approximately one month later than the hardy kinds, or mid-April to early May. Earliest sowings are best made, where possible, in a somewhat protected or sheltered location.

Earlier flowering may be obtained with the half-hardies by starting them indoors or in a frame three to five weeks earlier than they would be sown in the open. Where this is not convenient, or in the case of such species as do not transplant well (notably California-poppy, Candytuft, and Nigella), they may be advanced by starting the seeds under plastic starters (see page 101).

Tender

This group—much greater in number than the hardies and half-hardies—includes those species, mostly from tropical and subtropical climes, which will perish at a slight touch of frost. Even if not killed by frost, they make little growth at low temperatures and may be so severely checked that they fail to recover and achieve normal development. Nothing is gained, therefore, through trying to rush the season with them by early sowing in the open.

Surprisingly, some of the tender annuals occasionally self-sow; the seeds, dropped where the plants have grown, surviving the winter and germinating in the spring. Among these are Balsam, Petunia, Nicotiana (Flowering Tobacco), and Torenia. These belong to a group of plants which might be designated as "self-timers"—that is, they remain dormant in the ground until conditions are right for germination and safe aftergrowth. Tomatoes and Squash (both ex-

Many annuals, because of their compact growth and continuous bloom, are ideal for window boxes, hanging baskets, roof gardens, and other uses where planting space is restricted.

Backgrounds often make the picture. ABOVE *Petunia Crown Jewels silhouetted against a wall and with a hedge above it.* BELOW *The late autumn color of Alyssum Royal Carpet harmonizes with the purple-gray of field boulders.*

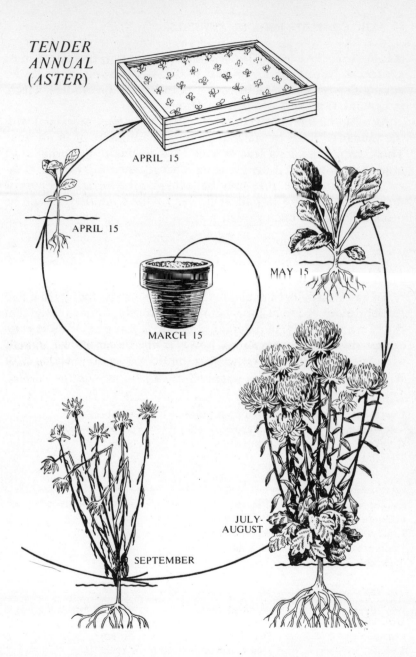

TENDER
ANNUAL
(*ASTER*)

APRIL 15

APRIL 15

MARCH 15

MAY 15

JULY-
AUGUST

SEPTEMBER

ceedingly sensitive to frost) are examples of this type familiar to most gardeners. Nevertheless, it is best to delay the sowing of all tender annual flowers until conditions for planting are favorable—which, in general, is about Corn-planting time.

As with the half-hardy annuals, much time may be gained with the tender varieties by starting them early, indoors or in a frame. Those requiring a long season from seed sowing to flowering must indeed be so started if the gardener is to get their full benefit. If facilities are adequate, they may be transplanted (usually to pots or dirt bands) and had in bud or flower by the time they should be transferred to the open garden.

EXAMPLES

As has already been explained, the terms hardy, half-hardy, and tender cannot be too definitely employed, for the simple reason that the same plant may, in different sections, fit any one of these categories. As ordinarily employed, however, the better-known annuals are classed as follows: (Others are metioned in the Catalogue of Annuals, page 179, and on pages 68 to 69.)

HARDY

Centaurea cyanus	Evening-primrose	Rudbeckia
(cornflower)	Larkspur	Sweet Alyssum
Coreopsis	Poppy	Sweet Pea
Dianthus		

HALF-HARDY

California-poppy	Cleome	Phlox Drummondi
Calendula	Gaillardia	Salvia
Candytuft	Mignonette	Scabiosa
Centaurea americana	Nigella	Stock
(Basket Flower)		

TENDER

Ageratum	Morning-glory	Salpiglossis
Browallia	Nasturtium	Sunflower
Celosia	Nicotiana	Torenia
Lobelia	(Flowering Tobacco)	Zinnia
Marigold	Petunia	

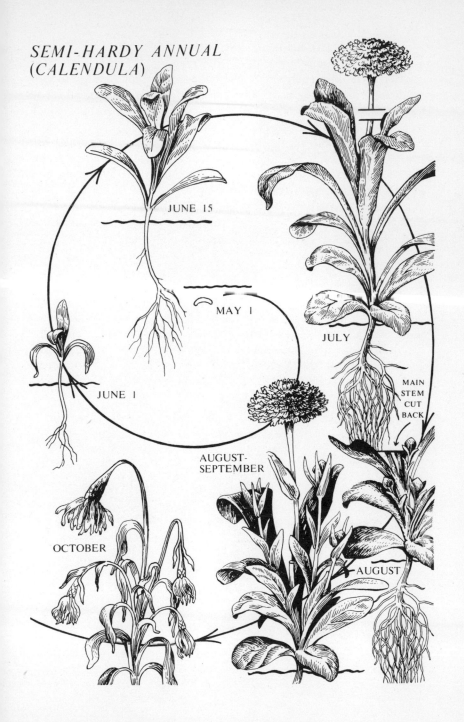

SEMI-HARDY ANNUAL
(CALENDULA)

JUNE 15

MAY 1

JUNE 1

JULY

MAIN
STEM
CUT
BACK

AUGUST-
SEPTEMBER

OCTOBER

AUGUST

CHAPTER 3. *Other Plants Grown as Annuals*

BIENNIALS, PERENNIALS, TENDER SHRUBS, BULBS

From the point of view of the gardener, there are certain members of other groups of plants which he treats as annuals even though, botanically speaking, they are not annuals at all. Some of these are biennials, some perennials; others are bulbs and shrubs too tender to remain out of doors in a cold climate during the winter.

Among these are to be found some of the most pleasing and the most continuous-flowering of all "one-season" plants. As they are adapted in most respects to the same pattern of culture as true annuals, they are given consideration here.

Biennials

As already explained (see page 29), these are plants which normally require parts of *two* seasons to complete their cycle of growth. Seed sown in one year develops plants which live over winter and produce blossoms and seed during the following year. Most of them, however, *if sown sufficiently early*, will give some flowers the first season and still live over winter to complete their life cycle the following year. The list of biennials includes:

Bellis	Evening-primrose	Pansy
(English Daisy)	Foxglove	Sweet William
Cheiranthus	Myosotis	(Dianthus barbatus)
(Siberian Wallflower)	(Forget-me-not)	

Perennials

Perennials that are often treated as annuals include half-hardy and tender species. In northern gardens we cannot otherwise take

Many tender perennials, shrubs, and bulbous plants are grown as annuals. In this small pool, a tropical Water-lily pinch-hits as an annual.

advantage of all they have to offer in form and color, to add variety and interest to our list of single-season flowering and foliage plants. Perennials to be grown as annuals are handled in three ways:

From seed. The first is to sow them very early—in some cases as early as January or February—and so obtain strong pot-grown plants to be set out in spring, either with the half-hardy annuals when hard frosts are past; or a few weeks later when frost danger is over. The timing, of course, depends upon the character of the particular species or variety involved. Usually this method is practical only when a greenhouse or other exceptional facilities for starting and growing on the plants are available. Examples are:

Cobaea scandens	Glaucium	Nicotiana
(Cup-and-saucer Vine)	(Horned-poppy)	(Flowering Tobacco)
Dianthus	Heliotrope	Nierembergia caerulea
Gerberia	Hibiscus Manihot	Salvia splendens
(Gerbera)	Hunnemannia	(Scarlet Sage)
	(Tulip poppy)	Verbena

Still another group of perennials, often grown primarily for a single season's bloom, includes those which, in too severe or otherwise unfavorable climates, are short-lived. They are handled as biennials, being sown in late spring or midsummer to form plants that will produce their best bloom the year following. Among these are Delphiniums (in the Northeast), Violas, some of the Campanulas, (Canterbury Bells), and Sweet William.

Wintering over. The second method is to take up the perennial plant at the end of the season, carry it over winter under suitable conditions, and then replant it in the spring. Some species—such as not-quite-hardy Chrysanthemums, Tritomas, and Snapdragons —may be over-wintered in a cold frame in a dormant state.

From cuttings. A variation of this method is to take cuttings of the desired plant and grow these on through the winter, repotting as required, and thus obtain a supply of new plants for setting out each spring. This method is often employed with such tender perennials as *Begonia semperflorens,* Geranium, Heliotrope, *Impatiens sultani*, Nierembergia.

Shrubs

A number of the tender shrubs, generally used as greenhouse plants, serve excellently in the outdoor garden. Being of quite different character in plant form and foliage from most annuals, and having a prolonged flowering season, they provide additional variety and interest to the plantings of annuals. Familiar examples in this category are Flowering-maple (*Abutilon hybridum*), Fuchsia, Lantana, Lemon-verbena, with its indescribably delicious aromatic foliage, and the almost equally delightful Rosemary.

All of these make much more rapid growth when set out in the open garden than they do in pots indoors. We have had, by the end of September, Flowering-maple four feet tall from plants set out

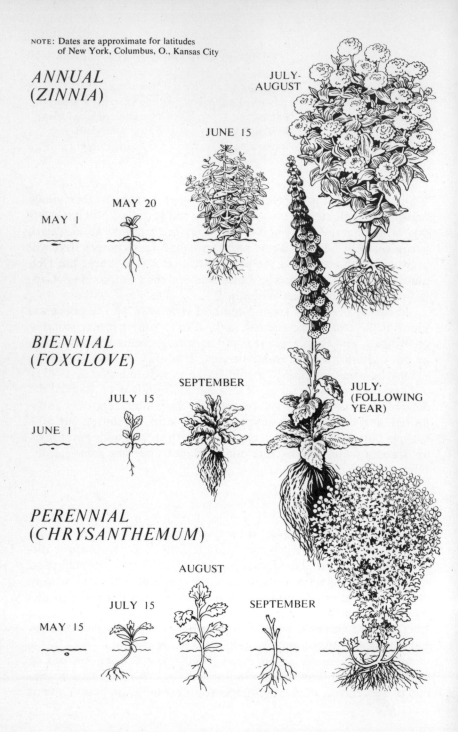

NOTE: Dates are approximate for latitudes
of New York, Columbus, O., Kansas City

ANNUAL
(ZINNIA)

JULY-
AUGUST

JUNE 15

MAY 20

MAY 1

BIENNIAL
(FOXGLOVE)

SEPTEMBER

JULY 15

JULY-
(FOLLOWING
YEAR)

JUNE 1

PERENNIAL
(CHRYSANTHEMUM)

AUGUST

JULY 15

SEPTEMBER

MAY 15

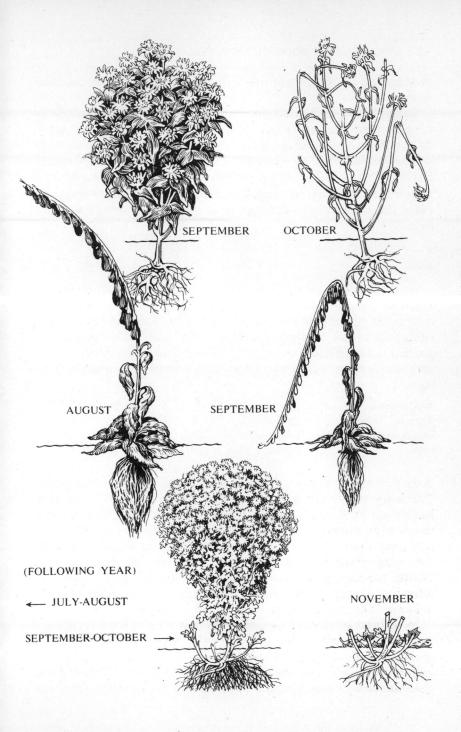

SEPTEMBER

OCTOBER

AUGUST

SEPTEMBER

(FOLLOWING YEAR)

← JULY-AUGUST

SEPTEMBER-OCTOBER →

NOVEMBER

in May, and Lantanas grown into dense, knee-high shrubs two feet or more across.

Such plants may be cut back to mere stubs, given a bit of rest by keeping them on the dry side, and then started into growth again. But this is not practical for house culture, and even in a fairly large greenhouse they will be demanding a good deal of space by spring, just when room is most at a premium. It is, however, an easy matter to root cuttings in late August or September (in the North) and carry the young plants through as suggested for perennials. (See page 39.)

Bulbs

Most bulbs that are not winter-hardy in the North are treated as annuals. They are indispensable in providing tall, spire-like effects in a mixed planting of annuals and are more harmonious with annuals than with most perennials. (The term "bulb" is here used in its general sense and includes corms, tubers, and fleshy roots.) A list of those readily available and easily grown would take in the following:

Acidanthera	Canna	Montbretia
Begonia, Tuberous	Dahlia	Tigridia
Caladium, fancy-leaved	Gladiolus	Tuberose
Calla	Ismene	

A few of these—notably Bedding Dahlias and Tuberous Begonias —if sown early, will produce flowers the first season from seed, but for the most part they are all purchased as "bulbs," planted outdoors after danger of frost, and then taken up in the fall when first frosts nip the tops, and stored over winter, to be planted again the following spring. Some of the more tender subjects, especially in the North, are started into growth in pots or flats indoors and set out after the ground has thoroughly warmed up. These include Caladiums, Tuberous Begonias, Callas, and Tuberoses.

In sections of moderate winter temperatures the hardiest of these bulbs may be left in the ground and heavily mulched—*after* the ground freezes an inch or so deep. With such treatment the chances are that they will come through safely, but one runs the risk of loss if an unusually severe winter is encountered. We have had Gladiolus and even Dahlias survive unscathed, without protection, in northern Connecticut; but such cultural practice is not to be recommended.

Even in southern areas, where the chance of frost injury is slight, the plants soon develop large clumps so crowded that there is no chance of top-quality flowers being produced.

For complete details on the culture of tender bulbs, the reader is referred to the authors' *The Complete Book of Bulbs.*

If you wish annuals and any of the other plants grown as annuals to do the most they are capable of doing to beautify your garden and grounds, you must give some thought—yes, considerable thought—to where and how you are going to use them. There is a mistaken but all too widely held assumption that annuals are merely pinch hitters, to be stuck in here or there where other plants have not yet been established or have failed. Learn to look upon annuals as one of the most important of the several different types of plant materals you can use to create a well-rounded *and constantly colorful* home landscape, and you will find them indeed rewarding.

HAVE A PLAN

This involves, on your part, some definite decisions as to the effects or the results you wish to obtain; and following that, careful planning as to *what* to use and *where* to use it. All this spells out one thing: the making of a plan.

It is true that many gardeners, even experienced ones, do not take the trouble to work out such a plan. It is also true, however, that those who do, get the most satisfactory results. Moreover, the making of a plan saves both time and cash: time, because when it comes to planting, the gardener knows just where each packet of seeds or group of plants is to go, and can have prepared the ground for them in advance; money, because it will not have been spent for surplus seeds or extra plants that cannot be fitted into the space available.

There are two other big advantages in making a carefully considered plan. The first is the fun to be had from doing it; the second is that mistakes may be found, *and corrected*, on paper in a mere fraction of the time that would be involved when the gardener is actually doing the work.

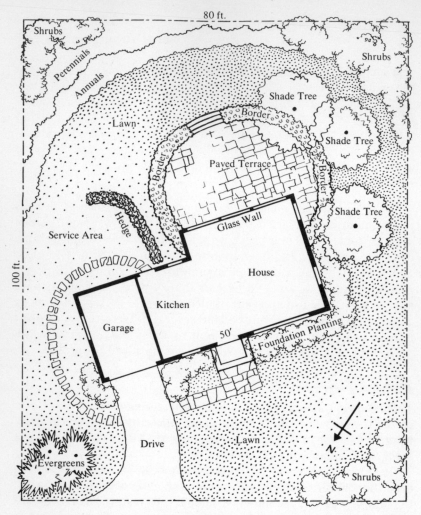

Without a plan your plantings must be more or less hit or miss. This will result in getting tall-growing species or varieties in front of lower-growing ones, thus partially or completely hiding them from sight; in making it impossible to carry out any preconceived color scheme or even to assure pleasing combinations of color; and in spots of flowerless foliage here and there, in a mixed border, through having kinds with the same blooming season placed next to each other. So much for reasons for making a plan. Now: how to set about it.

We have found that most beginning gardeners have a sort of psychological dread of attempting to make a plan. They seem to feel that a course in engineering and another in landscape architecture are essential prerequisites for attempting anything so complicated. Their fears are groundless. They may bolster their hesitant spirits by saying it's "a poor thing but mine own." And the very fact that it is his own will add immeasurably to its value for the gardener. Nobody can make such a plan without acquiring a good deal of valuable information about the different plants involved in its component parts.

In the making of a plan, there are two steps. The first is to decide on the different areas to be planted and the general size and shape of each. The second is to work out the details for each area.

So here is the process, step by step:

1. Procure a few sheets of cross-ruled paper from a stationery store. Attach a sheet of it to a piece of heavy cardboard or light plywood for convenience in carrying it about and marking on it.

2. Next, indicate the boundary lines of the property, using a scale of one eighth inch to a foot, or one quarter inch to five feet, or whatever may be convenient. After the boundary lines are in, locate on the plan the residence, garage, driveway, paths, large trees, rocks, outdoor fireplace, service area, and other fixed objects. If some landscaping has already been done, the flower beds and borders are probably already "fixed."

3. Now comes the first step in planning. Indicate in a general way the areas to be assigned to different uses: lawn, play yard, service yard; vegetable plot and/or cutting garden; main flower borders; any small areas for special treatment, such as bulbous plantings, shady garden, rock garden. (See plan on page 48.)

The preliminary work is done, and you are ready to get down to brass tacks; i.e., a detailed plan for each area where annuals are to be used. These will be your planting sheets, ready to save you no end of time, uncertainty, and confusion when the garden eventually is made and planted.

4. To prepare these, it is easier and better to make a separate sheet for each area. This makes it possible to use a much larger scale— possibly up to an inch to the foot—so you can get a very good picture of how any particular bed or border is going to shape up.

Long borders, straight or curved, should be at least three feet from front to back, and better a foot or two more. If the front is arranged in a series of sweeping curves, providing a succession of

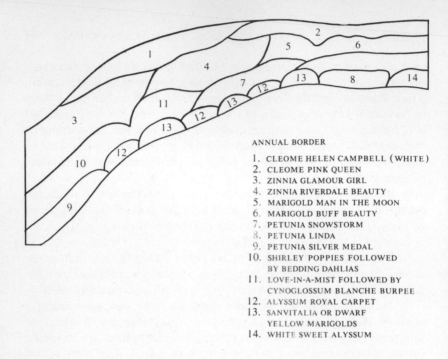

ANNUAL BORDER

1. CLEOME HELEN CAMPBELL (WHITE)
2. CLEOME PINK QUEEN
3. ZINNIA GLAMOUR GIRL
4. ZINNIA RIVERDALE BEAUTY
5. MARIGOLD MAN IN THE MOON
6. MARIGOLD BUFF BEAUTY
7. PETUNIA SNOWSTORM
8. PETUNIA LINDA
9. PETUNIA SILVER MEDAL
10. SHIRLEY POPPIES FOLLOWED
    BY BEDDING DAHLIAS
11. LOVE-IN-A-MIST FOLLOWED BY
    CYNOGLOSSUM BLANCHE BURPEE
12. ALYSSUM ROYAL CARPET
13. SANVITALIA OR DWARF
    YELLOW MARIGOLDS
14. WHITE SWEET ALYSSUM

small bays and promontories, the effect will usually be much more pleasing than if it is made a straight line. Not only will the front edge actually be longer but to the eye it will appear longer still. (See photo page 49.)

If the whole design is to be formal in character, then beds rectangular in shape or of some fixed geometric pattern will of course be in order.

New we are ready to begin filling in the details.

To get effective masses of color and also to avoid a spotty appearance, several plants of each variety should be placed in a group. In a large border these groups may be repeated as often as desired. Never less than three and preferably at least half a dozen plants should be used in each group or unit. (The few exceptions to this rule are such large or dominating species as Ricinus (Castor-bean) and the big Sunflowers. Except in very formal beds, the spaces devoted to each variety should be irregular in shape and size. The size of each space will be determined by the size and number of the

As a rule, a curved or irregular edge enhances the appearance of a flower border, especially if it can be made, as here, to fit the contours of the land. BELOW:
Annuals are indispensable, especially in a first-year garden, in base planting
against the house.

plants to be placed within it and also by the over-all dimensions of the bed or border; the larger the border, the larger should be the size of the individual units of color (that is, the number of individual plants in each group) comprising it. The typical plans on pages 46 and 48 give an idea of the distribution of planting spaces.

Talls to the rear!

Whether annuals are used by themselves in an all-annual border or as supplementary material in a mixed border, it is all-important to keep in mind the *height* to which each species or variety used will grow. Unless this is done, the border will be a jumbled jungle, ragged in appearance and with a large proportion of the flowers hidden by taller plants in front of them. As annuals vary in height from six inches to six feet, the importance of this can readily be understood.

On the other hand, any appearance of stiff regimentation is to be avoided. Rank behind rank of flowers of even height would be quite as bad, if not worse, than the jumble we're trying to avoid. A band of gypsies is much more picturesque than a phalanx of goose-stepping soldiers!

Keep them coming!

The next step in fitting annuals into the garden plan is to consider the *period of bloom* of the various species, and of individual types and varieties. Although many annuals will continue in flower over very long periods (especially if not allowed to form seeds), there are some which can be counted upon for only short periods. In the all-annual border, care should be taken to avoid having too many short-season bloomers next to each other, and also to see that each section of the border contains some early-season, some mid-season, and some late-season kinds near each other. The lists on pages 63 to 81 will enable you to make selections to accomplish this end. Where annuals are mixed through the perennial border, less precaution in this respect is required.

Color

Much has been written about color in the flower garden—with belabored suggestions for an all-white, pink, mauve, or what have you effect. It is always a tempting topic for apartment-house garden authors. Such elaborate color schemes may have their place in the field of professional landscape architects planning things on a large scale for anemic clients, but they are more than likely to prove disappointing to the average home owner. In many years of looking we have found very few such plantings that came off to any satisfactory degree. Usually the more important factors of good "facing down" (graduated heights of plants) and bloom sequence are sacrificed to the color scheme.

The border of annuals planned for analagous color harmony— that is, in tones, shades, or tints related to a chosen key hue—is more satisfactory; but even such a border is subject, in lesser degree, to the same limitations. Max Schling, an erratic but certainly a remarkably successful enthusiast in flower art, always maintained that any flower colors used together would harmonize if sufficient white, gray, or green were mixed with them. But the if, it must be noted, is most important. Green foliage is certainly an excellent blender. (Study the color illustration facing page 3.)

All this, however, does not imply that color is not to be taken into consideration when you select your flowers. Two important facts should constantly be kept in mind.

The first of these is that the stronger (purer) a color is, the less will it be compatible with neighboring colors. Pastel tints and deep shades will give little trouble.

The second is that the closer two colors are placed in conjunction, the more marked will be their harmony or their discord.

The practical application of these two single principles will make a great difference in the degree of charm which your plantings of annuals will have for yourself and for others—and their application is not difficult.

It will mean, in practice, that you will avoid using strong, aggressive colors—such as purple, magenta, scarlet, and orange—near together unless they are toned down by nearby white or gray, or by plenty of green foliage; or unless combined with the complementary colors (the exact opposite of each on the color wheel)—an accomplishment which, for the beginner, is more difficult.

It will mean, too, that you will be on the lookout for "little harmonies" in your flower borders, or in small groups—planned combinations of two or three different flowers that get along so happily together that any observer will stop to exclaim, "What a charming effect!"

You cannot expect, at your first attempt, to get perfect results. But you can be certain that if you try for them you will come off infinitely better than if you merely go at the task by chance, trusting to luck for results. And in the course of a season or two you will find your plantings improved surprisingly.

Your progress will be speeded by the simple device of keeping a record, through the course of the summer, of sour notes and of sweet ones in your garden picture. This applies not only to color combinations but also to the season of bloom and the relative heights of those annuals which come to be your favorites. And there will always be the fascination of new species and new varieties with which you wish to experiment. You'll find yourself embarked in a never-ending, always exciting and changing game.

MAKING USE OF ANNUALS

So much for the considerations to be kept in mind in combining different annuals in group plantings. Now we return to that planting plan which, for the moment, we left sort of dangling on the drawing board.

After the locations of the several areas have been determined, the next step is to decide the position and the size of each planting that will contain annuals, either by themselves or combined with other flowers. These plantings will include several of the following:

Color masses, to be effective over a fairly long season of bloom, can be created more effectively with annuals than with any other group of plants. They are employed by landscape architects in the designing of fairly large grounds and in public plantings in parks, but much less frequently on moderate-sized places. The purpose—as the term implies—is to obtain a dramatic spot of color in a general planting scheme. Frequently only a single variety of annual is used, —one which grows uniformly to an even height, the plants being set with mathematical precision in beds of rectangular or geometric design. Everyone is familiar with the flaming carpets of Scarlet Sage or the massed beds of Marigolds that are still to be seen in public grounds.

Zinnias are used to provide a mass of color against green lawns.

While, as already implied, this method of using annuals is of little concern to the average home owner, nevertheless he will occasionally find it possible to use small and less formalized masses of color about his grounds as highlights in his general planting scheme. A group of some colorful blooms—such as tall Marigolds, Lupines, or Cosmos—against evergreens or rhododendrons may prove to be a very happy combination. While such plantings are not ordinarily seen, they do open an intriguing avenue of experiment to the adventurous gardener.

Design bedding is a variation of the color-mass idea in which plants with flowers or foliage of contrasting colors but of uniform height are employed. Oldsters will recall the meticulously barbered beds of Coleus and/or Achyranthes (Alternanthera) that used to decorate sizable lawns but are now—happily—seldom encountered. A less objectionable modern form of this type of planting is often to be seen today in borders or narrow beds of Ageratum, Sweet Alyssum, and dwarf Marigolds planted in one bed in symmetrical rows or blocks.

The annual border provides the most spectacular way of using annuals. In this, annuals alone are used, and a good selection of them will provide a mass of brilliant colors stepped down from four to

A small bed of annuals always shows off to much better advantage when planted against a wall or a hedge—and also is well protected from winds and driving rains. BELOW: An abundance of flowers for both display and cutting are assured for this short-season summer home by combining shrubs, perennials, and annuals.

six feet at the rear to from six to ten inches at the front. A well-planned arrangement of the various species and varieties provides a fairly constant succession of bloom from late spring until frost.

In planning a border of annuals, the number of different kinds used should be in proportion to the size of the bed—the smaller, the fewer. One of the most common mistakes of the beginner is to use too many kinds. Even in a fairly large border more artistic effects can be had if the number of species and varieties is resolutely kept limited. The size of the individual groups can be increased in a large area and the various combinations repeated.

If you have an urge to grow a whole catalogue of annuals, try out the ones with which you are not familiar in rows in a garden for cutting, and work them into your border planting only as you have become sufficiently familiar with them to be able to judge what they will do for the border.

The mixed border, in which annuals are employed to supplement perennials, provides the gardener with a chance to test his skill. Unless one has considerable space available and either plenty of time or the services of a professional plantsman (or both), it is very difficult to maintain that continuous succession of bloom which writers and lecturers so happily prate about. Cleverly used, annuals can go far toward filling the holes and bridging the gaps ordinarily encountered at different periods in the average perennial border.

This is not meant to imply that such a border should be a continuous "riot of color" from one end of the season to another. A solid sheet of bloom—such as one often sees displayed in flower-show gardens and in the assembled garden scenes of slick-magazine color photographs—would be neither possible nor desirable. But stretches of foliage without a bloom in sight and bare spots where plants are going into dormancy or have already disappeared are far from inspiring to behold, and it is here that the annuals have an important role to play.

To use them most effectively for this purpose, the annuals should be grown in advance, ready to be moved into place when their services are needed. This will require some well-considered planning. The most satisfactory results can be obtained only on the basis of experience—experience gained in one's own garden. Nevertheless, even the beginner, working pretty much at random for his first season, will find the effort richly rewarding; especially so if he

A pleasing foundation planting of annuals between drive and house.

has a first-season perennial border which, in the nature of things, will be long on empty spaces and short on bloom while the perennials are getting really established.

Plants of annuals for filling in may be started in a frame or in a seed bed and either transplanted directly to the border or transferred first to pots or dirt bands. In the latter case they may be held for weeks until needed, and may even be had in bud or flower to give immediate results when transferred to the border. A list of plants especially well suited for use in the perennial border is given on page 73, and methods of growing them are described in Chapter 7.

After spring bulbs the annuals are even more indispensable than in the perennial border. Wherever Tulips, Daffodils, Hyacinths, and other Dutch bulbs are used by themselves or predominate in a planting, the flowering season is followed by a period of foliage growth and ripening off. For the good of the bulbs the *foliage should never be removed* before it begins to turn yellow. This presents a problem in unsightliness. But the solution is simple: merely have annuals ready to set out among the bulbs, and supplement these by patches of seed of annuals that will continue to bloom on into the fall. (see list on page 73.)

In the rock garden, too, annuals have an important part to play

A spot "fill-in" with annuals against shrubs.

Sweet Alyssum and Portulaca—two excellent flowers to use where rocks are involved.

in maintaining a modicum of color during summer. A real rock garden is a spring garden, with alpine plants its chief denizens; and the simon-pure rock gardener is quite likely to suffer from shock at any suggestion of employing common garden annuals in the sacred precincts.

For many who are more concerned with their rock gardens merely for such additional beauty or out-of-the-ordinary interest as they can provide, the idea of using annuals does not seem too horrendous a breach of horticultural etiquette and will not prevent their sleeping soundly o' nights.

They will, however, be careful to select such things as are in scale with the rock-garden setting and in harmony with its general design: plants, for the most part, which are creeping or mat-forming in habit. (See list, page 74.) For *temporary* effects the first year, such things as Summer-Cypress (*Kochia*) or Mexican Fire-Plant (*Euphorbia heterophylla*) may simulate dwarf evergreens and shrubs while the latter are becoming established.

In walls and on banks the same types of plants may be used, often with surprisingly charming results. Try two or three plants of Petunia, Alyssum, dwarf Ageratum, or Sanvitalia placed near together in the crevices of a dry wall.

Bedding Petunias along a low wall make an attractive binding for a carpet of lawn.

Problem: a sloping bank and a bare, high foundation. Solution: a small rockery —better if stones had been laid flat—and colorful annuals.

Edging or low borders are employed not only for the fronts of borders but also along walks or drives. Here plants that are low-growing and—for some purposes—neat and compact are sought. Ageratum, dwarf Marigolds, Sweet Alyssum, and others mentioned in the list on page 71 fit in here.

Hedges and screens are sometimes wanted quickly but at slight expense, especially for new properties that are just being whipped into shape. Fast results for a season or two may be achieved with dense-growing annuals of medium height such as Summer-cypress, Hedge Marigolds, and Scarlet or Welwyn Hybrid Sage. (See list on page 72.) For a tall screen to assure a fair degree of privacy or to shut out an objectionable view, Castor-bean *(Ricinus),* Tithonia, and Polygonum, or a Gourd or other rapid-growing vine on a trellis, will answer the purpose. (See list on page 75.)

Accent plants are of striking form, size, or habit, employed in garden design to provide emphasis by contrast. Usually individual species are chosen for this purpose. A list of suitable plants will be found on page 72.

Lesson in backgrounds. Note how the single plant of Globe-thistle silhouettes the fragile white Nicotiana flowers which otherwise would have been lost against the stucco wall.

Here very compact, low-growing annuals have been cleverly employed to demark the long walk without interrupting the wide sweep of lawn.

BUYING THE BEST

In closing this chapter let us add just a few words about buying seeds and plants.

The cost of seed—no matter how high-priced a packet may be—is slight compared with the time, trouble, cost of plant foods, preparation of the soil, and other items that go to make a successful garden. It doesn't pay to skimp on a few pennies where seed is involved. Buy where you have good reason to believe you will get top quality—and where you can have a good range of varieties to select from. Keep in mind that good germination is not enough—it's what the plant does after it germinates that is important.

In general, mixtures are best avoided unless they are made up of named varieties. Some things, of course, may be had only in mixtures. But where possible, learn to know your varieties.

When it comes to purchasing growing plants of annuals, most beginners will select the largest available, especially if they are in flower. Often smaller, younger plants, in bud rather than in bloom, are better. The seed shops and roadside stands, for instance, every spring sell millions of baskets of Pansies that have been in full bloom for several weeks—and which, a few days after the purchaser sets them out, will look like something the cat dragged in—while younger plants full of buds but with few blooms are passed by. It's much the same with Geraniums and other flowers handled as pot plants.

If you are purchasing seedlings from a flat, insist that they be re-be removed with some soil about the roots rather than merely pulled out, as is often done for the unwary customer. Even at a higher price small plants in individual dirt bands are well worth the difference. (See photograph page 106.)

PLANTS USED AS ANNUALS—BY COLOR

White

Ageratum
Arctotis
Babys-breath
Balsam
Begonia semperflorens
Browallia
Campanula
Candytuft
Cape-marigold
China-aster
Chrysanthemum
Clarkia
Cleome
Cobaea scandens
Cornflower
Cosmos
Cynoglossum
Dahlia

Datura
Dianthus
Evening primrose
Everlasting
Geranium
Gilia
Godetia
Immortelle
Larkspur
Lavatera
Lobelia
Love-in-a-mist
Lupine
Lychnis
Mallow
Mentzelia
Mesembryanthemum
Moonflower

Morning-glory
Nemesia
Nicotiana
Pansy
Petunia
Phlox Drummondi
Poppy
Portulaca
Prickly-poppy
Scabiosa
Snapdragon
Statice
Stock
Strawflower
Swan River Daisy
Sweet Alyssum
Sweet Pea

Pink or rose

Babys-breath
Balsam
Begonia semperflorens
California-poppy
Campanula
Candytuft
Celosia
China-aster
Clarkia

Cleome
Collomia
Cornflower
Cosmos
Dahlia
Dianthus
English Daisy
Everlasting
Flax

Four-o'clock
Geranium
Godetia
Hollyhock
Larkspur
Lupine
Lychnis
Mallow
Mesembryanthemum

Moonflower
Morning-glory
Nasturtium
Nemesia
Nicotiana
Petunia
Phlox Drummondi

Poppy
Portulaca
Salvia Welwyn
 Hybrids
Sand-verbena
Scabiosa
Silene armeria

Snapdragon
Star-of-the-desert
Statice
Stock
Strawflower
Sweet Pea
Virginia-stock

Red

Adonis
Alonsoa
California-poppy
Celosia
China-aster
Collomia
Coreopsis
Cosmos
Cuphea
Cypress Vine
Dahlia
Dianthus
Echium

Emilia
Gaillardia
Geranium
Gilia
Globe Amaranth
Godetia
Hollyhock
Larkspur
Lavatera
Love-lies-bleeding
Lychnis
Maskflower

Mexican Fire-plant
Monkey Flower
Morning-glory
Nasturtium
Nicotiana
Pansy
Petunia
Phlox Drummondi
Poppy Mallow
Poppy
Portulaca
Salpiglossis

Purple or lavender

Anoda
Balsam
Campanula
Candytuft
Centaurea
China-aster
Clarkia
Cleome
Collinsia
Dahlia
Gilia
Heliotrope

Immortelle
Lantana
Larkspur
Lobelia
Lupine
Lychnis
Malope
Morning-glory
Pansy
Petunia
Phacelia
Phlox Drummondi

Salpiglossis
Sand-verbena
Scabiosa
Star-of-the-desert
Statice
Stock
Sweet Alyssum
Sweet Pea
Virginia-stock
Verbena
Torenia

Dominating colors should be employed with care. Petunia Comanche, which wars with most other hues, is balanced by a mass of the soft gray foliage of Snow-in-summer (Cerastium tomentosum) to give a pleasing effect. BELOW Double Portulaca, an ideal rock-garden annual.

A dwarf, spreading French Marigold, Yellow Pygmy, ideal for edging and good for rock work. BELOW *Plants of annuals grown in dirt bands of wood veneer.*

Blue

Ageratum
Anagallis
Anchusa
Arctotis
Blue Lace-flower
Blue Woodruff
Browallia
Campanula
China-aster
Cobaea scandens
Collinsia
Cornflower
Cynoglossum
Datura

Echium
Felicia
Flax
Forget-me-not
Gilia
Godetia
Heliophila
Larkspur
Linaria
Lobelia
Love-in-a-mist
Lupine
Lychnis
Morning-glory

Nemophila
Nierembergia
Nolana
Pansy
Phacelia
Salpiglossis
Salvia farinacea
Scabiosa
Stock
Swan River Daisy
Sweet Pea
Tahoka-daisy
Torenia

Yellow

California-poppy
Calendula
Canary-bird-vine
Cape-marigold
Celosia
Chrysanthemum
Coreopsis
Cosmos
Dahlia
Datura
Evening-primrose
Everlasting
Feverfew
Four-o'clock

Gaillardia
Gazania
Gilia
Hunnemannia
Lantana
Lupine
Marigold
Mentzelia
Monkey Flower
Nasturtium
Nemesia
Pansy
Poppy
Portulaca

Rudbeckia
Sanvitalia
Scabiosa
Sea-poppy
Snapdragon
Star-of-Texas
Statice
Strawflower
Sunflower
Sweet Sultan
Tassel-flower
Thunbergia
Zinnia

Orange

California-poppy
Calendula
Cape-marigold
Coreopsis
Cosmos
Dahlia

Emilia
Gazania
Globe Amaranth
Hunnemannia
Marigold

Nasturtium
Poppy
Strawflower
Tithonia
Zinnia

ANNUALS ACCORDING TO HEIGHT

Tall, 3 to 6 feet

Anoda (Snowcup), 3'
Antirrhinum:
　Giant, 3'
　Rust Resistant, 3'
　Tetra, 3'
Calliopsis, Tall, 3'
Castor bean, 4 to 6'
　Red Spire
Celosia:
　Tall Plumed, 3'
　Feathered, 3'
　Gilbert's Maple
　　Gold, 3'
Centaurea (Cornflower),
　to 4'
Cleome:
　Helen Campbell,
　　white, 4'
　Pink Queen, 4'

Cosmos:
　Sensation, 3–6'
　Fiesta, 3'
Datura, to 5'
Hollyhock, Indian
　Spring, to 5'
Lavatera, to 6'
Larkspur:
　Steeplechase, 5'
　Supreme, 6'
　Wonder, 3½'
　Regal, 3'
Marigold, Tall, to 3½'
Mexican Fire-plant, 3'
Salvia:
　Bonfire (early), 3'
　Welwyn Hybrids, 3'

Scabiosa:
　Blue Moon, 3'
　Mixed, 3'
Summer-cypress, to 5'
Sunflower, to 12'
Sweet Pea:
　Cuthbertson, 6'
　Heat Resistant, 6'
Tithonia, 4 to 6'
　Torch, 3½'
Zinnia:
　Burpee hybrids, 3'
　Dahlia-fl'd. 3'
　Giant cactus fl'd. 3'
　Giant fl'd, 3'
　Luther Burbank, 4'

Medium, 15 to 24 ins.

Ageratum Tall Blue, 18–24"
Anchusa Blue Bird, 18"
Antirrhinum, Semi-tall, to 24"
Arctotis, 24"
Bells-of-Ireland, 24"
Browallia, to 24"
Calendula:
　Apricot Beauty, to 24"
　Art Shades (pastels), to 24"
　Lemon Giant, to 24"
　Orange Giant, to 24"
California-poppy, to 24"
Calliopsis Drummondi, 20"
China-aster, 20–24"
Celosia, Crested: 15"
　Flame of Fire, 18"
　Gilbert's:
　　Harlequin, 24"

　Rose Beauty, 24"
　Green Gold, 24"
Centaurea (Sweet Sultan), 24"
Cynoglossum:
　Blanche Burpee, 24"
　Firmament, 15"
Gaillardia:
　Fiesta, 15"
　Gaiety, 15"
　Sunshine, 18"
Globe Amaranth, 18"
Hunnemannia, 24"
Marigold:
　African, to 24"
　Carnation fl'd, to 24"
　Red & Gold Hy., 18"
　Rusty Red, 18"
　Tangerine, 15"

Mignonette, to 18"
Nasturtium, Fragrant Gleam, 15"
Nicotiana:
    Daylight, 18–24"
    Sensation Mix., 18–24"
    Affinis hybrids, 24"
Nigella, to 24"
Poppy, 24"
Petunia:
    Balcony, 18"
    Bedding, to 24"
    Fringed, to 24"
    Hybrids, to 24"
    Ruffled, to 24"
    Single, to 18"
Phlox Drummondi:
    Tall Giant, 10"

Tall Large, 15"
Tetra, 20"
Rudbeckia, 24"
Salpiglossis, Emperor mix., to 24"
Salvia farinacea, Blue Bedder, 24"
Sideritis candicans, gray foilage, 20"
Stock:
    Giant Imperial, to 24"
    Trysomic, to 24"
Sweet William, Newport Pink, to 24"
Tahoka-daisy, 24"
Vinca rosea, 18"
Zinnia:
    Cut-and-Come-Again, 24"
    Lilliput, 18"
    Persian Carpet, 10"

Low, 4 to 12 ins. ─────────────────────

Ageratum:
    Midget Blue, 3"
    Blue Ball, 6–8"
    Imperial Dwarf Blue, 7"
    Imperial Dwarf White, 7"
Alyssum, Sweet:
    Carpet of Snow, 4"
    Little Gem, 4"
    Royal Carpet, 6"
    Violet Queen, 6"
Anagallis, 6"
Antirrhinum, Magic Carpet, 6"
Begonia semperflorens:
    Carmen, 6–8"
    Mixed, 6–8"
Bellis (English Daisy), 6"
Brachycome (Swan River Daisy), 12"
    Dwarf, 6"
Candytuft, 12"
Celosia, Dwarf:
    Plumed, 9–12"
    Crested, 9–12"
Lobelia:
    Blue Gown, 4"

Crystal Palace, 4"
Gracilis Blue, 10"
Marigold:
    Dwarf doubles, 12"
    French singles, 12"
    Yellow Pygmy, 6"
    Butterball, 8"
    Cupids, 6"
    Lemondrop, 9"
Mignonette, dwarf, 6"
Nasturtium:
    Dwarf Giant double, 12"
    Dwarf single, 12"
Nolana, 3–6"
Petunia, dwarf singles, 12"
Portulaca, 8"
Phlox Drummondi, fringed, 12"
Salvia, Fireworks, 12"
Sanvitalia, 6"
Torenia, to 12"
Verbena:
    Giant fl'd, 8–12"
    Dwarf compact, 8–12"
Zinnia, Cupid, 12"

Tender bulbs

TALL	MEDIUM	LOW
Acidanthera	Caladium	Dahlia
Canna	Calla-lily	Oxalis
Dahlia	Ismene	Tuberous Begonia
Galtonia	Montbretia	(basket type)
Gladiolus	Tigridia	Zephyranthes
Tuberose	Tuberous Begonia	

ANNUALS ACCORDING TO HARDINESS

Hardy annuals

Adonis	Gaillardia	Pansy
California-poppy	Glaucium	Polygonum
Candytuft	Gypsophila	Poppies
Centaurea	Larkspur	Rudbeckia
Collinsia	Limnanthes	Snow-on-the-mountain
Coreopsis	Love-in-a-mist	Sweet Alyssum
Dianthus	Lunaria	Sweet Pea
Evening-primrose	Lupine	

Half-hardy annuals (zone 6, and north)

Arctotis	Godetia	Petunia
Calendula	Hunnemania	Phlox Drummondi
Cape-marigold	Hyacinth-bean	Portulaca
Cleome	Lavatera	Rudbeckia
Cosmos	Linaria	Salpiglossis
Cypress Vine	Lobelia	Salvia
Datura	Lupine	Scabiosa
Dusty Miller	Lychnis	Snapdragon
Everlastings:	Marigold	Statice
Immortelle	Mexican Fire-plant	Stock
Strawflower, etc.	Mignonette	Summer-cypress
Flax	Nasturtium	Tahoka-daisy
Gaillardia	Nemesia	Thunbergia
Gilia	Nicotiana	Verbena

Tender annuals (zone 6, and north)

Ageratum	Cobaea scandens	Salpiglossis
Amaranth	Datura	Sanvitalia
Anagallis	Everlastings	Scarlet-runner Bean
Balsam	Heliotrope	Schizanthus
Begonia	Immortelles	Snow-on-the-mountain
Bells-of-Ireland	Lobelia	Star-of-Texas
Blue Lace-flower	Mesembryanthemum	Statice
Browallia	Monkey Flower	Strawflower
Castor-bean	Moonflower	Sunflower
Celosia	Morning-glory	Tassel-flower
China-aster	Nasturtium	Tithonia
Chrysanthemum	Nemophila	Torenia
Clarkia	Phacelia	Zinnia

Annuals (and others) to start early under glass

Ageratum	China-aster	Marigold
Althea	Clarkia	Myosotis
Antirrhinum	*Cobaea scandens*	Nicotiana
Begonia (Wax)	Coleus	Nierembergia
Browallia	Cosmos	Petunia
Calendula	Dahlia (bedding)	Salvia
Campanula	Datura	Sideritis
Celosia	Gerberia	Verbena
Cheiranthus	Impatiens	Zanthisma
Chrysanthemum (annual)	Lobelia	Zinnia

Tender summer-flowering bulbs which can be treated as annuals

Acidanthera	Galtonia	Oxalis
Caladium	Gladiolus	Tigridia
Calla-lily	Gloriosa	Tuberose
Canna	Ismene	Tuberous Begonia
Dahlia	Montbretia	Zephyranthes

ANNUALS FOR SPECIAL PURPOSES

Ornamental grasses

Brome Grass or Quake Grass   Cloud Grass
  (*Bromus brizaeformis*)   (*Agrostis nebulosa*)

Fountain Grass
   (Pennisetum Ruppeli)
Hare's-tail Grass
   (Lagurus ovatus)
Job's Tears
   (Coix lachryma-Jobi)
Love Grass
   (Eragrostis interrupta)

Quaking Grass
   (Briza major)
Rainbow Grass
   (Zea japonica quadricolor)
   (Zea japonica variegata)
Squirrel-tail Grass
   (Hordeum jubatum)

Vines

Allegheny Vine
   (Adlumia)
Austrailian Pea
   (Dolichos lignosus)
Balloon Vine
   (Cardiospermum halicacabum)
Balsam-apple
   (Momordica balsamina)
Balsam-pear
   (Momordica charantia)
Canary-bird-vine
   (Tropaeolum peregrinum)
Cardinal Climber
   (Quamoclit sloteri and hybrids)
Cup-and-saucer Vine
   (Cobaea scandens)
Cypress Vine
   (Quamoclit pennata)

Gourds, in variety
Hyacinth-bean
   (Dolichos lablab)
Japanese Hop
   (Humulus japonicus)
Kenilworth-ivy
   (Cymbalaria muralis)
Maurandia
Moonflower
Morning-glory
Nasturtium
Scarlet-runner Bean
Sweet Pea
Thunbergia
Wild-cucumber
   (Echinocystis lobata)

For bedding

Arctotis
Balsam
Begonia semperflorens
Browallia
Calendula
Campanula, annual
Candytuft
Cape-marigold
China-aster
Celosia
Cigar Flower

Cineraria
Clarkia
Coleus
Cynoglossum
Datura
Geranium
Gerberia
Gilia
Heliotrope
Hunnemannia
Lantana

Lobelia (tall)
Marigold
Mignonette
Nasturtium
Pansy
Patience Plant
Perilla
Petunia
Phlox Drummondi
Poppy, Iceland
Poppy, Shirley

Poppy, Tulip
Rudbeckia
Salpiglossis
Salvia
Scabiosa
Schizanthus
Spur-valerian
Star-of-Texas

Star-of-the-desert
Swan River Daisy
Tahoka-daisy
Torenia
Ursinia
Verbena
Zinnia

TENDER BULBS

Caladium
Calla-lily
Gladiolus
Montbretia
Oxalis
Tigridia
Tuberous Begonia

For edging

Ageratum (dwarf)
Anagallis
Begonia semperflorens
Briza
Candytuft (dwarf)
Campanula
Celosia (dwarf)
Cheiranthus
Coleus, Trailing Queen
Dianthus
Dusty Miller
English Daisy
Felicia
Forget-me-not

Gamolepis
Gazania
Heliophila
Linaria
Lobelia
Marigold (dwarf)
Mesembryanthemum
Nemophila
Nierembergia
Pansy
Petunia (dwarf)
Phlox Drummondi (dwarf)
Platystemon
Portulaca

Sand-verbena
Sanvitalia
Snapdragon (dwarf)
Sweet Alyssum
Thunbergia
Tolpis
Torenia
Verbena
Virginia-stock
Zinnia, Cupid

TENDER BULBS

Oxalis
Zephyranthes

For foliage

Castor-bean
Coleus
Dusty Miller
Love-lies-bleeding
Mexican Fire-plant

Ornamental Grasses
  (see page 69)
Perilla
Sideritis
Snow-on-the-mountain

Summer-cypress
Unicorn Plant

TENDER BULBS

Caladium

For green house and window garden

Balsam
Begonia semperflorens
Blue Lace-flower
Browallia
Calendula
Campanula
Canary-bird-vine

Cape-stock
Cigar Flower
Cineraria
Clarkia
Cobaea scandens
Coleus
Diascia

Felicia
Geranium
Gerberia
Godetia
Heliotrope
Kenilworth-ivy
Lantana

Marigold (French, dwarf)
Maskflower
Maurandia
Mentzelia
Mignonette
Morning-glory
Nasturtium (dwarf)
Nicotiana
Nierembergia
Pansy

Petunia
Patience Plant
Penstemon gloxinioides
Schizanthus
Snapdragon (dwarf)
Sweet Alyssum
Sweet Pea
Thunbergia
Torenia

Venidium

TENDER BULBS

Calla-lily
Ismene
Gladiolus
Montbretia
Oxalis
Tuberous Begonia

For ground covers

California-poppy
Calliopsis
Collinsia (shade)

Forget-me-not (shade)
Kenilworth-ivy
Poppy, Iceland

Portulaca
Thunbergia
Vinca rosea

For hedges

Anoda (Snowcup)
Balsam
Celosia (tall)
Cleome
Datura
Four-o'clock
Grasses (see page 69)

Lantana
Lavatera
Love-lies-bleeding
Marigold (tall)
Marigold, Spanish Gold
Mexican Fire-plant
Polygonum

Rehmannia
Salvia Welwyn Hybrids
Scarlet Sage
Strawflower
Sunflower
Zinnia (giant)

For landscape accents

Castor-bean
Celosia (tall)
Chrysanthemum
Cleome
Cosmos
Datura
Hibiscus
Hollyhock
Larkspur
Lavatera
Love-lies-bleeding

Lupine
Malope
Marigold (tall)
Moonflower
Morning-glory,
    Heavenly Blue
Poppy, Shirley
Poppy, Tulip
Rehmannia
Salvia Welwyn Hybrids
Snapdragon (tall)

Sunflower
Zinnia (tall)

TENDER BULBS

Caladium
Calla-lily
Dahlia
Gladiolus (tall)
Tuberose
Tuberous Begonia

For the mixed border

Adonis
Ageratum
Anchusa
Anoda
Balsam
Bells-of-Ireland
Blue Woodruff
Calandrinia
Calendula
California-poppy
Calliopsis
Cape-stock (Heliophila)
Catananche
Celosia
Centaurea
Chrysanthemum
Cleome
Cosmos
Datura
Dianthus
Diascia
Dusty Miller
Echium
Emilia
Evening-primrose
Feverfew

Flax (Linum)
Four-o'clock
Foxglove (shade)
Gaillardia
Gilia
Godetia
Gypsophila
Helenium
Heliotrope
Hunnemannia
Lantana
Larkspur
Layia
Love-in-a-mist
Love-lies-bleeding
Lupine
Lychnis
Mallow
Malope
Marigolds
Mentzelia
Mexican Fire-plant
Mignonette
Nemesia
Nicotiana (shade)
Petunia

Poppy, Iceland
Poppy, Shirley
Poppy, Tulip
Poppy-mallow
Prickley-poppy
Rehmannia
Rudbeckia
Salvia farinacea
Salvia patens
Salvia splendens
Salvia, Welwyn Hybrids
Schizopetalon
Sideritis
Silene armeria
Snapdragon
Snow-on-the-mountain
Statice
Sunflower
Tahoka-daisy
Zinnia

TENDER BULBS

Dahlia
Gladiolus
Montbretia

Overplanting for bulbs

Ageratum
Arctotis
Babys-breath
Begonia
Browallia
Calendula
California-poppy
Celosia (dwarf)
Cleome
Coleus
Cynoglossum
Dahlia (bedding)

Dianthus
Flax
Heliotrope
Lobelia
Love-in-a-mist
Marigold (dwarf)
Marigold, French
Pansy
Petunia
Phlox Drummondi
Poppy, Iceland
Poppy, Shirley

Portulaca
Sanvitalia
Star-of-Texas
Sweet Alyssum
Sweet William
Thunbergia
Torenia
Verbena
Vinca rosea
Zinnia (dwarf)
Zinnia, Mexican

For pool sides

Allegheny Vine
Balsam
Blue Woodruff
Campanula (annual)
Clarkia
English Daisy
Forget-me-not
Foxglove

Gentian
Hibiscus (Mallow)
Kenilworth-ivy
Maskflower
Monkey Flower
Nemophila
Nicotiana
Pansy

Virginia-stock
Torenia

TENDER BULBS

Calla-lily
Caladium
Montbretia

For rock gardens and walls

Abronia
Anagallis
Babys-breath
Blue Woodruff
Calandrinia
Campanula (annual)
Candytuft
Cape-marigold
Cheiranthus
Collinsia
Dianthus
Diascia
English Daisy
Felicia
Forget-me-not
Gazania

Gentian (annual)
Gilia
Kenilworth-ivy
Limnanthes
Lobelia
Lychnis
Mesembryanthemum
Monkey Flower
Nemophila
Nierembergia
Nolana
Oxalis
Pansy
Phacelia
Phlox Drummondi
Platystemon

Portulaca
Poppy
Sanvitalia
Saponaria
Snapdragon, Miniature
Swan River Daisy
Sweet Alyssum
Thunbergia
Torenia
Ursinia
Verbena
Virginia-stock
Vinca rosea

TENDER BULBS

Zephyranthes

For porch and window boxes

Ageratum
Begonia semperflorens
Browallia
Campanula fragilis
Celosia (dwarf)
Coleus
Dusty Miller
Geranium
Kenilworth-ivy
Lantana (trailing)

Lobelia
Marigold (dwarf)
Maurandia
Perilla
Petunia, Balcony
Nasturtium
Nierembergia
Nolana
Snapdragon (dwarf)
Sweet Alyssum

Thunbergia
Torenia
Verbena
Vinca rosea
Zinnia (dwarf)

TENDER BULBS

Oxalis (for sun)
Tuberous Begonia (for shade)

For screens

Allegheny Vine	Hyacinth-bean	Prickly-poppy
Balloon Vine	Japanese Hop	Scarlet-runner Bean
Balsam-apple	Lavatera	Sunflower
Cardinal Climber	Love-lies-bleeding	Sweet Pea
Castor-bean	Mallow	Tithonia
Cleome	Moonflower	
Cobaea scandens	Morning-glory	
Gourds	Nasturtium (tall)	TENDER BULBS
Hollyhock	Polygonum	Canna

For sweet scent

Ageratum	Lupine (yellow)	Stock
Calendula	Lychnis	Sweet Alyssum
Candytuft	Marigold	Sweet Pea
Centaurea	Mentzelia	Sweet William
Cheiranthus	Mignonette	Unicorn Plant
Cleome	Moonflower (night)	Ursinia
Dianthus	Nasturtium	Verbascum (night)
Evening-primrose	Nicotiana (night)	Verbena
Feverfew (pungent)	Pansy	
Geranium (pungent)	Petunia	TENDER BULBS
Heliotrope	Scabiosa	Acidanthera
Hibiscus	Schizopetalon	Ismene
Limnanthes	Snapdragon	Tuberose

For cutting

Amaranthus	Chrysanthemum	Forget-me-not
Amberboa	Clarkia	Gaillardia
Arctotis	Cobaea scandens	Geranium
Bells-of-Ireland	Coleus	Gerberia
Blue Lace-flower	Cosmos	Glaucium
Browallia	Cynoglossum	Grasses (see page 69)
Calendula	Dahlia	Gypsophila
Calliopsis	Datura	Heliotrope
Castor-bean	Dianthus	Hunnemannia
Cape-marigold	Dusty Miller	Larkspur
Catananche	Euphorbia	Lavatera
Celosia	Everlasting (see page	Love-in-a-mist
Centaurea	140 for drying)	Lupine
China-aster	Feverfew	Marigold

Mignonette
Moonflower
Nasturtium
Nicotiana
Nierembergia
Pansy
Perilla
Petunia
Phacelia
Poppy, Shirley
Poppy, Tulip
Prickly-poppy
Rudbeckia

Salpiglossis
Salvia farinacea
Scabiosa
Schizanthus
Sideritis
Snapdragon
Unicorn Plant
Stock
Star-of-Texas
Sweet Pea
Tahoka-daisy
Tassel-flower
Tithonia

Verbena
Zea
Zinnia

TENDER BULBS

Caladium
Calla-lily
Dahlia
Gladiolus
Ismene
Montbretia
Tigridia
Tuberous Begonia

For drying (See also Chapter 11)

Catananche
Celosia
Cobaea scandens
Evening-primrose
Everlastings:
  Ammobium (Winged Everlasting)
  Helipterum Humboldtianum
  Helipterum Manglesi
   (Swan River Everlasting)
  Helipterum roseum
   (Acroclinium roseum)

Globe Amaranth
Gourds in variety
Grasses (see page 69)
Gypsophila
Honesty
Immortelle
Silver-leaf Sunflower
Statice
Strawflower

ANNUALS—WHERE TO SOW

Plant these where they are to grow

Adonis
Anchusa
Babys-breath
Balsam
Blue Lace-flower
California-poppy
Calliopsis
Callirhoe
Campanula
Candytuft
Cape-marigold

Centaurea
Collinsia
Collomia
Cynoglossum
Echium
Emilia
Evening-primrose
Flax
Four-o'clock
Gilia
Godetia

Hunnemannia
Larkspur
Lavatera
Limnanthes
Linaria
Love-in-a-mist
Lupine
Lychnis
Malope
Mignonette
Morning-glory

Nasturtium
Nemophila
Phacelia
Phlox Drummondi
Platystemon
Poppy, Iceland
Poppy, Shirley

Poppy, Tulip
Portulaca
Prickly-poppy
Rudbeckia
Scarlet-runner Bean
Sea-poppy

Snow-on-the-mountain
Sunflower
Swan River Everlasting
Sweet Alyssum
Sweet Pea
Virginia-stock

Start these indoors

Abronia
Ageratum
Alonsoa
Begonia semperflorens
Browallia
China-aster
Clarkia
Cobaea scandens
Cuphea
Dahlia
Datura

Echium
Everlasting
Flax
Gerberia
Heliotrope
Hunnemannia
Lantana
Limonium
Lobelia
Mesembryanthemum
Nemesia

Nierembergia
Pelargonium
Petunia (hybrids)
Salpiglossis
Scabiosa
Senecio
Snapdragon
Sweet Sultan
Tithonia
Verbena

Annuals which self-sow

Ageratum
Babys-breath
Balsam
Browallia
Calendula
California-poppy
Calliopsis
Candytuft
Centaurea
Clarkia
Cleome
Cosmos
Four-o'clock

Foxglove
Gaillardia
Godetia
Honesty
Kenilworth-ivy
Larkspur
Love-in-a-mist
Love-lies-bleeding
Marigold
Morning-glory
Nicotiana
Pansy
Petunia

Poppy, Iceland
Poppy, Shirley
Portulaca
Prickly-poppy
Salvia
Snapdragon
Snow-on-the-mountain
Summer-cypress
Sunflower
Sweet Alyssum
Torenia
Virginia-stock
Zinnia (especially Mexicans)

ANNUALS WITH SHORT SEASON OF BLOOM
(Make Successive Plantings)

Babys-breath
Calliopsis
Candytuft
Cape-marigold
Cornflower
Love-in-a-mist

Love-lies-bleeding
Mignonette
Phlox Drummondi
Swan River Daisy
Sweet Alyssum

Short Season Biennials

Cheiranthus
English Daisy
Foxglove
Sweet William

ANNUALS FOR SPECIAL CONDITIONS
Dry and Hot

California-poppy
Calliopsis
Cape-marigold
Celosia
Cleome
Cornflower
Four-o'clock
Gaillardia
Gourds
Gypsophila

Mesembryanthemum
Nolana
Perilla
Phacelia
Phlox Drummondi
Poppy
Portulaca
Prickly-poppy
Rudbeckia
Sand-verbena

Sanvitalia
Scarlet Sage
Snow-on-the-mountain
Star-of-the-desert
Star-of-Texas
Statice
Summer-cypress
Sunflower
Tassel-flower
Zinnia (Mexican)

Moist and Cool

Anchusa
Blue Lace-flower
Blue Woodruff
Calendula
Campanula (Annual
   Canterbury Bells)
Candytuft
Datura

Dianthus
Forget-me-not
Hibiscus (Mallow)
Maskflower
Monkey Flower
Nemesia
Nemophila (Baby
   Blue-eyes)

Nicotiana
Oenothera
Polygonum
Sweet Pea
Summer-cypress
Torenia
Verbena

Full Sun

Ageratum
Anagallis
Arctotis
Babys-breath
Bells-of-Ireland

Browallia
California-poppy
Castor-bean
Datura
Everlasting

Gaillardia
Gilia
Godetia
Gourds
Hunnemannia

Love-in-a-mist
Marigold
Mignonette
Moonflower
Morning-glory
Nasturtium
Petunia
Poppy, Iceland
Poppy, Shirley

Poppy, Tulip
Portulaca
Salpiglossis
Scabiosa
Scarlet Sage
Sea-poppy
Silene armeria
Star-of-Texas
Stock

Summer-cypress
Sunflower
Swan River Daisy
Sweet Pea
Thunbergia
Tithonia
Vinca rosea
Zinnia

Part Shade, Light

Anchusa
Begonia semperflorens
Calliopsis
Calendula
Campanula
China-aster
Celosia
Centaurea
Clarkia
Cleome

Cosmos
Cynoglossum
Dianthus
Dusty Miller
English Daisy
Evening-primrose
Feverfew
Honesty
Larkspur
Lobelia

Lupine
Petunia
Phlox Drummondi
Salvia farinacea
Salvia patens
Schizanthus
Snapdragon
Sweet Alyssum
Tassel-flower
Verbena

Part Shade, Heavy

Balsam
Collinsia
Forget-me-not
Foxglove

Godetia
Lobelia
Monkey Flower
Nemophila

Nicotiana
Pansy
Torenia
Virginia-stock

Rich Loam

Arctotis
Candytuft
Castor-bean
Celosia
China-aster
Cobaea scandens
Datura
Helenium
Marigold
Nicotiana

Pansy
Salpiglossis
Salvia farinacea
Salvia patens
Salvia splendens
Snapdragon
Summer-cypress
Sweet pea
Verbena
Zinnia

TENDER BULBS

Caladium
Calla-lily
Canna
Dahlia
Ismene
Tuberous Begonia
Tuberose

Sandy Loam

Anoda
Babys-breath
Balsam
Cape-marigold
Clarkia
Chrysanthemum
Cosmos
Cynoglossum
Gaillardia
Godetia
Hunnemannia
Larkspur (rich soil)

Mesembryanthemum
Mignonette
Nigella
Phlox Drummondi
Poppies
Poppy Mallow
Prickly-poppy
Silene armeria
Snow-on-the-mountain
Star-of-Texas
Stock (rich soil)
Sunflower

Sweet Alyssum
Tahoka-daisy
Tithonia

TENDER BULBS

Acidanthera
Gladiolus
Montbretia
Oxalis
Tigridia

Tolerate Poor Soil

Balsam
Blue Woodruff
California-poppy
Calliopsis
Celosia
Centaurea
Cleome

Four-o'clock
Gaillardia
Godetia
Love-lies-bleeding
Mentzelia
Mesembryanthemum
Morning-glory

Moss Verbena
Nasturtium
Perilla
Poppies
Portulaca
Sweet Alyssum

Tolerate City Conditions

FULL SUN

California-poppy
Celosia
Four-o'clock

Geranium
Marigold
Morning-glory

Portulaca
Zinnia

PART OR LIGHT SHADE

Anchusa
Begonia semperflorens
Calliopsis
Celosia

China-aster
Cleome
Cobaea scandens
Cornflower

Forget-me-not
Lobelia
Petunia
Torenia

For Seashore

Candytuft
Cheiranthus
Chrysanthemum
Cornflower
Cosmos

Dianthus
Dusty Miller
Gaillardia
Godetia
Hibiscus

Horned- or Sea-poppy
Larkspur
Lupine
Marigold
Mesembryanthemum

Mignonette
Petunia
Portulaca
Scabiosa
Snow-on-the-mountain
Statice

Sweet Alyssum
Sweet Pea
Sunflower
Tassel-flower
Vinca rosea
Zinnia

TENDER BULBS

Calla-lily
Gladiolus
Montbretia
Tigridia

PART TWO
— GENERAL CULTURE

CHAPTER 6. *Soils and Fertilizers*

Of the several groups of garden flowers, annuals are the most easily satisfied so far as soil is concerned. Most of them are comparatively shallow-rooting and do not require as deep a soil as is needed for perennials, bulbs, and shrubs. Feeding near the surface, they are more easily supplied with plant food and with moisture.

Annuals have an additional advantage, too, in that under adverse conditions most of them will not die or fail to produce flowers but struggle along even if stunted in growth, and manage to bloom. Such is their inherent urge to carry out Nature's command to reproduce their kind that they will usually flower and set some seeds even when they attain but a small fraction of their normal size.

Some annuals, in fact, must be restricted to a rather meager diet if they are to bloom bountifully. Nasturtiums, Portulaca, and Morning-glories are cases in point. Most annuals can easily be overfed to a degree which will prevent their flowering as freely as they should. Only last summer I was visiting the garden of a new and sometimes overenthusiastic gardener who proudly showed me a large bed of Marigolds growing about as luxuriantly as Skunk-cabbages in a swamp. When we asked if we might take a photograph of it she said, "Oh, not now. Wait until it is in full bloom."

"But," I said, "it never will be in full bloom." We wanted a picture showing what *not* to do. These plants had been entirely too well taken care of. She didn't believe us; even made a bet. But when we visited the garden again some weeks later there were few if any more flowers and she sadly conceded with the remark, "Live and learn," that we had been right.

SOIL TYPES AND THEIR IMPROVEMENT

This is not the place to go into an extensive discussion of soils and how to handle them, but for the benefit of the beginner who

Overfeeding with fertilizer high in nitrogen often results in luxurious foliage but few flowers.

may have had little experience in this field, a brief discussion may be in order.

Let us state at the very beginning that, wherever you live, and whatever type of soil you have, there will be some—yes, many—annuals that you can grow. The list of annuals now available to gardeners includes species from all parts of the world. Most of them are extremely obliging in the way they adapt themselves to conditions other than those under which they naturally grow. Plant breeders, working patiently and persistently through the years, have created hybrids or selected strains and sports, extending still further the amazing tolerances already possessed by most species of annuals. Cosmos, for instance, normally a long-season plant requiring twelve to fourteen weeks to come into flower, is now to be had in early-flowering strains that require only about ten.

But let us return to our soils.

There are three general types of soils: sand, clay, and loam. The latter is a mixture of the other two. Where sand predominates, we speak of a sandy soil; and where clay predominates, of a clayey soil. Sometimes the latter is referred to as a "heavy" soil. This term is due not to the relative weights of the two materials but to the fact that clay retains moisture and is tenacious and difficult to dig or plow, while sand loses water rapidly, is open and porous and therefore easy to "work."

This brings us to the very important factor of drainage. To function properly, plant roots need water; but they also require air, a fact which many gardeners, even experienced ones, often fail to realize fully. A loam soil, having the characteristics of both sand and clay, permits surplus water (which excludes air from the soil) to drain off freely while at the same time retaining a sufficient amount to support normal plant growth.

Subdrainage is quite as important as drainage in the top layer of soil. Sometimes the subsoil is so dense or so hard that it prevents the escape of water that has drained down through the surface layer. In extreme cases—fortunately not frequently encountered—this may result in the actual drowning of plants or even large trees. In such circumstances a system of drainage tile to carry the water off to some lower level must be resorted to. Ordinarily, however, the simple expedient of making raised beds with paths between them on a level four to eight inches lower will serve.

The improvement of small areas of soils which are too sandy or too clayey is usually not a very difficult matter. The addition of heavier soil or of ordinary topsoil to the former or of sand to the latter will accomplish the purpose. It need merely be spread over the surface two to four inches deep and forked in. Raw ground limestone, oddly enough, will improve the mechanical structure of both sandy soils and clay soils. The application may be as heavy as ten to twenty pounds per hundred square feet. Half the amount should be applied and dug well under; the other half spread on the surface and lightly forked in. This will assure more even distribution than when the full amount is applied at one time. Lime, however, should not be applied where the soil is already alkaline—that is, if it shows a pH reading of 7 or more; or where plants requiring an acid soil are to be grown. The degree of acidity or alkalinity of a soil is denoted by what is known as the pH scale, in which readings bleow pH 7 indicate the degree of acidity, and those above pH 7 (which is neutral) the degree of alkalinity. Various simple soil-testing kits with which the home gardener can do his own testing are available. Or a sample of soil may be sent to one's local county agent or state experiment station for a report.

Humus, like lime, is helpful in improving the texture of both sandy soils and clay soils. Humus is a general term applied to vegetable or other organic matter in a state of partial decomposition. May be purchased in the form of peatmoss, of commercial humus obtained from old lake bottoms or drained swamp areas, or from the gardener's own compost pile. The ideal form of humus is partly decomposed stable manure; but this, of course, except in rural areas, is extremely difficult to procure in these days. A layer of peatmoss or of commercial humus, two to four inches thick, applied to the surface and then forked into the top six inches of soil, will go far toward assuring an excellent growth of annual plants. In addition to its beneficial effect in improving the texture of the soil itself, it will absorb and hold for future use surplus moisture that would otherwise drain away, and will also retain, along with this moisture, soluble plant foods. When you add humus to the soil, you open a bank account for your plants. They can draw against the deposit whenever the need arises.

PLANT FOODS FOR ANNUALS

When these steps have been taken, you have set the table for the feast you wish to prepare for your annuals. The next step is to bring on the food—keeping in mind, of course, that, as has already been suggested, it is possible to provide too rich a diet.

All growing plants require certain chemicals in the soil. There are a dozen or so of these, but all except three of them are usually present in sufficient quantities in most soils.

The big three which need concern you most are nitrogen, phosphorus, and potash. The plant scientists tell us that nitrogen is especially important in producing succulent growth and that it delays maturity; that phosphorus hastens maturity and encourages the development of flowers and the production of seeds; that potash helps to control too great a tendency toward succulence and the consequent brittleness of stalks and stems, and also tends to intensify flower colors.

This knowledge is extremely helpful to us in planning the main course in the banquet we wish to provide for our plants, and also the side dishes which it may be desirable to present to them later on as they grow and develop.

Much is written these days about organic *versus* chemical plant foods—the ones which are ordinarily referred to as "fertilizers." In our book there is no such word as "versus" in this connection. The phrase should be organic *and* chemical fertilizers.

It is perfectly true that excellent flowers (and fruits and vegetables as well) can be grown without the use of chemical plant foods—particularly if one lives where animal manures are available. It is equally true that just as fine flowers can be grown with chemical plant foods alone *if* the soil contains a sufficient amount of humus. We believe that the sensible gardener, under conditions usually encountered, will employ both organic and chemical materials. To back up this position, we have had, between us, something over a hundred years' experience.

Applying humus and plant food

As a general rule, the further in advance of seed sowing and of planting, humus and fertilizers can be applied and the deeper they can be worked down into the soil, the better. In each case, however, there is one important exception. Fertilizers that contain quickly available nitrogen—such as nitrate of soda, ammonium sulphate, tankage, and the quick-action high-nitrogen soluble fertilizers now recommended as "plant starters" in transplanting—should be applied only shortly before seeds are sown or plants set out, or during the early stages of growth.

In very light, sandy soils so open in character that water is carried down through them quickly, it is best to keep fertilizers near the surface, as otherwise much of the nutrients they contain will be carried away and lost through leaching.

As for the amount to apply, in the case of humus it is almost impossible to get too much. Peatmoss, humus, sawdust, and similar materials should be put on at least two inches thick; double that amount is even better. This is dug or otherwise worked into the surface of the soil about four inches deep if the soil is very light and sandy, or to twice that depth in heavier soils.

The standard rate of application for chemical fertilizers is three to five pounds per hundred square feet. Most soils will benefit from the heavier application, particularly for the first year or two. After that, if growth is entirely satisfactory, the amount may be reduced. Where seeds are to be sown or plants set out it is always desirable to get the soil prepared two or three weeks in advance. This gives an opportunity for the weed seeds which may be present to germinate; then when the surface is given a final raking over just before sowing or planting, the weed seedlings will be destroyed thus giving the flowers a running start with little competition from weeds until the flowers become well established.

CHAPTER *7. Starting Seedlings*

While the seeds of most annuals can be sown in the open ground, the gardener will find many advantages in starting some of them indoors and thus having a supply of growing plants ready to set out in the open. The equipment required to accomplish this is neither complicated nor expensive. No greenhouse is needed, and even a cold frame, while desirable, is not essential.

One reason for starting annuals indoors is that there are several very desirable ones which require a long season of growth before they come into flower and which, if sown in the open in northern latitudes, are likely to be cut off in their prime by early frosts. Among these are Aster, Salvia, Tithonia, and Verbena.

Then, too, the gardener likes to have some show of color in his garden as early as possible. Many of the faster-growing annuals—such as Alyssum, Lobelia, Marigold, and *Phlox Drummondi*—can, if started under glass, be had in bud or bloom by the time they are set out in the open garden.

It is true that one may buy growing plants from a florist or a road-side market. But in the first place this is more expensive; and in the second it usually is not possible to get just the varieties one may want, for the commercial grower naturally is limited as to the number of varieties he can handle and must stick to those for which there is the greatest popular demand.

Furthermore, if you grow your own plants, you have them on hand, properly hardened off, and ready to set out when conditions are just right—a matter that may mean the difference between success and failure.

Above all else, however, are the fun you will get out of growing your own plants and the increased knowledge concerning them which you will acquire. These can be obtained in no other way.

The time when seed should be sown indoors is dictated by several different factors. First of these is the climate in which they are being grown. Usually six to eight weeks are required, after seed sowing, to produce plants large enought to set out. Hardy species, which will withstand some frost, may therefore be started six to eight weeks before outdoor planting can be begun.

In the latitude of New York, Chicago, and Kansas City, where soil is usually ready for planting about April first to fifteenth, the date for indoor sowing of *hardy* seeds would be about February fifteenth to March first. Further south or north it would be proportionately earlier or later. Tender varieties would be started two to three weeks later than the hardy sorts, except for those requiring an unusually long time to come into flower.

Annuals wanted for immediate bloom in the garden should be started as early as mid-January to mid-February. These will usually require a second transplanting and proportionately more space indoors or in a hot bed.

The place. The directions for starting annuals given in the following pages apply to procedures which can be carried on in any house that has one or more windows that receive direct sunshine for the greater part of the day. In fact, many enthusiastic gardeners manage to start their plants without benefit of sunlight by employing electric lights. This method has indeed several distinct advantages, in that heat and moisture can be more readily and more uniformly controlled, and the work can be carried on in a cellar or a storeroom without the danger of "mussing up" living quarters. The details of such an indoor plant nursery are illustrated on page 101.

A greenhouse is, of course, the ideal place in which to grow plants. Not everyone, however, is so fortunate as to possess a greenhouse, but the number of those who manage, through one method or another, to obtain one is increasing rapidly. As a substitute for a greenhouse the electrically heated hotbed, which can either be bought as a unit or constructed by any handy tinkerer, finds favor with many. Any gardener with a few pieces of board and some 2 x 4 stakes can knock together a coldframe of sorts. Old window sash will answer for a cover; or one of the plastic substitutes for glass now available, tacked to a wooden frame, will do. Many dozens of seedlings can be started in a single sunny window. The pinch comes when they reach the stage at which they should be transplanted.

This is usually late enough so that even the crudest kind of a cold-frame, if it is fairly tight, will keep out the late frosts likely to be encountered.

EQUIPMENT REQUIRED

Before seed sowing is begun it is advisable to provide some sort of table or bench in the sunniest spot available on which the flower-pots or flats in which the seeds are to be started may be kept while they are germinating and growing to transplanting size.

To prepare the mixture in which the seeds are to be started, the following materials are required:

Sifted, light garden loam, peatmoss, and sharp, gritty sand (the type used by masons for mixing cement). To these may be added, for special purposes, sphagnum moss and vermiculite, but the beginner will not need them.

To hold the soil mixture in which the seeds are to be sown several flowerpots or, better still, bulb pans (which are merely shallow flower-

Here's what you need for starting seeds—mixed compost, containers, drainage material, labels—and, of course, seeds.

pots), ranging in diameter from four to six inches, and flowerpot saucers to go under them are needed. Small, shallow boxes or flats, two to three inches deep and of any convenient size, may be used in lieu of the bulb pans, but for small quantities of seed, such as single packets of a variety, we have found the bulb pans both more convenient and better suited to the job.

Pieces of glass or plastic or, much better, plastic caps or domes such as are used for covering tender seeds sown in the open are needed for covering the planted seeds. These domes can be obtained from most seed houses. If they are not readily available, a satisfactory substitute can be made from kitchen-type Pliofilm, with rubber bands to hold it in place. For very fine, "difficult" seeds, a cake container with a tight plastic cover is ideal.

Sowing

The medium in which seeds are to be sown should be one which will readily absorb and hold moisture and at the same time be so open and porous that any surplus water will quickly drain away. In a soggy, wet soil seeds will rot or fail to germinate; in one that dries out too quickly they are likely to shrivel up and die during the period of emergence from the soil, or during the few days following it, when their minute root systems are just being formed.

To obtain a seed-starting medium which will be sufficiently absorbent to retain moisture and at the same time let the surplus water drain away, mix together soil, peatmoss, and sand. The rule-of-thumb recommendations usually given are one third of each ingredient. If these proportions are taken by volume, there is likely to be more sand than is needed. If they are made by weight, with the sand dry and the soil and peatmoss slightly moist, the result will be about right. Much depends, however, upon the quality of the soil used and how much clay it contains. A clay soil requires more sand to counteract it. Personally, instead of soil we use a sifted compost from a heap to which some soil is added as it is built, and consequently the proportions of peatmoss and sand are somewhat reduced. With a little practice the gardener can tell when enough sand has been added to "cut" the soil mixture so that it will always remain loose and friable.

In recent years many experiments have been made in the use of

Calendula seedlings started in soil-peatmoss-sand compost and (at extreme right) in garden soil. Difference in roots retained in transplanting is noticeable.

various media, such as sphagnum moss, vermiculite, pure sand, and other materials, for starting seedlings. We have tried all of these and have yet to find one more satisfactory, all things considered, than the mixture described above. And we find that most experienced gardeners, especially in the commerical field, where seedlings are started by the hundreds of thousands, agree with us. Pure vermiculite has the two advantages of being entirely sterile (thus preventing the possibility of soil-borne diseases and pests) and of providing excellent drainage. Its chief disadvantage is the fact that as soon as seeds come up they must be watered regularly with a plant-food solution, as there is no nourishment in the sterile vermiculite itself.

Sterilizing the soil, to eradicate weed seeds and for certain disease organisms, may be accomplished in any of three ways. The simplest is to heat the compost—thoroughly moist but not wet—in a deep pan in the oven for forty-five minutes at a temperature of 200 to 250°. (Keep ventilating fan going; the odor is not too pleasant!)

Or fill an ordinary florist's flat (about 13 x 20 x 3") with the compost, sprinkle it with one teaspoonful of formaldehyde, and mix thoroughly. Then sow seeds, subirrigate, and cover with several layers of moist newspaper for twenty-four hours. Flat may then be removed to a suitable place for germination.

Or prepare containers, sow seeds, and sprinkle surface with solution of Anti-damp, 1 part to 100 parts water.

With the soil mixture prepared, the next step is to fill the containers. Ordinarily the use of "crocking"—a layer of broken flowerpot shards over the bottom of the bulb pan—is recommended. We have found a layer of any coarse material, such as compost screenings, gravel, or lumps of sphagnum moss, equally good. This may be an inch or so in depth. On top of this the prepared soil mixture is filled in to within half an inch of the rim. Then this is pressed down with any convenient tamper—the bottom of a flowerpot will answer—until it is firm and smooth on the surface.

In the case of extremely fine seeds such as those of Petunia or Begonia, we sift the top half inch of soil through an old sink strainer to get an extra-fine, smooth surface.

Now we are ready for the delicate job of sowing the seed. Perhaps the most common of all mistakes which beginners are likely to make is that of sowing too thickly. Once a packet of seed is opened, they hate to "waste" any of it by not using every seed. The result is overcrowded and spindly seedlings, most of which may have to be thrown away while even those that are saved are not so good as they should be, and may never recover from the slum conditions they had to contend with in infancy. Fairly large seeds, such as those of Zinnia, Dahlia, and Calendula, should be dropped one eighth to a quarter of an inch apart; medium-sized ones (Aster, Marigold, and Balsam), somewhat less; and very fine seeds (Petunias, Begonia, and Portulaca), one sixteenth to one eighth of an inch apart. Always keep in mind that the seedlings, no matter how soon they are transplanted after they come up, need more space than the seeds themselves occupied.

Garden of annuals on a slope—brilliant color for weeks on end.

Don't sow too thickly. *If you do, you may get a thick mat of spindly seedlings (as at right) instead of seedlings with room to develop (left).* BELOW: *Fairly large seeds may be spaced evenly in rows instead of being scattered.*

Never attempt to sow seeds by sprinkling them from the package. It is next to impossible to get even distribution if you do this. If you have many seeds to sow, we strongly recommend that you add to your equipment a gadget for sowing seed by hand. Most seed houses list one of the several which are available. A sheet of stiff, smooth paper cut in the shape of a long V and folded to form a miniature trough will prove helpful in getting even distribution.

Disinfecting. A disease of seedlings known as "damping-off" is the seed starter's greatest enemy. As a precaution against this and other seed- and soil-borne diseases, we treat all seeds with Arasan, Rootone, or one of the other protectants available. The cost is infinitesimal, and the smallest-sized package or jar will treat scores of packets of seed. Most seedlings will come through all right without your taking this precaution, but the one or two lots it may help to save will be worth all the trouble involved.

Covering. After the seeds are sown they are pressed down firmly into the soil so that they are in close contact with it rather than just lying on the surface. Now we again make use of the sink strainer to sift over them a layer of the starting mixture with some extra sand added to it. Large seeds are covered an eighth of an inch or slightly more, and medium-sized ones about half this depth.

When it comes to extremely fine seed, however, the soil covering is omitted and in its place we use sphagnum moss or, if that is not available, vermiculite. The moss should be fairly dry so it can be rubbed through a fine screen. We use the sink strainer, letting the moss fall in place until the seed—which has been pressed down lightly into the soil surface—is covered from sight by a layer scarcely more than a sixteenth of an inch thick. The advantages of the moss are that it is sterile, light, and above all retains moisture just *at the surface,* thus preventing the very minute seedlings from being inadvertently dried off during the first critical days, when even a few hours without moisture may cause them to perish. Vermiculite may be used in the same way, but we prefer the moss.

Moisture. This question of moisture in relation to seed starting can hardly be overemphasized. It is, however, dangerous to get the surface so wet that in drying out it may form a crust. To prevent this, after the seeds are sown we water from the bottom up instead of from the top down. This is accomplished by setting the seed pans or flats in water two or more inches deep until the soil in the con-

Pans or flats are best moistened—after seed is sown—by letting water soak up from below.

tainers has absorbed all it will hold and moisture *begins* to show on the surface. Then they are removed, allowed to drain for an hour or so, and transferred to the places allotted them. From then on until the seedlings are large enough to transplant they are never watered from the top, but either kept in saucers where they can be subwatered as needed or again given a drink in the pan or the kitchen sink. With a little experience one soon becomes conscious of the difference in weight as the soil begins to dry out and can readily determine when another drink is needed.

As a further precaution against the surface drying out, the bulb pan or flat may be covered with a pane of glass or plastic or, better yet, one of the plastic domes or a sheet of pliofilm previously mentioned. (See illustrations pages 93 and 101.) Such a covering for the seed pan is particularly desirable where seedlings are being started in a living room where central heating—especially steam— keeps the air constantly dry.

Temperature. The seeds of most hardy annuals (and biennials and perennials) will germinate readily in a temperature of 45 to 60 degrees. The semi-hardy and tender kinds appreciate ten degrees or so higher. The lower temperatures in most cases result in slower germination.

In starting seeds in a house the problem more often is to find a place that is cool enough rather than one that is warm enough. Too high a temperature is sure to result in spindly and weak seedlings. Often there is available somewhere a cooler spot where some sort of enclosure, such as a large box with a sliding door, can be rigged up to take the containers in which the seeds have been planted and within which the temperatures can be regulated as desired by means of electric light bulbs. An extension cord with a double socket and two 60-watt bulbs, one or both of which can be turned off part of the time, will usually provide sufficient control without the necessity of using a thermostat. If a considerable number of plants are to be started and grown up to transplanting size, two fluorescent tubes, one blue and one white, so arranged that they can be kept about twelve inches above the growing plants, give satisfactory results.

Bottom heat. Where proper conditions for getting the seedlings to germinate are not readily available, the bulb pans or flats in which they have been sown may be set in some warm place *just until the germinating plants break through the soil.* A couple of bricks placed on top of a radiator or the furnace, supporting a board on which the containers are placed, will do the trick. Containers should be kept covered to retain moisture and keep soil surface moist.

Light. While most seeds germinate readily in the dark or in subdued light, they must be given full light and preferably direct sunshine just as soon as they get aboveground. Even two or three days' neglect in this respect is likely to cause them to be so weak and gangling that they will never develop into first-class seedlings. Even when placed in a window in full sunshine, they draw toward the light. The seed pans or flats should therefore be turned frequently to maintain an upright, even growth.

Air. In nature, plants grow in the open and learn to accommodate themselves to rather extreme fluctuations in temperature.

Bottom heat—supplied here by placing seed pans over radiator—hastens germination. Saucers provide moisture for soil. Surface soil is kept moist by plastic domes, which maintain humidity. Fluorescent light overhead pinch-hits for sunshine until seedlings are well started.

After your seedlings are well up, use every opportunity to supply them with all the fresh air you can. A draft from an open window will not harm them, provided the temperature does not fall below freezing. On warm, sunny days they may be set on a window sill (where there is no danger of their being knocked off!) or even in a sheltered spot out of doors.

TRANSPLANTING AND GROWING ON

In from two to four weeks, under favorable conditions, the little seedlings will have begun to develop their true leaves and be ready for transplanting. The earlier this is done, the better, even if the seedlings are not crowded. If they are crowded, delay in transplanting may result in failure.

Seedlings transplanted into flat of prepared compost. True leaves, between spatula-shaped seed leaves (cotyledons), have just begun to develop.

Transplanting is usually done into flats, but where only six to a dozen plants of a variety are wanted, a six-, seven-, or eight-inch bulb pan will make a convenient container. If the seedlings are not crowded, they may be allowed to go somewhat longer and then transferred directly to individual small pots. In this case, however, they will take up much more room.

The soil used for transplanting is the same as that used for starting the seedlings, except that the sand may be reduced in amount or entirely omitted. Also, as they will now be ready to make rapid growth, they will need abundant plant food. Our own method of supplying this is to mix one part of bone meal with three of Driconure or Bovung and add one quart of this to a half bushel of the transplanting soil, mixing it thoroughly. Many gardeners use other fertilizers or special formulas for this purpose, but over the years we have found nothing more satisfactory. Too much nitrogen at this stage of the game should be avoided, as it will result in quick, succulent growth instead of the short-jointed, tough, stocky plants that better withstand being transferred to the open later on.

For a day or two before transplanting we withhold water so that the soil in which the seedlings are growing is on the dry side. This is contrary to the instructions often given, but we believe that thirsty plants will take hold much more quickly when transferred to their new environment.

In removing the seedlings from their seed bed, much care must be taken to avoid injuring the delicate root systems. Never pull a seedling from the soil, as this will strip it of the tiny feeding root hairs.

To remove the seedlings from the soil in which they have been growing, we use a homemade transplanting stick which is flattened to a thin spatula shape at one end and tapered to a blunt point a little larger than a lead pencil at the other. The flat end is convenient for removing seedlings in a group of a dozen or so at a time, and when these have been carefully separated the other end is used for making holes in which the seedlings are inserted. (See photograph page 102.)

There are two serious mistakes which the beginner at transplanting is likely to make. The first is failure to get the seedlings into the

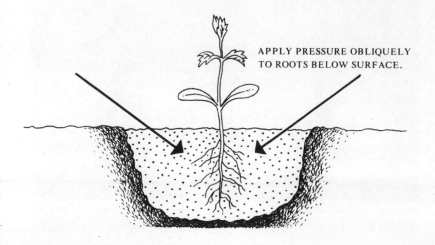

APPLY PRESSURE OBLIQUELY
TO ROOTS BELOW SURFACE.

soil as deep as they should go, and the second is firming the soil about the stem at the surface instead of making sure that it is pressed close around the roots *below* the surface. The diagram on page 103 shows how the job should be done.

If you are transplanting into a flat, fill it level-full of the prepared soil, press the surface down firmly but not too hard to a half inch below the rim, and mark off rows two inches apart with the edge of a foot ruler or a long wooden label. The seedlings should be spaced about two inches apart in the rows. Spacing will depend both on the character of the particular plants being grown and upon whether they will be given a second transplanting (usually into pots or dirt bands) before being transferred to the open ground. In the latter case they may be set more closely together.

The soil in the flat or bulb pan to which the seedlings are being transferred should be sufficiently moist so that the holes will not crumble and fill up with soil before the seedlings are lowered into them to the proper depth. Immediately after transplanting, we give a thorough subwatering by placing the pans in an inch or two of water and leaving them until moisture *begins* to show on the surface. Then

Flat and seed pans watered from bottom.

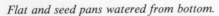

they are promptly removed and drained. No overhead watering is given until the seedlings have become firmly established and are capable of withstanding spray from a hose or watering can without being knocked over.

During the first few days after transplanting, the seedlings should be kept shaded from direct sunshine. As soon as they have recovered sufficiently to show no indication of wilting, they are given all the direct sunshine possible.

Second transplanting

Seedlings which have been started very early—such as those species which require a long season to come into bloom or those which it is desired to have in flower as early as possible out of doors—may be given a second transplanting from flats into pots or dirt bands. Dirt bands are merely bottomless boxes of wood veneer or treated tar paper which can be packed shoulder to shoulder into a flat. They have several advantages over flowerpots in that they are much less expensive, hold more soil in proportion to their diameter, and fit closely together, so that they dry out much less rapidly than flowerpots. Furthermore, they may be used as protectors against cutworms when the plants are set in the garden. (See page 106.)

After transplanting, your little plants will require about the same care as they did before; i.e., all the sunshine you can give them and fresh air on every possible occasion.

If a coldframe has been provided, as soon as the plants have become well established and growth has been renewed—which should be in a week or so—they may be transferred to the frame. A supply of old burlap bags or an old blanket or two should be kept handy to cover the glass on nights when the thermometer is likely to drop below freezing. This is particularly important in the case of tender species. The hardy kinds, after they have been out for a few days, will not be injured by a few degrees below freezing within the frame.

Hardening off. Before either hardy or tender plants are transferred from the frame to the open garden they should be given less and less protection and finally left for a few days and nights with the glass sash entirely removed, so that they may become inured to the conditions they will encounter after being set out.

Seedling Petunia plant grown in dirt band. Lateral shoots beginning to develop.
BELOW: Seedling plants in dirt bands, placed in flats, transferred to coldframe
for hardening-off period.

Where no coldframe is available, the same procedure should be followed: the plants are transferred from indoors to an open porch or a very protected spot against a fence or a building for a few days and nights before they are set out in the open garden.

Digitalis seedlings in bulb pan.

Removed, ready for transplanting. BELOW: *Seedlings in both pots* from same sowing: *compare untransplanted ones (left) with those removed and transplanted (right.)*

CHAPTER 8. *Sowing and Planting*

Important as the advantages are, for special purposes and in special places, of getting a running start by planting seeds indoors, nevertheless the general practice is to sow them in the open ground where they are to bloom.

How to prepare the soil and the advantages of preparing it as early as possible in the season have already been discussed, so we can assume that the gardener, with seed packets on hand and his or her green thumb twitching to begin actually getting some seeds into the ground, is growing impatient.

What is the signal for starting?

We used to say that the really hardy annuals could be planted as soon as it was safe to plant garden peas. But nowadays, when very few people know anything about planting peas (or, for that matter, what real peas taste like, being familiar only with the frozen or canned product), it may be better to shift the signals and suggest that they watch for the first opening crocus cups or bursting buds on Forsythia or Japanese Quince. The semi-hardies may follow two or three weeks later and the really tender ones about the time last frosts are to be expected. As it will be a week or ten days before these seeds germinate, it is not essential to wait until *after* the last possible frost date.

The seed bed

Successful germination depends principally upon two factors. The first of these is the condition of the soil immediately around and in contact with the seeds, and the second is the maintenance of a constant supply of moisture just at and immediately below the surface until the seeds have sprouted and seedlings have commenced to grow. The smaller the seeds are, the more imperative these conditions become.

If the soil has already been prepared in accordance with the suggestions given in Chapter 7, all that will be needed now is a final going over with a steel rake (or, for very small areas, with a finger-type hand weeder) to break up any crust that may have formed and to destroy sprouting weed seedlings. This should leave a smooth, finely pulverized surface. If, however, the soil is inclined to remain rough and lumpy, further preparation will be required if you want to be sure of success in getting good germination with your flower seeds, particularly with those that are very small. This consists in scooping out the soil for a depth of two or three inches in the areas where seeds are to be sown, and filling these depressions with a compost similiar to that suggested for starting seeds indoors. This means a little extra work, but it will be time well spent. Where seeds are to be sown over fairly large areas, much the same result can be obtained by adding a couple of inches of peatmoss and/or vermiculite and then working it into the surface soil. This of course saves some labor as compared with the other method but will not give quite as sure-fire results.

Pre-watering

It sometimes happens that the gardener must do his seed sowing when the soil is much drier than it should be for best results. Or-

When sowing in dry soil, open furrow and soak thoroughly before *distributing seed. Here porous canvas hose (Soil-soaker) is used to saturate soil.*

dinarily he sows the seed and then waters the surface afterward. If he gives only a light sprinkle, this does little good. If he attempts to give a thorough soaking, the surface of the soil is likely to be puddled and, with an ordinary hose spray, some of the seed is apt to be washed out.

A much better method is to give the soil a thorough soaking a day or so in advance of planting. If the seed is to be sown in rows, a furrow three inches or so in depth may be opened up and flooded with water two or three times in succession until it will not readily absorb more. Then fine soil is filled in to bring the row almost level with the surface, and the seed is sown. Where surface areas are watered heavily in this way, it is desirable to rake them over gently to break up any crust that may be forming before sowing the seed.

SOWING

It is a good plan when seed packets are received to separate them into hardy, half-hardy, and tender groups and then place all the packets of each type in separate boxes, or at least fasten them together with rubber bands. This saves time and confusion when it comes to sowing. Another time-saving step is to have labels prepared in advance so that you will not have to bother with making them out during planting operations.

If a planting plan has been prepared as advised earlier in this volume, you will know just where each variety is to go and the approximate space it will occupy. After final preparation has been given the surface of the seed bed, these areas may be marked off with a pointed stick; or if you wish something more permanent that will remain until all the seeds have germinated, narrow ribbons of sand may be applied with a watering can from which the sprinkler head has been removed.

For sowing operations, select a time when there is no wind stirring. This is most likely to be early in the morning. A further advantage of early-morning sowing is that the distribution of fine seeds can be observed more readily than during the midday hours.

While not essential, it is desirable to treat all seeds with a protectant such as Arasan or Rootone (see page 97). The remarks made in the previous chapter about distributing the seed, the depth to which it should be covered, and precautions against sowing too

Always thin out seedlings left to grow in rows! Seedling at right from thinned-out row; those on left from unthinned row, same variety sown at same time.

thickly apply also to sowing seeds out of doors. The danger of too thick sowing out of doors is, if anything, more disastrous than indoors, for the little seedlings in most instances will not be transplanted and in this way given more space in which to develop. Even when seed is sown as scantily as it should be, a considerable thinning out of surplus plants is likely to be necessary in order that all those remaining will have the amount of air and elbow room they require. If seedlings come up "thick as hair on a dog," the job of thinning will be an extremely tedious and time-consuming one, and the plants which are to be left are quite likely to be mauled in the process. Where thinning is needed, it should be done at the earliest possible moment: every day's delay increase both the difficulty and the danger involved.

Where the thinning operation has been a severe one, wilting of the seedlings which remain may result. In this case, give a light, very fine mist spray and keep them covered for a day or two with sheets of newspaper held down at the edges with small stones.

Seedlings sown in compost in frame. BELOW: *Thinned out once, now ready for transplanting.*

Extra aids to Sowing

While the suggestions given above, if carefully followed, will result in success with most annuals and biennials, there are some species which are exceedingly fine and others which, regardless of size, are "difficult." With these it will pay to take some extra precautions.

Mixing very tiny seed with fine sand at the rate of one pint to a packet of seed will help in getting more even distribution. The seed, of course, should be very thoroughly mixed with the sand.

Peatmoss rubbed through a fine screen may be used in place of soil or compost for covering the seed after it is distributed and pressed into the soil. The peat, after being put on, should be thoroughly moistened with a mist spray and kept moist until germination takes place.

Heavy, beating rains sometimes pack the surface hard over the seeds, especially those that are slow to germinate, or may wash them out. Pieces of light building paper cut to suitable size or two or three thicknesses of newspaper laid over the planted area will afford protection until germination takes place. If newspapers are used, they should be kept moist. If this type of protection is resorted

Soil-soaker hose applies water directly to roots, without waste.

Supplex hose, with mist-like spray, used for watering seedlings started under hotkaps; and (below) for newly transplanted seedlings.

to, the utmost care must be taken to remove the covering as soon as the seedlings push aboveground.

Surest and safest of all is the use of plastic domes to cover small areas where seeds have been sown. These serve not only as protection from beating rains but also as miniature greenhouses, keeping the soil surface moist and admitting light, so that they do not have to be removed until the seedlings have made a good start.

If you are a beginner, it will be a good idea to read over these suggestions two or three times until you are thoroughly familiar with them. In fact, you will find it well worth while to rehearse the several operations involved by going through all the motions and using radish seeds (which will germinate in four or five days) to make sure that everything operates smoothly. Above all, keep in mind the three important things *not* to do.

Do not sow too thickly.

Do not cover too deeply.

Do not allow the surface of the soil to dry out during the germinating period—even for a day.

SETTING OUT PLANTS

So much for sowing seeds in the open. Now how about those little baby plants raised indoors which we left—at the end of the last chapter—basking in the sunshine in a glass-covered frame to keep their little green noses from being nipped by the cold on a frosty night?

The hardy species, if they have been given suitable exposure to wind and weather, can be transferred to the open ground ten days to two weeks after the first hardy seeds are planted outdoors. We have never found any evidence that planting by the moon— though it has many advocates—produces any outstanding results. We do, however, confess to transplanting by the moon to this extent: time and again—so often that it seems to be more than a mere coincidence—we have observed that the last hard frost occurs at or very close to the full moon. And so when setting-out time arrives we wait a few days if necessary until the old lady has passed her "full" before entrusting our little plants to the vagaries of wind and weather. Our favorite time for "settin' out" is just in advance of a warm, rainy spell, when the ground is sufficiently dry to handle nicely but with a prospect that Nature will do the first watering for us.

Spacing

The distance apart at which annuals are planted varies all the way from four to six inches to two to four feet. The former apply to dwarf plants such as Lobelia, Ageratum, and Alyssum, particularly when they are used for continuous edging; the latter for vigorous tall growers like the giant Zinnias and Marigolds. Annuals usually are planted in fairly large groups or for mass color effects, so that some overcrowding is not only permissible but often desirable. In general, twelve to eighteen inches apart will do even for such vigorous growers as the big Zinnias and Marigolds. Where plants are grown primarily for cut flowers, it is advisable to give them more space than would be required for a show of color in the garden.

Preparation of planting holes is not required if the garden is in good tilth and well enriched. In new ground or in poor soils, better results will be had by digging out a hole where each plant is to go and incorporating a trowelful or two of good compost with the soil in the bottom before setting in the plant. While this will help give the individual plants a stronger start, it will not take the place of using fertilizer over the whole area, because by the time the plants are half grown they will have filled the entire area with roots.

Setting the plants is a simple operation and yet frequently it is improperly done. To begin with, care should be taken in removing the plants if they are growing in flats, to procure with each a good ball of soil about the roots. The soil in the flats should be fairly moist, so that when cut into squares between the plants it will lift out without crumbling off. A small mason's trowel, which has a flat blade, is ideal for this purpose. Wanting that, an old kitchen knife may be used. The ordinary garden trowel is so shaped that it is not a good tool for this particular job.

To remove the plants growing in pots, turn the pot upside down, with the fore and middle fingers of the left hand on either side of the stem, and tap the edge sharply against any wooden surface. Once plants have been removed, they should be got into the planting holes as soon as possible.

Seedlings (above) grown in 2½" "Jiffy" pots; (below) same age, in clay pots.

If seedlings have been grown on in peatmoss composition pots, pot and all can be planted, as roots grow through sides and bottoms.

In setting out the plant, get it well down into the ground so that the soil surface will slightly cover the root ball. Plants that have been grown too close together and as a result are rather lanky may be set considerably deeper, to just below the first leaves. Set them firmly, pressing down and around the root ball with the fingers and/or knuckles, but do not break it apart. A well-set plant should be so firmly embedded in the soil that it cannot readily be pulled up without breaking it.

If at all possible, avoid transplanting in sunny, windy weather. A cloudy day, preferably with anticipated showers, is the ideal. If transplanting must be done when the soil is dry or the sun bright and hot, prepare planting holes in advance and fill them with water, allowing it to soak away before the plants are set in. If despite such precautions as may be taken the plants are inclined to wilt badly, protect with newspapers either spread over the tops or, for individual plants, made into small open-end tents held in place by soil placed along the edges. Old berry baskets can also be used for this purpose.

Plants set out under favorable conditions should take hold quickly and continue to grow without any serious wilting. If wilting does occur, a light wetting with a fine mist spray will help to correct the situation. In very hot or very windy weather it may be desirable to give two or three light waterings per day for the first few days. Soaking the ground with a heavy hose spray until it is a mass of mud, as is done so frequently, is likely to result in more harm than good.

CHAPTER *9. Keeping Them Happy*

With seedlings that have been given a robust start, indoors or out, and that have been properly transplanted or thinned out, the battle for success in growing annuals is more than half won. Their cultural requirements from now on will be simple and demand little time. Many of them, in fact, will grow so vigorously as to be able to hold their own even against weeds and drought. But the gardener who seeks perfection must continue to minister to them in such ways as he may.

The first step in this direction is a light stirring or cultivating of the soil between the plants to establish a fine, loose surface. The operations of transplanting or even of thinning out will have left the soil more or less packed down in spots, especially if it was on the moist side when this work was done. To develop properly, the roots need air as well as moisture and plant food. A loose, friable soil admits air freely. Furthermore, it will quickly absorb and retain rainfall or water applied with the hose.

The most convenient tool for this first light working of the soil around small plants is the finger weeder (of which there are several types), which may be obtained with either a short handle or a longer one to permit its use without kneeling or bending over. We use both types, for sometimes one is more convenient and sometimes the other. Such cultivation should be given frequently enough to prevent the formation of a hard crust, and to destroy weeds while they are still very small—ordinarily once every two weeks or so.

Extra feeding may prove desirable, particularly on new soil. This may be given in the form of a light side dressing three or four weeks after the plants have been set out or thinned out. Use a complete plant food at the rate of two to three pounds per one hundred square feet. Additional feeding is most likely to be needed on new soil which has not been well fertilized and conditioned in previous years. Among commercial growers, the practice of using several supplementary applications of plant food during the growing season has been rapidly gaining in favor, and the home gardener is not likely to overdo in this respect. Slow growth and foilage that is light green or yellowish in color generally indicate that the plants are getting too little nitrogen. In such circumstances an application of a high-nitrogen fertilizer or even of nitrate of soda will prove helpful. Care should be taken, however, not to overdo in this matter, as has already been pointed out.

Out of the mud

Many annuals have a tendency to grow with a single tall center stalk. Except in cases where maximum height is to be desired—for instance, when annual Hollyhock, Cosmos, or Snapdragon may be wanted for a background—it is much better to keep them low and stocky in growth. Single tall stems have two disadvantages. In the first place, they are too likely to be blown over or bent over in heavy rains, with the result that the blooms will be spattered with mud; and in the second, the single tall stems are likely to give one burst of bloom and then cease flowering in short order.

The remedy in such cases is a simple technique known as "pinching back." This is accomplished by merely pinching out the tip of a growing seedling when it has attained three to five true leaves or pairs of leaves. The result of such a check to the plant's aspiring ambitions will be to encourage the development of side branches on the lower parts of the stem. Usually a bud will start in each leaf axil. Plants started early and grown on in pots in order to provide bloom shortly after they are transferred to the garden are pinched back when they are potted up or soon thereafter.

Supports

Every grower of annuals has encountered at one time or another the harassing experience of having a sudden storm more or less wreck the garden—and all too often such a tragedy occurs just a day or two before the flower show at which one envisioned winning a basketfull of blue ribbons!

Such diabolical aberrations on the part of kindly Mother Nature can neither be foreseen nor entirely protected against. Damages from such sources may, however, be mitigated, chiefly by providing supports of one sort or another.

For tall upright plants there are various types of wooden stakes, some with wire gadgets to do away with the necessity of tying. Some are painted or stained green to "harmonize" with the foliage. In most cases, however, the green will prove to be of a particularly virulent shade that does anything but harmonize. If wooden stakes are used, it is a good plan to paint them with Cuprinol, a penetrating preparation available in either brown or green, which is decidedly effective in preventing wood from rotting where it is placed in contact with the soil.

The supports we have found most satisfactory are Tonkin bamboo stakes. These come in various lengths, from two to six feet. (These are not to be confused with the split bamboo sold for florists' use in greenhouses.) Even better for very tall plants are heavy wire stakes which can be bought in (or cut to) any desired length. Unlike wooden or bamboo stakes, these will bend slightly in a high wind, and as a result there is much less danger that the stem of the attached plant will be broken. The illustration on page 31 shows the proper method of tying a plant to a stake. Only raffia or very soft cord should be used for this purpose, as hard twine is likely to cut the stems.

For plants of medium height, and particularly for those that are naturally of a spreading or bushy growth, small twiggy branches will be found much more satisfactory as supports than staking and tying. We find pea brush quite ideal for this purpose. Such supports should be put in place long before they are needed, so that the plants can grow up through them naturally, gradually hiding the supports from sight. The main stems of such branches should be very firmly fixed in the soil, as otherwise they may blow or fall over just when most needed.

Climbing annual vines—such as Sweet Pea, Morning-glory and Cardinal Climber—will of course require substantial support. While a permanent trellis of wood or metal may be desirable under some circumstances, our preference for general use is the treated, weather-resistant netting sold under the trade name of Trainettes. These may be had in lengths of six, eight, or fifteen feet, five feet wide, and may be stretched either horizontally or vertically. Climbing plants take kindly to the soft twine meshing. Supports of chicken wire, often used, are unsightly, difficult to put up, and in direct summer sunshine may become so hot as to be injurious to tender growth.

Mulching

The use of mulches in growing annuals is desirable both as a cultural aid and also to provide additional protection from deface- ment of the blooms by spattering mud. A mulch applied when the plants have started to grow vigorously, but before they have begun to touch each other, will practically eliminate the necessity for any further cultivating or weed pulling, and in addition will keep the surface of the soil open and porous and do a wonderful job of conserving moisture already in the soil.

Our method of using mulches is to apply them just after the first supplementary feeding. For most purposes we prefer buckwheat hulls. These are a good color, are slow to disintegrate, and will stay put even though they do not form a matlike surface. Rain or artificial watering will penetrate them and seep into the soil much more readily than is the case when peatmoss and some other types of mulches are used. Rather coarse semi-decomposed compost is also excellent, as are pine needles, sawdust, ground corncobs, and similar materials readily available in some localities. With most of these a mulch two inches thick will serve. In using any mulch it is wise to guard against getting it either so deep or so compact in character that water will not readily penetrate it.

TO THE END OF THE SEASON

This brings us to the subject of watering in general, one of the most important, if not *the* most important, factor in the successful growing of annuals in the home garden.

If one wishes not only to have fine annual flowers but to have them for as long a season as possible, the only way to accomplish this is to keep the soil in which they are growing well supplied with moisture. There are of course exceptions to this general rule. Some annuals—such as Portulaca, California-poppy, Mesembryanthe- mum, and Sand-verbena—will continue to grow and bloom in soil that is so dry that it seems as though they must perish. But the great majority of them, and particularly modern horticultural varieties that are far removed from their wild ancestors, will not, without resentment, tolerate too-long-continued thirst.

Nature's objective for an annual plant is to produce seed and thus continue the existence of the species. If growth must be made in abnormally dry soil, the plants will come into flower prematurely, produce seed quickly, and then die long before what would be their maximum period of growth with a normal water supply to keep them growing.

An abundance of humus material in the soil, plus mulching, will help to maintain soil moisture. The importance of these measures has already been stressed, but in most seasons and in most climates the time will arrive when such moisture as Nature may have provided will become exhausted and must be supplemented by artificial means.

Just how such watering is done will have a great deal to do with its efficacy. Here the two points of moment are: (1) to supply a sufficient quantity of water so that it will thoroughly moisten the soil to a depth of at least four or five inches or, still better, six or more; and (2) to apply it slowly enough so that it will be absorbed as it falls, instead of forming a wet, muddy surface resulting in a hard, caked crust after it dries out. (A mulch mitigates the latter danger but does not entirely prevent it.)

These two requirements for the adequate watering of annuals rule out the ordinary hose and nozzle sprinkling. Most circular sprinklers apply the water much too rapidly, and also unevenly. An oscillating sprinkler, which supplies the water in fine rainlike drops and which, turning slowly from one side to the other, permits each "wave" of rain to penetrate the soil before it is followed by another, does an adequate job.

Recently there has been developed a flat plastic hose formed of three parallel tubes, each of which is punctured at intervals with minute holes. This applies water in an almost mistlike spray and can be left in position for hours, if necessary, so that the soil may be wet to a great depth without any puddling of the surface. The spray is so fine that even small seedlings or freshly set out transplants will not be beaten over by it. A further advantage is that it may be laid out in curves or angles to fit almost any shape of bed or border. We have recommended this to many gardeners and have yet to find one who was not pleased with its performance.

This type of hose has another great advantage. When turned up-side down on top of a mulch, the tiny needle-like sprays quickly force their way through it, thoroughly moistening the soil beneath.

The beginning gardener seldom has any idea of how much water it requires to moisten soil to a depth of several inches once it has become thoroughly dry. We suggest that as an important lesson in gardening he try the experiment of watering an area of dry soil un-til he thinks it is sufficiently wet and then taking a trowel and dig-ging down into the soil to ascertain just how far the moisture has actually penetrated. If he does this he will soon realize that nothing is saved either in time or in the amount of water used by allowing the soil to become really dried out before water is applied. Further-more, plants make much better growth when the amount of soil moisture can be kept at somewhere near an even level. Alternate extreme drying out and soaking are serious handicaps to growth.

Cutting back

As has already been pointed out, the annual's aim in life is to produce seed. Anything that hastens seed production will shorten the life of the plant; and, conversely, anything that delays seed pro-duction will prolong it. No annual should be allowed to set seed if the gardener desires the longest possible period of bloom.

For this reason all faded flowers should be removed. With some free-flowering species such as Petunias and small-flowered Mari-golds, it is not always possible to carry out this rule, particularly when they are grown in masses, but the nearer one can come to observing it the better.

Cutting back the plants by removing branches or side stems that have "flowered out" will, in the case of many annuals, encourage new side growths, which in turn will flower and carry on the de-sired display. The generous cutting of flowers for indoor decoration will have much the same effect, particularly if they are taken just as the buds begin to open.

Shearing back is a still more drastic treatment that may be used to renew the life of some species, particularly such spreading or trail-ing ones as Pansies, Nasturtiums and Sweet Alyssum. In shearing back, the old procumbent stems are removed until little is left but the main stem or central crown of the plant. If the roots and central stems are still in good condition, new growth will be rapid. If such shearing is done in "two bites," first removing about half of the old stems and then, about three weeks later, cutting off those that are left, there will be only a short period, if any, when the plants are without some flowers.

Cutting for indoor use

If you are going to cut flowers to make your rooms indoors as colorful and gay as the beds out of doors, make a practice of cutting them before they are fully open. Such blooms will develop perfectly and, in addition, will last two or three times as long as those allowed to open fully and perhaps remain in the garden for two or three days before they are gathered.

Cutting is best done either very early in the morning or late in the afternoon.

Welcome to spring. Same garden as shown in frontispiece, with bulbs and early-flowering perennials providing color until the annuals take over. BELOW Petunias atop a newly constructed wall provide an immediate effect.

For bold, long-season masses of color, annuals are unequaled. ABOVE *Zinnias in a roadside planting.* BELOW *A border of Marigolds at Gray-Rock.*

CHAPTER *10.* *Keeping Them Healthy*

Most annuals give the gardener little to worry about in the way of injury from insect pests or diseases. There are a few, it must be admitted, that are definitely associated with certain troubles. If you grow Nasturtiums, for instance, you may expect, more often than not, to encounter black aphids; if you plant China-asters, you may escape the wilt disease by buying the resistant varieties, but even so you will probably have the voracious blister beetle in black and shining armor to contend with.

With comparatively few exceptions, however, you may anticipate going through the entire season with little use for spray gun or duster. And if by chance you do encounter serious trouble with one species or another, the loss is not too great. The affected plants —unless the attack has occurred late in summer—may be replaced by some other species. And as all annuals die anyway at the end of the season, there is, in most cases, not the same danger of a carry-over to another season as with perennials or shrubs.

Equipment

The effectiveness of dusting or spraying for the control of pests or diseases depends largely upon the equipment used. Of equal importance is the fact that the time and effort involved in applying control materials are doubled or trebled with inadequate equipment.

We feel that these points can hardly be stressed too strongly, for in addition to our own experience we have met with scores of cases where poor control was due to failure to get complete and even coverage of plant surfaces with the dust or liquid being used.

Moreover, in most home gardens the time required to do a spraying or dusting job often determines whether or not it will be done when it should be; often whether it gets done at all. A difference of a few days, sometimes of a few hours, in attacking the enemy may mean complete control, with little or no damage done, or only partial control, with much damage done.

The cheapest dusters or sprayers cost from one to three dollars each. They are tedious to operate, apply materials so unevenly that foliage is frequently injured, and seldom remain in working condition for more than a season or two.

Really efficient ones cost from five to fifteen dollars, apply materials much more rapidly and evenly, and with good care will last ten years or longer. In the end they are in reality by far the least expensive.

Most catalogues list several types of dusters and sprayers, and others are to be found in the advertising pages of garden publications. The low-cost dusters are of the plunger type. Repeated thrusts of the plunger eject the dust in a series of spurts, giving very uneven distribution and resulting in waste of materials and often in foliage injury. The bellows type is somewhat easier to work and does a better job.

We have found the crank type, in which a rotating fan blows the dust out in a continuous cloud, the most satisfactory. With this the *undersides* of foliage can be covered—something which is most important and almost impossible to achieve with either of the other types of duster.

In sprayers there are three types available: the plunger or "squirt gun," the trombone, and the compressed air. The first of these is open to the same objections as the plunger duster.

The trombone, which consists of one tube rod operating inside another with a back-and-forth motion, gives a very forceful spray or a long stream—to a distance of twelve to fifteen feet. It is used in connection with any ordinary pail or bucket to hold the liquid, or is available with a gallon container for the spray material and equipped with a shoulder strap. It is not likely to get out of order and is easily cleaned. We have found trombone sprayers entirely satisfactory for most of our spraying, which includes several hundred rose plants.

The closed tank or compressed-air type of sprayer, when it must be operated by one person, has the great disadvantage of constantly varying pressure behind the spray, making even coverage very difficult. For a large garden, the compressed-air sprayer equipped with an electric motor is the ideal, but of course this involves a considerable outlay.

For small-scale operations where only a few plants are involved, there are now available insecticide bombs or pressure cans (similar to those designed for control of moths and other household pests) which release a mistlike spray at the pressure of a button. These are easy to use and effective, but of course relatively expensive.

Dusting vs. spraying

As for the effectiveness of spraying compared to dusting, it is generally considered that for most purposes the former gives more reliable control. However, for small-scale operations where only a few plants are to be treated, dusting has several decided advantages. The job can be done with dust in the time it would take to mix up a liquid spray, let alone apply it. Moreover, the dust gun can be kept loaded, while the sprayer cannot; and a duster does not have to be carefully washed out and cleaned, as a sprayer should be, after each time it is used.

Hand picking

For many troubles the simple remedy of hand picking can be employed effectively—if it is used in time. But the "if" is most important! A few colonies of aphids at the tips of new growths, a few diseased leaves, *removed at once,* may forestall further trouble. We keep several tin cans half filled with water and kerosene at convenient points around the garden, ready for instant use. Into these are dropped any unwelcome plant guests. It's not difficult to capture most of them—or knock them into the cans with a small wooden paddle—early in the morning before they become active. Diseased foliage should be burned.

In any case, the gardener should learn to keep a keen eye open for the least sign of anything unusual about any of his plants. The curling of a leaf, the wilting of a growth tip, the lopsided opening of a flower bud—these and many other things that might ordinarily pass unnoticed—to the practiced eye of the gardener are advance signals of possible trouble ahead. And he will not be content until he has discovered their cause.

Fortunately the modern combination "all-purpose" (or, more accurately, *almost* all-purpose) dusts and sprays, many of them with residual or long-lasting effect, have in recent years made it much easier for the flower lover to combat his or her enemies. The insecticide bomb or pressure can is a wonderful aid in caring for a few plants or "spot-treating" an initial colony, such as a group of aphids or whitefly.

HOW TO USE THE LISTS

On the following pages are four health-control lists:

1. ANNUALS: THEIR TROUBLES AND TREATMENT
   A. Annual plants, pests most likely to attack them, and controls
   B. Annual plants, diseases most likely to attack them, and controls
2. PESTS OF ANNUALS AND THEIR HOSTS
3. DISEASES OF ANNUALS AND THEIR HOSTS
4. MATERIALS FOR CONTROL OF ANNUAL PLANT TROUBLES

To make use of this information, in case you encounter trouble:

FIRST: *Check through List 1 for the insects or diseases apt to attack the particular kind of plant in question, and decide which one it probaby is, and its control.*

SECOND: *Look up insect or disease in Lists 2 or 3 to find out more about it.*

THIRD: *Consult List 4 for description of the recommnded control (if your are not already familiar with it).*

The subject of insect and disease controls must, in a book such as this, be treated in rather condensed form. Gardeners who are interested in following the matter further will be helped by one or more of the following books:

> *Garden Enemies,* by Cynthia Westcott
> *The Gardener's Bug Book,* by Cynthia Westcott
> *Modern Gardening,* by P. P. Pirone.

1. ANNUALS—THEIR TROUBLES AND TREATMENTS

A. Annual plants, pests most likely to attack them, and controls

PLANT | PEST AND TREATMENT

PLANT	PEST AND TREATMENT
Ageratum	Whitefly · Malathion spray
aster, China-	Beetle,
	Asiatic Garden · DDT dust or spray
	Blister · DDT dust or spray
	Borer, Stalk · DDT dust and hand kill
	Lace Bug · Lindane spray
	Root Aphid · Chlordane. Treat soil
	Tarnished Plant Bug · Chlordane spray
Calendula	Aphids · Black Leaf 40 spray
Chrysanthemum	Aphids · Black Leaf 40 spray
(annual)	Tarnished Plant Bug · Chlordane spray
	Thrips · Lindane spray
Coleus	Mealybug · Malathion spray; or swab with rubbing alcohol
	Whitefly · Malathion spray
Coreopsis	Beetle, Spotted Cucumber · DDT or rotenone dust
Cosmos	Beetle, Asiatic Garden · DDT dust
	Japanese · DDT spray or dust
	Spotted Cucumber · DDT or rotenone dust
	Borer, Stalk · DDT dust, and hand-kill
Dahlia	Beetle, Asiatic Garden · DDT dust or spray
	Japanese · DDT dust or spray
	Spotted Cucumber · DDT or rotenone dust
	Borer, Stalk · DDT dust, and hand-kill
	Leafhopper · DDT dust or spray
	Tarnished Plant Bug · DDT dust or spray
Foxglove	Red Spider · Aramite spray
	Thrips · DDT dust or spray
Geranium	Mealybug · Malathion spray
	Mite, Cyclamen · Di-mite spray
	Whitefly · Malathion spray
Gourds	Beetle, Spotted Cucumber · Rotenone or DDT dust
	Striped Cucumber · Rotenone or DDT dust
	Whitefly · Malathion spray
Heliotrope	Whitefly · Malathion spray
Hibiscus	Caterpillars · DDT dust or spray

PLANT   PEST AND TREATMENT

PLANT	PEST AND TREATMENT
Hollyhock	Beetle, Japanese · DDT dust or spray
	Borer, Stalk · DDT dust and hand-kill
	Red Spider · Aramite spray or sulphur dust
	Slugs · DDT dust or spray; or metaldehyde
Impatiens	Whitefly · Malathion spray
Lantana	Mealybug · Malathion spray
	Whitefly · Malathion spray
Larkspur	Aphids · Black Leaf 40 spray
Lupine	Aphids · Black Leaf 40 spray
Mallow	Beetle, Japanese · DDT dust or spray
Marigold, African (Odorless)	Beetle, Japanese · DDT dust or spray
Moonflower	Beetle, Tortoise · DDT dust or spray
Morning-glory	Beetle, Tortoise · DDT dust or spray
Myosotis	Beetle, Flea · DDT dust or lindane spray
Nasturtium	Aphids · Black Leaf 40 spray
Pansy	Slugs · Chlordane. Dust soil
Petunia	Beetle, Flea · DDT dust or lindane spray
	Mite, Cyclamen · Di-mite spray
Poppy	Aphids · Black Leaf 40 spray
Rudbeckia	Aphids · Black Leaf 40 spray
Snapdragon	Mite, Cyclamen · Di-mite spray
Stock	Beetle, Flea · DDT dust or lindane spray
Sweet Pea	Aphids · Black Leaf 40 spray
	Leaf Miner · Lindane spray
Verbena	Beetle, Asiatic Garden · DDT dust or spray
	Japanese · DDT dust or spray
	Borer, Stalk · DDT dust and hand-kill

B. Annual plants, diseases most likely to attack them, and controls

PLANT	DISEASE AND TREATMENT
aster, China-	Rust · Fermate and sulphur. Dust.
	Wilt · Purchase seeds of resistant strains.
	Yellows · Spray leafhopper carriers with DDT.
Dahlia	Mildew, powdery · Sulphur. Dust.
	Mosaic · Burn infected plants.
	Wilt · Burn infected plants
Geranium	Botrytis blight · Cut away affected parts. Reduce water.

PLANT	PEST AND TREATMENT
Hollyhock	Rust · Sulphur. Dust regularly throughout season.
Larkspur	Crown rot · Burn affected plants. Soak surrounding soil with bichloride of mercury.
Marigold	Botrytis blight · Remove and burn affected flowers.
Myosotis	Crown rot · Burn affected plants. Soak surrounding soil with bichloride of mercury.
Pansy	Botrytis blight · Burn affected plants. Scab · Fermate. Spray. Or burn affected plants.
Petunia	Mildew, powdery · Sulphur. Dust. Mosaic · Burn affected plants
Poppy	Blight · Burn affected plants. Replant elsewhere.
Snapdragon	Rust · Purchase resistant varieties.
Stock	Mosaic · Burn affected plants.
Sweet Pea	Anthracnose · Arasan. Treat seeds before planting. Mildew, powdery · Sulphur. Dust.
Sweet William	Fusarium wilt · Burn affected plants. Replant elsewhere.
Verbena	Mildew, powdery · Sulphur. Dust.
Zinnia	Mildew, powdery · Sulphur. Dust.

2. PESTS OF ANNUALS AND THEIR HOSTS

Pest and Description	Annuals attacked
APHID (Plant Lice): Small, soft, sucking, black, green, red, grayish, or pinkish insect found on young growth, buds, and undersides of leaves.	Calendula Chrysanthemum Larkspur Lupine Nasturtium Poppy Rudbeckia Sweet Pea
ROOT: Bluish-green. Attacks roots.	Aster
BEETLE	
ASIATIC GARDEN: A night-feeding brown beetlle ⅜ inch. Eats leaves.	Aster Cosmos Dahlia Zinnia
BLISTER: Long, thin black beetle. Eats flowers and foliage.	Aster

Pest and Description	Annuals attacked
FLEA: Small, roundish, dark jumping beetle. Eats small round holes in foliage.	Myosotis Stock
JAPANESE: One-half inch metal-green and bronze beetle. Eats flowers and foliage.	Cosmos Dahlia Hollyhock Mallow Marigold, African (Odorless) Zinnia
SPOTTED CUCUMBER: Black-spotted greenish-yellow beetle. Eats flowers.	Coreopsis Cosmos Dahlia Gourds
STRIPED CUCUMBER: Black-striped yellow beetles ⅕ inch. Eats leaves, flowers, and fruit.	Gourds
TORTOISE (Gold Bug): Glistening gold beetle, ¼ inch dotted or striped black. Eats leaves.	Morning-glory Moonflower
BORER, STALK: Inch-long brownish-gray caterpillar. Tunnels flower stalks.	Aster Cosmos Dahlia Hollyhock Zinnia
CATERPILLAR: Soft, wormlike larva. Chews foliage.	Hibiscus
LACE BUG: Sucking insect with lacy wings. Attacks undersides of leaves.	Aster
LEAFHOPPER: Winged, hopping insect. Attacks undersides of leaves.	Dahlia
LEAF MINER: Chewing insect makes tunnels in leaves.	Verbena
MEALYBUG: Soft, reddish, scale-like insect covered with white, wooley protective substance. Sucking. Found at joints and on undersides of leaves.	Begonia Coleus Geranium Lantana
MITE, CYCLAMEN: Minute insect which stunts and distorts leaves and buds, turning them dark.	Geranium Petunia Snapdragon
RED SPIDER: Minute mite which discolors leaves and makes webs on undersides.	Foxglove Hollyhock
SLUGS: Shelless snails leaving slimy trails. Eat large holes in foliage at night.	Hollyhock Pansy
TARNISHED PLANT BUG: Brownish ¼-inch bug which attacks foliage and buds, causing them to wilt and darken.	Aster Chrysanthemum Dahlia

Pest and Description	*Annuals attacked*
THRIPS: Minute insects. Attacks buds and flowers.	Chrysanthemum
	Foxglove
WHITEFLY: Small, white, winged, sucking insect. Attacks undersides of leaves and lays eggs there.	Ageratum
	Coleus
	Geranium
	Gourds
	Heliotrope
	Impatiens
	Lantana

3. DISEASES OF ANNUALS AND THEIR HOSTS

Disease and Description	*Annuals attacked*
ANTHRACNOSE: Causes wilting; stems and leaves die. Spread by handling plants in wet weather.	Sweet Pea
BOTRYTIS BLIGHT: A fungus disease causing gray mold to form on affected plants.	Geranium
	Marigold
	Pansy
CROWN ROT: Crown of plant rots. Surrounding soil may be covered with reddish, mustard-seed-like bodies.	Larkspur
FUSARIUM WILT: Causes plants to turn yellow and die.	Sweet William
MILDEW, POWDERY: Fungus which forms a white growth on foliage, stems, and buds of affected plants. Aggravated by nitrogen overfeeding.	Dahlia
	Petunia
	Sweet Pea
	Verbena
	Zinnia
MOSAIC: Spots, mottling, and stunting. Causes wilt.	Dahlia
	Petunia
	Stock
RUST: Deep orange areas on stems and undersides of leaves.	Hollyhock
SCAB: Foliage spotted with brown.	Pansy
WILT: A fungus in soil causes wilting and death of plant.	Aster
YELLOWS: Plants stunted and yellow. Flowers greenish. Virus carried by leafhoppers.	Aster

4. MATERIALS FOR CONTROL OF ANNUAL PLANT TROUBLES

Commercial sprays and dusts are accompanied by analyses of the ingredients and specific directions for use. READ AND FOLLOW DIRECTIONS CAREFULLY.

ARAMITE: A non-poisonous miticide.

ARASAN: A disinfectant for the treatment of seeds to safeguard against damping-off and other seed-borne diseases.

BICHLORIDE OF MERCURY *(Deadly Poison!)*: Soil disinfectant for crown rot. Dilute 1 to 1000.

BLACK LEAF 40: Contact spray most effective against aphids.

CHLORDANE: Contact and stomach-poison spray or dust effective against ants, beetle grubs, leaf miners, thrips, etc.

DDT: Contact and stomach-poison spray or dust effective against beetles, borers, leaf miners and leafhoppers, thrips, etc.

DI-MITE: A miticide.

FERMATE (FERBAM): An excellent fungicide for anthracnose, botrytis blight, downy (*not* powdery) mildew, etc.

LINDANE: A contact and stomach-poison spray for aphids, lace bugs, leaf miners, etc.

MALATHION: A phosphate spray for mealybugs, mites, etc.

METALDEHYDE: Stomach poison for slugs.

PARATHION: A spray for the control of mealybugs, mites, nematodes, and scale. *Not* suitable for use by the amateur, as a gas mask, gloves, and complete protection for the skin are necessary.

ROTENONE: A contact and stomach-poison spray or dust, harmless to man.

SULPHUR: A fungicide dust.

TRI-OGEN: An all-purpose rose spray or dust which can safely be used on other garden flowers. Controls aphids, beetles, red spiders, and diseases such as black spot and powdery mildew.

WILSON'S O.K. PLANT SPRAY: A nicotine spray for the control of aphids, etc.

CHAPTER *11. Dried Annuals and Everlastings for Winter Bouquets*

Drying and curing fresh flowers, foliage, seed pods, nuts, grasses, ferns, and even some vegetables for use in winter arrangements are a fascinating hobby for flower lovers.

The woman who has an attic full of carefully dried plant material need not worry about the high cost of florist's flowers in mid-winter.

The arranging of such material is an art in itself. The creation of good designs by wise blending of forms and textures and the clever use of the muted colors present a real challenge. Those who have mastered this art find it rewarding not only because of the fine effects which can be achieved but because, unlike arrangements of fresh flowers, dried bouquets last almost indefinitely.

Annual flowers, seed pods, and foliage, of course, constitute only a small part of all material suitable for drying. With these, branches, seed pods, and berries of evergreen and decidous shrubs; perennial material and fern fronds are used, as well as exotic items like palm hearts and the foliage of Aspidistra, Dracaena, and other tender tropical foliage plants. Driftwood, bare branches, and vine stems often form the main lines or skeleton.

CUTTING, DRYING, AND STORING

Cutting and preparation

In general, material for drying should be cut after the dew is off it, on a clear day of low humidity. As dried material shrinks to almost half its original bulk, cut twice as much as you expect to need.

Blossoms are best cut *as soon as they have opened.* Overmature blooms do not dry satisfactorily. Strip foliage at once from flowering stems.

Material like Poppy seed heads, Salvia, Snapdragon, or Liatris, with long stems; Broom, Siberian Iris foliage, Aspidistra, and Dracaena leaves, and Pussy Willow branches can be wired or bound with cord before drying, in such a way as to form the curves which will later lend themselves to arrangement.

Wash broad foliage leaves after cutting.

Drying Methods

Erect. Place stems of cut material in a Mason or other jar, flower heads erect. Leave in a dry, airy, shaded room, attic, or barn until dry.

Upside down. Stretch stout cords the length of room, attic or barn and from these suspend single heavy sprays, branches, or small bunches of light material, flower heads down. If you have sufficient space, leave material hanging until needed.

Sand, sifted sea sand only. Fill a pan or box to a depth of three or four inches. Place flowers, head down, on this. Cover by pouring more sand gently over flower heads and stems. Label plainly. Store for two weeks in cool, dark, dry place. Then pour sand gently from pan, brush each bloom with a camel's-hair brush, and store in boxes or erect in open jars.

Borax, sifted only. Use as sand. Place flower sprays horizontally or flower heads upside down on bed of borax before covering as with sand method. Remove after twenty-four to seventy-two hours. Experiment by removing one flower after twenty-four hours. Do not leave too long, as petals may discolor.

Storing. Materials dried by the upside-down or erect methods may remain hanging or standing where they are until needed, or they may be stored in clearly marked boxes, one species or type of material to a box. Seed pods may be stored in labeled boxes, jars, or tins.

AVAILABLE ANNUAL MATERIAL FOR DRYING AND HOW TO HANDLE EACH

Ageratum—Place stems in water for twenty-four hours. Then use upside-down method.
Babys-breath—Stand branches erect in jar.
Balsam blossoms—Borax or sand method.

Begonia semperflorens seed pods—Upside-down method.
Calendula flowers—Erect method.
Campanula (Canterbury Bells) spikes—Borax or sand method.
Candytuft—Borax or sand method.
Cape-marigold—Borax or sand method.
Castor-bean seed pods and stalks—Upside-down method.
Celosia blooms—Cut with dew on them. Erect method three days. Then up-
    side down.
Centaurea blooms—Upside-down method.
Catananche blooms—Upside-down method.
Cleome seed pods—Erect method.
Cohaea scandens seed pods—Erect method.
Coleus foliage—Borax or sand method.
Cornflower—Borax or sand method.
Cosmos—Borax or sand method.
Coreopsis seed heads—Erect method, then store in box.
Dahlia blooms—Borax or sand method.
Datura blooms and seed pods—Blooms, erect method. Store seed pods in
    box or tin.
Dianthus blooms—Borax or sand method.
Evening-primrose blooms—Borax or sand method.
Everlastings—Upside-down method.
Foxglove blooms—Borax or sand method.
Geranium leaves—Place between sheets of blotting or wax paper, under
    pressure, until dry.
Gilia blooms—Upside-down method.
Globe Amaranth flower heads—Upside-down method.
Gourds—Mature on vines before frost. Shellac surface.
Grasses, ornamental and wild—Erect method.
Hollyhock blossoms—Upside-down method.
Honesty seed pods—When dried on plant, cut, strip covering, and use erect
    method or store in box.
Hyacinth Bean pods—Store in tins or glass.
Immortelle blooms—Borax or erect method.
Larkspur spikes—Cut in bud. Let foliage remain. Upside-down method.
Liatris blooms—Upside-down method.
Lupine blooms—Borax method.
Marigold, double—Upside-down method.
Marigold, single—Borax or sand method.
Morning-glory blooms—Upside-down method.
Nicotiana blooms and stems—Upside-down method.
Okra pods—Erect method, or store in box.
Pansy—Sand method.

Polygonum—Erect method.
Poppy seed pods—Wire or bind stems in curves and store in box.
Poppy-mallow blooms—Borax or sand method.
Proboscis Plant, seed pods—Erect method.
Salvia spikes—Borax method.
Scabiosa blooms—Upside-down method.
Snapdragon spikes—Borax method.
Snow-on-the-mountain sprays, foliage and flowers—Borax or sand methods.
Star-of-Texas—Borax or sand method.
Statice—Erect method.
Stock—Borax method.
Strawflower—Erect method.
Sunflower flower disks—Erect method.
Sunflower leaves—Sand method.
Wild-cucumber seed pods—Pick when dry and store.
Zinnia, Fantasy type—Borax or sand method.

Seed pods of many kinds keep better, retain better color, are protected from insects and rodents, if dipped in clear shellac or sprayed with clear plastic.

MAKING, STORING, AND PRESERVING DRIED-FLOWER ARRANGEMENTS

Because the material is so frail, making a dried arrangement requires deftness and patience as well as the usual skills. Handling the material without damage soon becomes second nature, however, to the dried-arrangement enthusiast.

Needle-point holders may be used for low containers, as with fresh flowers. Tall vases may be packed with sand or floral-snow in lieu of a holder. Material should be firmly placed, as the arrangement will be in use a long time.

Several small flower heads, as those of Dianthus or small Zinnias, may be fastened together with a wire or Twist-em and substituted for one large round flower as a main element in the design.

Frail leaves or stems can be strengthened by binding them with floral tape to a thin stick or a heavy wire. Covered with brown florists' tape, wires are all but invisible in a dried bouquet.

See that your arrangement has depth—more than two dimensions. Even though it is planned for a console table, it should be constructed to be viewed from three sides, not one.

Combine interesting textures, forms, and subtle colors to create distinctive designs.

Keep your eyes always open for new dried material to add to those which you already have to work with. The meadow, the woods, and the hedgerows offer many possibilities to supplement materials from the borders in your own garden.

If desired, fresh flowers for focal interest and evergreen or other fresh foliage as accessory material may be used as part of an arrangement otherwise made up of dried material. For instance, I have a dried arrangement in an antique wooden mortar. The design is an S curve of Palm hearts and Wheat, with Yucca seed heads, Deodar and "wooden-roses," Sweet Gum pods, etc., for central interest. For an "occasion," I often remove the large Yucca heads and fill in this space with crimson Carnations, with a couple of Snail Begonia leaves to set them off. When the fresh flowers fade, back go the Yucca pods.

If a dried arrangement becomes dusty while on display or in storage, brush it with a camel's-hair brush. Or if generally bedraggled, place it in the bathroom on a board over the tub, turn on the hot water, and steam it as you would a velvet dress.

CHAPTER *12. Annuals*

for Window and Terrace Boxes

Window-box gardening, so important in most European countries, has in America become almost a lost art. True, it was part of the dying Victorian era. Along with many other customs that possessed a good deal of intrinsic value, it went "out of style" and as a consequence suffered a neglect that was not merited.

During recent years the popularity of the ranch type of home and the shrinkage in size of house plots in suburban areas have brought in a modernized form of window-box gardening which, for want of a better term, we may call terrace-box gardening. Whereas the window box was attached to the house—too often, it must be admitted, as a sort of afterthought excrescence having little or nothing in common architecturally with the building to which it was attached—the terrace box is usually built in as a planned part of the architectural design. In this respect it is of course a decided improvement.

Another difference is that the window box or porch box—which may still be seen at its best in parts of New England and in the residential sections of some large cities—was placed a considerable distance above the ground. Not infrequently window boxes were located beneath second or even third-story windows. Consequently trailing plants, particularly *Vinca major,* Balcony Petunias, and Ivy-leaved Geraniums, were much in vogue as plant material because they helped to hide the unattractive appearance of the box itself. The modern terrace box, on the contrary, is usually located at or slightly above ground level, often being merely a raised masonry-bound bed along part of the foundation of the house. Naturally it calls for a somewhat different type of planting, and it also has the distinct advantage of providing much more root room for the plants grown in it and consequently is better suited to accommodate plant material of a much more permanent character.

ANNUALS FOR BOXES

In planting window boxes and terrace boxes, annuals play an important part. For window boxes particularly, they are much less expensive than Geraniums, Ivy, *Vinca major,* and the other florists' plants generally used. They are easily and inexpensively replaced when they have bloomed out, and offer a wide range of color and form with which to create effects that will show some individuality.

Young plants of annuals may be purchased from a grower or raised from seed. A small reserve seed bed with plants coming on through the growing season provides a constant supply of replacements at a very low cost. If two or three small plantings are made a month or so apart, a supply of plants in flower or about ready to flower will be available to keep the window box in full bloom through late summer and autumn.

Before selecting species and varieties for window or terrace boxes, give careful consideration to the color scheme best suited to your home. A white frame house, for instance, will be enhanced by the bright blues of Ageratum and Lobelia, the cheery yellows and oranges of dwarf Marigolds, combined perhaps with white Sweet Alyssum trailing over the edge of the box to form a foil for the bright colors behind it. One nice thing about a white-wall background is that you can use any colors you choose in the plant material without fear of having them clash with it.

Brick walls, on the other hand, are particularly trying as background. Where one is encountered, special care should be taken in the selection of plant material. White and light colors in general are attractive and may be had with Petunias, Verbena, Sweet Alyssum, and others. *Vinca rosea* and *rosea alba* are particularly good because the masses of dark green foliage make a complementary harmony with the red of the bricks. With light-colored flowers one may use soft buffs and primrose yellows, such as those of Thunbergia and Sanvitalia, with an occasional accent of violet Pansies or Nierembergia. Another combination we have seen used is white Balcony Petunia with brick-red Petunia Comanche.

In the terrace box one is less likely to find an opportunity to use plants of trailing habit, so must turn to those of erect or moundlike form. Providing pleasing shades of blue are Ageratum Blue Ball, Blue Perfection, and Imperial Dwarf Blue. All these are usually less than a foot tall but grow a bit higher as a rule than the catalogue listings indicate. The very dwarf Midget Blue—two to three inches tall—is suitable for the front row of a box. Browallia Sapphire is like a neat miniature shrub and bears myriads of small deep blue flowers. This tolerates part shade, as does also Dianthus Westwood Beauty with its large single rose-red or carmine flowers on vigorous plants about eighteen inches tall. Lobelias are available in either moundlike or procumbent forms. Compact-growing varieties such as Blue Gown and Mrs. Clibran Improved are only about six inches tall. Lobelias, incidentally, are among the annuals which should be cut back quite severely in midsummer in order to produce new growth and flowers later in the season. Nierembergia Purple Robe forms dense plants a foot high and at least a foot across, bearing masses of lavender-blue cup-shaped blooms through summer and autumn. Plants can be cut back and carried through the winter indoors if desired.

A favorite of Grandmother's day, the Patience Plant (the real name of which is *Impatiens!*), is now available in salmon, brick-red, white, and soft pink. It is easily grown from either seeds or cuttings and is particularly valuable because it will endure considerable shade. By judicious pruning it can be held to a foot or so.

A real gold mine of material for the window or porch-box gardener is available in the many excellent new dwarf Marigolds. Among these are Yellow Pygmy and Butterball, six to eight inches high; Sunkist, orange, eight inches; Scarlet Glow, ten inches; and the somewhat dwarfer old favorite Spry, a blending of mahogany and yellow.

Pansies treated as annuals are always good for early and late color. Select named varieties like Delft Blue, Swiss Blue, or red Alpenglow. Part shade suits them admirably.

For a dry, sunny exposure Portulaca is excellent. The seeds can be planted right in the box, too. Single Jewel is a crimson, and there are pink, salmon, white, and yellow varieties; six inches. Torenia or Wishbone Flower, purple, blue, and gold, is for late bloom in shade. The neat bushy plants reach about twelve inches in height and the foliage colors up to a rich plum-red in autumn. They need plenty of moisture.

For ranch-type homes dwarf Celosias, either feathered or crested, have a modern feeling, especially varieties in separate colors such as Fire or Golden Feather, one foot; or Empress, only ten inches, with deep velvety crested crimson heads. Choose the color that blends or contrasts well with the house exterior.

Vinca rosea, previously mentioned, is a charming annual form with pink (Willie Winkie) or white (Purity) flowers and lush, dark green glossy foliage. It requires full sun and grows to one and a half feet.

Trailers and vines

The Petunia is probably the most important window-box annual because of its habit of growth and wide color range. The Balcony type, trailing to one and a half feet, is especially satisfactory for the purpose, with two-and-a-half- to three-inch single blooms in red, blue, rose, or white. Bedding types trail to some extent; while the ruffled, fringed, and double sorts are showy in the extreme for a large porch or patio box. Select varieties according to your need for color and habit of growth.

Sanvitalia, the so-called Creeping-zinnia, is not too well known but a lovely thing, its somewhat trailing branches covered with pert little buff-gold, double, Zinnia-like flowers. Thunbergia or Black-eyed Susan is a real vine, growing to five feet, but a dainty one. The attractive foliage forms a dense mat set with jewel-like dark-centered yellow, orange, buff, or white flowers, elegantly simple.

Mesembryanthemum criniflorum is an Ice Plant which can readily be raised from seed. Ice Plants are succulents well suited for hot, dry situations. In a sandy soil and bright sun they produce low mats of foliage with glistening dots which give the plant its common name. The brilliant rose, pink, buff, or white rayed flowers literally cover the plants. Use these in combination with Portulaca. Colors and growing conditions suit each other to a T.

Verbena in named varieties, Sweet Alyssum, dwarf Nasturtiums (select fragrant double varieties), trailing Lobelia, and Coleus Trailing Queen are other outstanding possibilities for the foreground.

In selecting plant material for window or terrace boxes, the matter of sun and shade should be kept in mind. The effects of both sun and shade are increased by the close proximity of the planting to the walls of a house, the former particularly if the wall is white or light-colored with a high reflection factor. Check the plants you think of using against the lists given in Chapter 5.

CONSTRUCTION OF WINDOW AND TERRACE BOXES

Window boxes may be as simple or as elaborate in construction as the gardener wishes to have them. In making or buying a box, however, it is well to keep in mind that the materials of which it is constructed will be subjected to the most trying conditions—constant contact with moist soil on the inside and subjected to extremes of heat or to more or less constant shade on the exterior. Many of the cheap metal plant boxes sold will rust out in a season or two and in the end prove much more expensive than a substantial homemade or custom-made one.

As to the materials to be used, we prefer either wood or a metal-lined wood box. A metal box in midsummer sun will become so hot that you cannot touch it. This heat, of course, is transmitted to the soil and the roots within the box.

The simplest, most practical, and least expensive type of plant box we know of is one of our own design. It consists merely of a bottomless box placed within a heavy galvanized metal tray two inches or so larger in both length and breadth. The box itself should

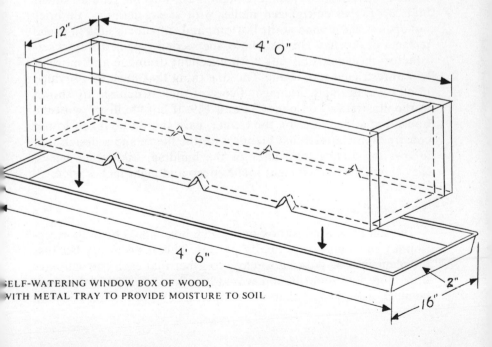

SELF-WATERING WINDOW BOX OF WOOD,
WITH METAL TRAY TO PROVIDE MOISTURE TO SOIL

be at least eight inches wide and eight inches deep (inside measurement) and as long as required. These dimensions can, of course, be varied to suit conditions, but anything less than the minimum dimensions suggested will mean overcrowded plants and very rapid drying out of the soil. The accompanying illustration shows the details of construction. We have had such boxes, with occasional repaintings, remain in good condition for more than fifteen years.

The woods most resistant to moisture are cedar, cypress, and redwood. Eastern white pine—now seldom available—is also excellent. Even these resistant woods should be given two coats of Cuprinol to increase their resistance to decay.

Supports for plant boxes, when they are to be attached to a building, should be substantial enough to prevent any possibility of their being torn out. Even a small boxful of soil, when wet by continued rain, will weigh as much as a man. See to it that your supports will hold any weight to which they can possibly be subjected. We know of one instance in which a person was killed by a falling plant box.

Built-in terrace boxes or recesses for planting are of all types and sizes, according to the ideas of the architect or the whims of the home owner. Some of them are made flush with the ground; others built up twelve or eighteen inches with stone, masonry, or brick but open to the ground at the bottom; and still others sunk in paved terraces or porches. On the whole, the second type is the most satisfactory because it affords both excellent drainage and more or less unrestricted root room. The one thing that must be provided in all cases is ample drainage. Types of such structures are shown in the illustrations on pages 32 and 149. If not "built in" with the house but added later by the owner, care should be taken to use construction material that blends with the house and a design that follows the architectural lines of the building. Like other boxes, they should be *at least* eight inches deep and eight inches wide.

Soils and Planting

The soil for a window box or a porch box should be both exceptionally rich and exceptionally porous. This is necessary because the plants will be growing so close together that each one will have little more root room than it would in a flowerpot. Also, there will be much more danger than in the open ground of the soil's becoming and remaining waterlogged to a degree that will prevent the free penetration of air, which is quite as essential to good plant growth as an abundance of plant food and moisture.

In filling the container, therefore, it is necessary to put in a bottom layer of rather coarse material to a depth of two inches or so —just as you would crock a flowerpot. If broken charcoal is mixed with this coarse material, so much the better. The soil itself should be a mixture of good loam, compost, and peatmoss in about equal proportions, enriched with driconure and bonemeal or other plant food. (See discussion of soils on pages 85–89.)

As the plants themselves, if taken from pots, will occupy much of the space within the box, fill the box only about half full before you begin planting, packing in additional soil as needed as the work progresses. The surface of the finished job should be a half inch or more below the rim of the container. When small plants are used, the exposed surface between them may well be mulched with sphagnum moss or peatmoss to help prevent rapid drying out until foliage covers the entire surface.

In planting it is well to begin along the front edge of the box so that any plants of trailing habit may be put in place first, then work toward the back with taller or upright plants. Each plant should be well firmed into the soil, and the whole, after planting, receive a thorough watering to settle the soil about the roots.

Where plants have recently been removed from the greenhouse or if the box is in a particularly windy or sunny location, it will be very helpful to give a mist spray daily or even twice a day for a week or so after transplanting until growth has been renewed.

CULTURE

Perhaps the greatest single danger in growing in window or porch boxes is that of having the plants subjected to alternate degrees of too much and too little moisture. Do everything possible to maintain an even degree of moisture in the soil. Where subirrigation can be arranged, it will help greatly in this respect. In any event, the plant-box gardener will do well to get into the habit of making a regular daily inspection of his window-box garden. This will require but a few moments and will be a very interesting task because it is fascinating to watch the growth of the plants from day to day even when they are not in bloom. It will also help to have a special watering can handy to use whenever needed for this particular purpose.

Feeding

To make certain that the plants in their somewhat crowded quarters will not lack for nourishment, a bimonthly or at least a monthly feeding with a liquid fertilizer is advisable. This, however, should not be overdone: too much nourishment will result in the production of leaves instead of flowers.

Trimming

As plants growing in boxes will at best be somewhat overcrowded, pruning knives should be kept sharp and used frequently. Some plants grow much more vigorously than others, and these will need to be controlled. Shoots that have bloomed may be cut out to make room for new ones eager to replace them and flower in their turn. Trailing plants especially may frequently be trimmed back for their own good. How often, for instance, does one see trailing, bare stems of Petunias, with a few flowers at their very tips, which should have been removed long before to encourage the growth of new flowering shoots from near the base of the plant?

HANGING BASKETS

The old-fashioned Victorian hanging basket filled with a few flowering plants and trailing vines is so seldom seen nowadays that one hesitates even to mention it. Nevertheless, it is not without certain merits and, in suitable surroundings, has a quaint charm of its own. Don't be afraid to try one, if you have the inclination, for fear your neighbors may laugh at you.

The basket is made of wire mesh supported by a stout wire handle. Suitably lined with a mat of sphagnum moss, it makes an oversize flowerpot to accommodate the few plants required. Most seed houses no longer list these baskets, but they may still be had. It is not difficult to make one yourself with quarter- or half-inch wire mesh. To have some fun and a sure-fire conversation piece, try your hand at a hanging basket!

CHAPTER *13. Annuals for*

Rock Gardens, Walls, and Pools

The use of annuals as supplementary material to enhance the attractiveness of rock gardens, walls, and pool sides has too long been overlooked—or perhaps "ignored" would be a better word. In fact, among many of the Rock Garden Society members and other simon-pure alpine plant lovers it still is derided. Among this sporting gentry it is considered just not cricket to employ a little old easily grown annual to get much the same effect in plant form and color as might be obtained with a rare and temperamental species from some high altitude.

For this attitude there is, to be sure, some excuse, because too frequently annuals have been misused in rock gardens and near water. This, however, is not the fault of the plant but rather of the unperceptive gardener. If the right annuals are used in the right way, they can add much to the planting and they are particularly valuable because they make it possible to carry color on through the summer and autumn, when in most rock gardens and wall plantings color is conspicuous only by its absence.

ROCK GARDENS

The fact that one may have seen somewhere a rock garden constructed of stones painted different colors and laid on the surface of a slope or a mound is no reason for not having any rock garden at all. Similarly, the fact that such plants as Scarlet Sage, Coleus, and large-flowered Zinnia may have occasionally been used, in so-called rock gardens, by insensitive gardeners is no reason for the exclusion of all types of annuals from the sacred precincts of the rock garden.

It really all boils down to a matter of selection. The perceptive

gardener—even if a beginner and not yet a skilled plantsman—
soon learns that certain types of plants look as though they "belong" in certain surroundings. Indeed, his observation of plants in
nature, if he possesses an inquiring eye, will have taught him this
even before he ever set his hand to a trowel handle. He can recall
without much effort that in rocky outcroppings he has not seen
such lush-growing plants as Skunk-cabbage, Bullrushes, and Pick-
erel Weed, but rather such tough (if sometimes frail-looking) miniatures as Saxifrage, Wild Columbine, and Creeping Phlox.

So when the gardener with annuals comes to select species or
varieties to use in his rock garden, he will try those that really look
at home in their proposed surroundings—and he can find many.
It might seem at first thought, for instance, that Zinnias would be
one of the last things to use in a rock garden. And certainly that
would be true if the Super Giant Colossal kinds growing three feet
tall were selected; but if one takes the trouble to read the Zinnia section of his catalogue beyond the big color plates, he will find a few
lines of small type devoted to *Zinnia linearis,* low in habit and with
very small flowers, and other dwarf forms such as Miniature, Cupid,
Tom Thumb, all of which look quite in place in a rock garden. A
list of other annuals and plants usually treated as annuals that are
suited to rock-garden surroundings is given in Chapter 5.

Quite as important as what to use, however, is *how* to use it. In
a rock garden the structural features, the rocks themselves, and the
ways in which they are arranged are quite as important as the flowers. In planting a rock garden, annuals—or any kind of plant material, for that matter—should be utilized in such a way that the rock
structure will not be hidden. Usually it is best to use only a few
plants of one variety in a place, and these should be arranged informally and irregularly, for the rock garden in its very nature
should *look* unplanned and unplanted. Often a single plant of a
kind may make an interesting point of accent.

Another precaution to be observed is that of keeping both the
plants and the plantings in scale with the area of the rock garden.
The smaller the area, the more important it is to use plants that do
not grow to large size and to limit the number in any one group.

Many of the annuals best suited to rock-garden planting do not
require a rich soil. Others—such as Verbena and Candytuft—
which do best in rich loam in the flower border will grow less vig-

Portulaca (Rose-moss) available in both single and double form, and in separate colors, is at home in the rock garden or along a wall.

Small rock garden on slope against a house.

orously but still flower satisfactorily in rather lean and gravelly soil in the rock garden and make good subjects.

Cutting back or trimming may be employed freely in the small rock garden to keep plants within their allotted bounds. Many plants which, left to themselves, tend to produce single upright spikes will, if severely pinched back, throw several shorter spikes. Snapdragons and Cheiranthus are examples.

FOR WALLS

Most of what has been said above applies to the use of annuals and pseudo-annuals in rock gardens. Many of the same plants are good wall subjects. In walls, of course, those of trailing habit are particularly effective. Many others will surprise the gardener, when planted in a wall, by forming a crown or tuft flat against the wall surface and then turning their flower stems upward at nearly right angles.

In "dry" or open-joint walls it is desirable to have the pockets in which the plants are to be inserted of generous size and filled with suitable soil containing a goodly percentage of peatmoss, as this helps to retain moisture about the roots. In watering plants in a

Hard long lines, whether of a building, hedge, wall, or curb, are readily made more attractive with a mixed planting of annuals.

wall, use a fine spray, applied for a long time, rather than the usual hose nozzle or sprinkler. The triple-hose irrigator mentioned on page 115 is ideal for this purpose, as it bathes the wall surface with a fine, mistlike spray.

In the case of masonry walls, planting must of course be done along the top rather than *in* the wall. Here such creeping or spreading annuals as Petunia and Nasturtium make a very pleasing and long-season picture. (See photograph page 59.)

For something a bit more out of the ordinary try a few of the other plants suggested on page 74. Ice Plant *(Mesembryanthemum crystallinum)*, despite its common name, is excellent for a wall in full sun. The annual form (*M. criniflorum* or Livingstone-daisy) is less vigorous in growth, but you can grow it from seed instead of having to buy plants.

FOR POOLS

Flowers that are most effective in creating pleasing pictures in combination with a pool are of two types: those of creeping habit,

In selecting annuals for pool-side planting, scale should be considered. This small pool has been smothered.

Here planting material around pool, largely annuals, has been well chosen for both variety and scale.

which make rambling growths that will run down over the edge to meet the water and perhaps send out a trailer or two to float upon its surface; and those that will produce blooms to be reflected in its mirror-like surface. The latter should be of moderate height, for tall plants near a pool will more or less conceal it from sight. Forget-me-not, *(Myosotis scorpidides)*, Mesembryanthemum, Verbena, and Sanvitalia or Creeping-zinnia are species of the first (trailing) type; Candytuft, Dianthus, Monkey Flower, Nierembergia, and Torenia, of the second type.

For larger pools with a considerable expanse of water, much larger and more vigorous plants will be in order. Such pools often have wet or moist margins, and perennials like Hibiscus, Cat-tails, Rushes, and Japanese Irsis are more satisfactory than annuals.

One word—or more accurately three—of caution should be observed in connection with moderate-sized pools: *do not overplant!* Keep in mind that the pool itself is the center of interest, the plant material about it only supplementary decoration. Also, plants grow, and the small plants or seedlings you set out in spring will soon take up several times as much space as at first. The same precaution should be observed with all plants—Water-lilies and various other aquatics—placed in the pool itself.

Annuals make satisfactory plant material for flower arrangement, by themselves or in combination with other flowers and foliage. Their bright colors, varied size, form, and stem length give great variety which the arranger may use to good advantage.

Outstanding annuals for arrangements are listed in Chapter 5. Here are special uses to which some are suited:

For main lines (skeletons or patterns) ――――――――――――――――

Amberboa	Cynoglossum	Nicotiana
Bells-of-Ireland	Geranium branches	Petunia branches
Castor-bean	Grasses	Salvia
Celosia	Larkspur	Snapdragon
Cobaea scandens	Lupine	Stock
Coleus	Nasturtium branches	Tassel-flower

For focal interest ――――――――――――――――

Calendula	Datura	Moonflower
China-aster	Gaillardia	Poppy
Chrysanthemum	Gerberia	Prickly-poppy
Centaurea	Hunnemannia	Tithonia
Cosmos	Lavatera	Zinnia (large)
Dahlia	Marigold, large	

For mixed bouquets ――――――――――――――――

Arctotis	Cape-marigold	Cynoglossum
Blue Lace-flower	Catananche	Dianthus
Browallia	Clarkia	Everlasting
Calceolaria	Cornflower	Feverfew
Calliopsis	Cosmos	Forget-me-not

Gerberia
Gypsophila
Heliotrope
Love-in-a-mist
Marigold (small)
Mignonette
Nicotiana

Nierembergia
Pansy
Petunia
Phacelia
Salpiglossis
Scabiosa
Schizanthus

Star-of-Texas
Sweet Pea
Tahoka-daisy
Torenia
Verbena
Zinnia (small)

Accessory foliage

Amaranthus
Castor-bean
Cobaea scandens
Coleus

Dusty Miller
Euphorbia
Grasses (see page 69)
Perilla

Prickly-poppy
Sideritis
Tassel-flower
Zea

Arrangements of a single species, using foliage, stems, and flowers

Cobaea scandens
Castor-bean
Dahlia
Geranium

Marigold
Moonflower
Nasturtium
Petunia

Sweet Pea
Verbena
Zinnia

Suggested combinations

Bells-of-Ireland
and Marigold Lime-
light, Buff Beauty,
Canary Bird
or Mayling
or Nasturtium
or Star-of-Texas
or Tithonia
or Calendula

Castor-bean
and Dahlia, small, red
or Poppy
or Tulip-poppy
or Tithonia
or Zinnia

Stock
and China-aster

Cosmos
Scabiosa
Salpiglossis
Snapdragon
or Lupine

China-aster
Clarkia
Schizantus
Tahoka-daisy
Gypsophila

Coleus
and Dahlia (small)
or Zinnia (small)

Tassal-flower
and Zinnia

Sideritis
and Star-of-Texas
or Calendula
or Scabiosa

Dianthus
Heliotrope
Mignonette
Verbena

Mignonette
Torenia
Verbena (pink)

Larkspur
Pansy
Petunia
Salvia farinacea

Compact, low-growing annuals—Ageratum, Alyssum, dwarf Petunias, used as neat edging for a brick walk. BELOW A mixed border, between an unsightly retaining wall and a curb, tempts customers to stop at a Cape Cod gas station.

Zinnias, formerly coarse-flowered and dull-hued, are now available in many types and sizes, and in a wide range of most attractive colors. ABOVE *Crown-of-gold retains the original broad, flat petals.* BELOW *The Cactus-flowered or Fantasy (Giant Hybrid variety).*

CUTTING AND CONDITIONING

Cut annuals for arrangement just as they are opening in early morning or in the early evening. Place the stems at once in deep, cool water and keep in a cool, dark room or cellar overnight or for at least six hours.

The tips of the stems of Poppies and Heliotrope should be seared in a gas flame as soon as cut and before hardening in water. If stems must be shortened as the arrangement is being made, stem tips should be researed.

The life of most annuals is prolonged by the use of one of the commercial plant preservatives now available. These materials both retard underwater decay of stems and foliage and supply essential nutrients. They are more effective than such methods as adding copper pennies or aspirin to the water.

During the time the arrangement is being made stems should be kept in water constantly. Every minute that a cut flower is out of water shortens its life expectancy.

Use containers large and deep enough to supply ample water to flower stems. Large flowers like giant Marigold and Zinnia need much more water than thin-stemmed annuals like Salpiglossis or Clarkia.

Fresh water may be added each day. If water becomes stale and discolored, remove it with a ball syringe and refill the container.

Keep arrangements as cool as possible at all times and out of direct drafts. If they must be in an overheated room while they are on display, remove to a cool place as soon as possible.

Individual faded blooms in an arrangement may often be freshened by removing them, recutting the stems, and placing them in hot water. Let them remain until water cools and then, if revived, replace in the arrangement.

FLOWER SHOWS AND EXHIBITING

The amateur gardener who decides—or is persuaded—to enter specimen flowers or arrangements in a flower show has much to learn. His or hers first effort may well end in disappointment or even humiliation unless time is taken to learn in advance the rules of the game.

First of all, plant material to be entered in a show must be the very best you are capable of growing. It is put in competition with other gardeners' entries for the purpose of winning prizes if possible. Therefore, it is better not to exhibit at all any spindly, diseased, or insect-ridden material. Any specimen offered in the horticultural classes should at least be healthy, with good foliage and typical blooms of good color. In an arrangement the material should be fresh and crisp and the foliage in perfect condition.

Your first entry in a flower show may be more or less accidental. You may have some fine flowers just at the time of the show and so dare, or be coaxed, to show them. After that first time, you will be wise to use every means in your power to produce the very best annuals you can for exhibition in horticultural or arrangement classes. (See pages 164–5.)

The show schedule should be studied carefully as soon as it is available. Mark the classes in which you wish to enter, and inform the chairman so that he or she can have entry blanks filled in and ready for you when you arrive at the show.

Cutting

Annual flowers for showing in horticultural or arrangement classes should be cut just as they are opening and placed at once in deep, cool water. For details of hardening, see page 161.

Grooming

Specimens to be exhibited should be groomed by removing any broken, bruised, or dead foliage and faded blossoms or petals.

Carrying

Care in transportation is essential. Pack with wax or tissue paper if material is to be carried in boxes. Heads of easily marred blooms may be wrapped separately in soft tissue paper and placed so that one bloom does not press upon another. If transported in buckets of water, each bloom should be held erect and away from other blossoms. See illustration, page 163.

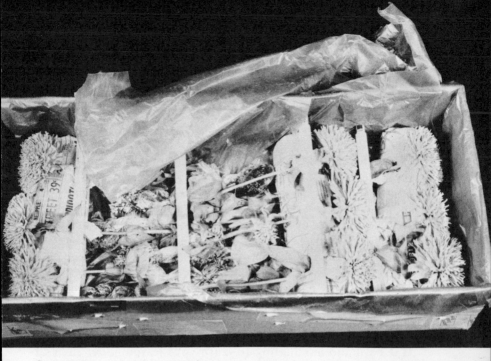

Giant Zinnias properly packed for shipping. Newspaper rolls under stems support heads, and cross slats hold stems in place. Bases of stems are wrapped in sphagnum, kept moist in pliofilm without wetting leaves.

Showing

A single specimen or even three specimens of Marigold, Zinnia, Salpiglossis, or Scabiosa will not look their best standing stiffly or at a crazy angle in a milk bottle or tumbler, awaiting the decision of the judges. If uniform containers are provided by the show committee, there may be nothing you can do about this other than suggesting that narrow-necked containers be supplied another year. If you are permitted to use your own containers, you may improve the appearance of your specimens by placing them in vases or containers, which will set each off to advantage.

When all your cut material is assembled, hardened, and ready for the show, get out the schedule once more and check it carefully with your entries. If the schedule calls for a class of three Zinnias of three different types, do not put in three Giant Dahlia-flowered in three colors. If a class calls for an arrangement in glass, do not use plastic or porcelain. If you ignore the limitations of a class, the judges will disqualify your entry.

Enter *exactly* what is called for in each class in the schedule in which you intend to compete. This is no time for independence or free thinking. After all your hard work, you do not want an entry disqualified.

We judged a show recently where one club had reserved all the spaces in one flower-arrangement class. There were eight arrangements in the class, all set up by members of this one club. The schedule called for a "composition," and the general instructions stated that the rules of the National Council of State Garden Clubs would be followed. According to those rules, a composition is "a flower arrangement, with one or more accessories." Only one entry had accessories. Therefore, seven entries had to be disqualified because they did not adhere to the schedule. The show chairman was distressed, but as she had emphasized the necessity of following the clearly stated rules, there was no other course open to her than to recommend their disqualification.

It is hard and humiliating to learn your lesson under such circumstances. A much better and more constructive method is to study the schedule closely well before the show opens. If you are in doubt about any class in which you want to enter, phone the proper chairman and get it straightened out in your own mind. Then when the time comes to enter, you will know just what you can and can't do.

After the prizes have been awarded, don't blame the judges if you failed to take a prize. Rather try to find out why they decided as they did. In arrangement classes especially, judges are generous in making notes for exhitbitors on what they did and did not like about the entries. These notes are invaluable to the beginner in show arrangement.

Judging

Remember that the judges are especially trained for their work. They often travel long distances and stand on their feet for several hours trying to do a conscientious job. Here are some of the things on which they base their decisions:

HORTICULTURAL CLASSES

Correct conformity of entry with requirements of schedule.

Color   Size
Form   Substance
Stem   Foliage

Where point scoring is used, scoring points vary with the flower being judged.

Uniformity: where a class calls for more than one specimen of a single species (as for instance three blooms of Larkspur), they should be as nearly as possible of one size, with equal stem lengths

ARRANGEMENT CLASSES

Correct conformity of entry with requirements of schedule.

Suitability in size to the space alloted. (Measurements of exhibition spaces or "niches" usually are given in the schedule).

Point scoring may or may not be used. In either case, the following items are considered. When point-scored, points are as noted:

Color combination	25
Relation to container	10
Design	25
Distinction and originality	20
Suitability of combination of material	10
Condition	10
Total	100

CHAPTER *15. Annuals*

for Winter Bloom Indoors

Much of the pleasure of growing annuals and other plants usually grown as annuals out of doors in summer can be carried on into the winter. This involves, to be sure, quite a different type of gardening, with its own special rewards and excitements. There will of course be no sweeps and masses of color, but a single slowly opening bloom in January or Ferbuary, when winter wraps the world in an ermine blanket and barren branches shake against the cold, may give to one's soul quite as much of a lift as a whole border of brilliant bloom in midsummer.

There are, too, some quite distinct advantages to the beginner at gardening in his venture into this new field. He will find that his relationship to his plants is on a much more intimate basis, and he will soon discover things he did not know before about their habits of growth; their reactions to varying conditions; their foibles, whims, and whimsies—which will prove invaluable to him in the growing of plants out of doors.

TYPES OF PLANTS FOR INDOOR GARDENS

There are, in general, two quite distinct types of plants suitable for growing indoors—and by indoors we here mean without benefit of a greenhouse.

First there are the annuals, and other plants which have some of the characteristics of annuals, which are usually grown indoors; i.e., commonly considered to be house plants. Among these are such species as Coleus, *Begonia semperflorens,* and Geraniums.

The second group includes annuals which, while commonly thought of as garden subjects, lend themselves also to indoor culture. Among these are Petunia, Ageratum, Calendula, Pansy and

Viola, Snapdragon, Mignonette, Dianthus, Lobelia, Browallia, and Torenia. There are many others. But usually available locations for growing plants indoors are such that medium size and height are prerequisites. Some annuals are available in miniature or dwarf types which make good indoor subjects. A list of these will be found on page 71.

The species mentioned in both of these groups of plants may be started from seed, although in some instances—as with Geraniums, Begonia, Coleus, and some others—several months may be saved if growing plants in pots are purchased.

OBTAINING THE PLANTS

When annuals that are ordinarily grown in the garden are wanted for the indoor winter garden, the grower has available four methods of obtaining his plants. He may start them from seed especially for winter bloom indoors; he may make cuttings to obtain new plants; he may take up old plants from the garden and pot them for continued growth indoors; or lastly, in some cases, he may find stray seedlings about the garden which can be potted and grown on.

Starting from seed is in general the best method. Its one drawback from a practical point of view is that it requires advanced timing and is likely to be overlooked until long after it should have been done. If you intend to grow plants from seed for winter bloom, get the seed early and mark planting dates on your calendar so that you will get them in in time. It is difficult to lure most annuals to bloom freely during the short days of very late fall and midwinter, and this should be taken into consideration. A few species, such as Sweet Alyssum, Candytuft, Ageratum, and dwarf Phlox, may be had in bloom in from ten to twelve weeks, but for most it is well to allow several weeks longer. The use of artificial lighting, where available, will of course cut down considerably the period of time before flowering.

A cold frame—no matter how crude and simple a one—will be found extremely helpful in getting the little seedlings started. Protection is required quite as much from the heavy driving rains of autumn as from frosty nights later on before the plants are brought into the house.

In sowing, keep in mind that only a few plants of any one kind

A stocky, branching plant of Ageratum—result of timely pinching back.

will be wanted. For this reason it is well to use only part of any one packet of seed at the first planting. Then if anything goes wrong you can make a second try.

The procedure in starting the plants is the same as that already outlined in Chapter 8. Special attention, however, should be given to the operation of pinching back the plants in order to secure dwarf, stocky growth. When giving the final potting up we prefer to use azalea pots rather than the taller, standard flowerpots, as they are much less likely to be accidentally tipped over; also, they dry out less rapidly. The size of pot to use depends both upon the character of the plant and the amount of space available in the indoor garden. Usually a four-inch pot is the smallest that should be used, and a five- or six-inch one is better. With the modern, highly concentrated fertilizers and very frequent feeding, excellent specimens can be grown in pots much smaller than were formerly considered essential.

Taking up stray seedlings and bringing them in for winter bloom are, for several reasons, much less satisfactory than sowing the seed.

Self-sown Viola seedlings. BELOW: *Taken up and transplanted.*

In the first place, you are getting a pig in a poke, because very few annuals will come true from seed. In the second place, they are much more likely to be smaller plants than those from seed sown at the proper time. The only advantage of stray seedlings is that they sometimes offer an "out" for the careless gardener who has neglected to sow seed especially for indoor bloom.

Making cuttings of plants which are wanted is, on the whole, easier and quicker than growing them from seed. If the frame is not available for use in rooting the cuttings, a cutting box can readily be made by using any fairly large box eight inches or so in depth and covering with a small sash or even a sheet of glass or plastic. It should be placed where it will not receive the full rays of the autumn sun—such as a spot north of a wall or hedge but free from drip. Also, it should be within reach of the garden hose so that a fine mist spray will be available. Good drainage should, of course be provided.

For a rooting mixture we like a half and half mixture, by bulk, of gritty sand and peatmoss or vermiculite. This can be placed either directly in the box or, if only a few cuttings are to be made, in azalea pots which (after the cuttings have been inserted), are set in the box and surrounded with damp peatmoss. The advantage of using the pots is that cuttings of each species can be handled separately and those which root quickest removed without disturbing the others.

The cuttings are made from new growth which is sufficiently firm

Cuttings of various summer plants—Geraniums, Heliotrope, and the like— trimmed and ready to insert in compost for rooting.

Geranium cutting ready for potting. Soil is pressed closely about bottom of stem, and top cut back.

so that it will snap like a string bean when bent between the fingers. The cut is made at or just below a joint and straight across the stem with a sharp knife so that no ragged edges are left. (Do not use scissors, as these are apt to bruise the flesh, thus inviting decay.) The cuttings are made just long enough, usually four to six inches, to carry at least three sets of leaves. The lower leaves are removed before the cutting is inserted in the rooting medium.

After the cuttings are made, the bases of the stems are dipped in Rootone or Arasan and then inserted almost up to the first set of leaves in the rooting medium. Use a lead pencil or a small round dibber to make holes to receive the cuttings, and after they are in place, firm the medium down around them with the fingers.

The cuttings are now ready for a watering sufficient to make the rooting medium thoroughly moist. This should be applied slowly in the form of a gentle spray. If the cuttings have been placed in pots, a better method of watering is to stand them in a pan or tray in an inch or two of water and allow them to remain until they have soaked up sufficient water from the bottom to make the surface slightly moist. From now on the rooting medium should be kept moist but never soaking wet. The tops may be moistened daily with a fog or mist spray. A special fogging nozzle that fits any ordinary hose coupling is excellent for this purpose.

A further aid to rooting may be given by keeping the cutting box or individual pots covered fairly tightly with cellophane or plastic tents. (See illustration page 101.) Such a covering forms a miniature greenhouse over the cuttings, keeps the air around them moist, and greatly reduces the care required for watering, as they may be left without attention in this respect for several days at a time.

Some cuttings will begin to form new roots very quickly—within ten days to two weeks. Others may require a month or more. As soon as the new roots are a half inch to an inch or so in length the cuttings should be removed and placed in small pots. It is decidely a disadvantage rather than an advantage to leave them until the roots grow longer. The more growth they have made, the greater will be the shock to the baby plants when they are transferred to pots.

Taking in plants from flower beds or borders—the fourth method for providing plants for the winter garden indoors—is in general much less desirable than growing them from seed or from cuttings. At first it may seem a quick and sure way to get plants for winter bloom, but in most cases it is not. Annually thousands of plants are taken up in late fall by enthusiastic inexperienced gardeners, crammed into pots several sizes too small for them (by a process which suggests the old rural problem of trying to get five quarts of cider into a gallon jug), and then—after a few weeks of overgenerous watering and hopeful prayer—finally thrown onto the compost heap.

If you decide to make the attempt to transfer plants from the garden to your window sills for winter bloom, realize first that they must be completely made over. A major operation is involved, and it will take the patient a long time to recover from it.

To begin with, the root system—which in the garden has roamed at liberty through the soil—must be reduced drastically to get it down to a size that can fit into a pot. This reduced root system cannot support the amount of top growth above soil which it has been carrying; therefore, the top also must be drastically reduced. In the case of fairly large plants—such as Geranium, Coleus, Patience Plant *(Impatiens)*, and others—the plants should be reduced,

An old Viola plant is taken up, potted, and trimmed back to stubs, ready to start new growth indoors.

to mere stubs. It may be possible to keep the root ball intact by cutting around it with a long-bladed knife, after moistening the soil sufficiently so that it will be less likely to crumble away from the roots, and then transferring this to a pot of suitable size. If the soil ball cannot be kept intact, it will be best to wash it off completely by sousing it gently in a pail of water and then trimming back the roots to suitable size. Then pot up, keeping the remaining roots, so far as possible, in their normal position. This is done by holding the plant suspended in the pot with one hand and gradually filling in the soil around the roots with the other. When the pot is filled, firm the soil about the roots by holding the pot with both hands and tapping the bottom rather severely several times against some surface that will not be likely to crack it.

When your collection of plants has thus been potted up, water them from the bottom until the soil is thoroughly moist (not soaking wet), and plunge them in soil or moist peatmoss in moderate shade. Thereafter water frequently enough to keep the soil in the pots from becoming dry, but avoid overwatering because at this stage of the game the roots will be taking very little moisture from the soil. At the same time care must be exercised to keep the tops from drying out. A frequent wetting with a fine spray, even if there are no leaves present, will help to accomplish this. It is better to place the newly potted plants in a closed frame in a shaded location until new growth begins to develop.

Timing

While potting up may be done just before frost, it is much better to undertake the operation a month or two earlier so that new growth will have started before the plants have to be brought indoors and thus subjected to the additional handicap of changed conditions. Earlier potting also means that you will not have to wait so long before you can begin to enjoy the returns from your labor.

GROWING CONDITIONS INDOORS

The factors that will determine your success—or lack of it—are light, temperature, and moisture. All three of these must be such as the plants you are growing require or your efforts will have been a waste of time.

Light

Almost all flowering plants and particularly annuals do best with all the direct sunlight they can get during the winter months. A south window is the preferred location. A north or west window—unless artificial lighting can be provided during the winter months —is pretty sure to bring nothing but disappointment.

Temperature

Contrary to what most beginners are likely to believe, indoor temperatures for growing plants are usually too high rather than too low. The majority of plants will thrive better at a temperature of 55 degrees at night and ten degrees higher during the day than they will at our usual modern living-room temperatures of seventy degrees or more. Abundant fresh air, too, is desirable, though the plants should never be exposed to direct cold drafts as from a nearby open window.

Moisture

The most difficult factor to control under average house conditions is that of moisture. It is an easy matter to water frequently enough to keep the soil moist, especially if pots are placed in saucers or in a tray on a bed of pebbles so that they may be sub-irrigated. Moisture in the air—humidity—is another matter. One of the main reasons why the old-fashioned country housewife so frequently had excellent specimens of flowering plants in her kitchen windows in winter was the constant supply of moisture in the air from her household operations. A kettleful of water was always simmering on the back of the range, distributing its steam through the air of the kitchen. Pans of water placed on or behind the radiators or on the windowsill itself where plants are being grown, are of considerable help—and the indoor gardener will be surprised at how frequently they have to be filled.

Plant Foods

The problem of keeping your indoor garden well fed is no longer a difficult one. There are a dozen or more brands of complete plant food under such trade names as Hyponex, Rapid-Gro, Instant Vigoro, and Plant Marvel, which are easily applied and odorless. One need merely follow directions carefully and avoid overfeeding, which may result in the too vigorous growth of stems and foliage at the expense of flower production.

Sanitation

Annuals grown indoors will profit by a weekly syringing of the leaves. Place the plants in a sink or laundry tub and spray the foliage with a fine mist.

At the same time, look over each plant carefully for possible pests. Aphids are apt to appear on the undersides of leaves and on opening foliage or buds. Mealybugs may be found under leaves or at joints. For control of these and other pests, see Chapter 10. If pests are discovered within a day or two of their appearance it is not hard to control them. Weekly inspection is therefore most important.

PART THREE
— CATALOGUE OF ANNUALS

In attempting to select the ten annuals most generally grown in the United States, in order to give these somewhat more detailed attention than can be accorded to every plant in this catalogue, we have been guided not merely by our own evaluation of their popularity. The list is based on the considered estimates of a group of leading authorities in the field, some commercial—for they certainly are in a position to judge—and others with nation wide experience.

Some of the results of this poll surprised us—Sweet Pea, for instance. But they are presented here in the order of the votes they received. Petunia and Zinnia nearly tied for first place, but the former won out by a narrow margin.

Here's how they ran:

PETUNIA	SNAPDRAGON
ZINNIA	LARKSPUR
MARIGOLD	SWEET ALYSSUM
CHINA-ASTER	PHLOX DRUMMONDI
SWEET PEA	MORNING-GLORY

PETUNIA

Among annuals, the Petunia is unquestionably every man's flower. North, south, east, and west it thrives in almost any type of soil and under widely varying conditions. The results which hybridizers have achieved in improving old varieties and developing new types are almost beyond belief.

And the end is not yet; the recent achievements in the work on F-1 Hybrids give promise of new strains and varieties which will surpass anything we have known up to now.

F-1 Hybrids, it may be explained *en passant,* are first-generation varieties which will not come true the second year from the seed which they produce, and which therefore can be obtained only by making the same crosses over again for each lot of seed. This involves a great deal of hand work and very meticulous care. Consequently such seed can be produced only at much additional cost and commands a much higher price than that of varieties which can be grown in the ordinary way. The greater vigor and other improved qualities of F-1 Hybrid varieties, of both flowers and vegetables, make their purchase worth while. This is particularly true of annuals for the home garden, where a few plants of superior quality are of much more value than a large number of less desirable ones.

Uses

Petunias, because of their wide variation in habit of growth, easy culture, freedom from pests and diseases, and extremely long season of bloom, lend themselves to many uses in the garden and even indoors.

Anyone who has ever driven through a suburban area knows how effective they can be for masses of color, either by themselves or in large beds with other flowers. They are unsurpassed as a succession planting for beds of spring-flowering bulbs, as they develop quickly, are shallow-rooted, and do not smother the ripening bulb foliage. The "Balcony" varieties, semi-trailing in habit, are excellent for low banks, along stone or masonry curbings, and of course in window or terrace boxes and for the old-fashioned hanging basket.

As Petunias will stand any amount of trimming and shaping, they are also excellent as pot plants, either for patios or terraces or for winter gardens indoors. While not usually thought of as flowers for cutting, Petunias neverless are outstanding for this purpose and quite ideal as one-flower arrangements for quick, easy, and long-lasting summer decoration. (See photograph page 225.)

Types

In ordering varieties, it is important to select those which will best fit into the uses you have in mind for them. Unfortunately for the gardener, there is no standard classification of types which covers today's innumerable ramifications and rapidly changing varieties. The old botanical classification of *parviflora, hybrida nana compacta, hybrida grandiflora, hybrida grandiflora fimbriata, flore pleno,* etc., is so obsolete as to be next to useless, and doubly confusing because the "hybrid" Petunias of today's catalogues are the F-1 Hybrids. So you will have to struggle through the lists of the various seedsmen and do the best you can.

The Balcony type, sometimes called Large-flowered Bedding, is fairly distinct, with trailing branches up to eighteen inches or more in length and two- to three-inch flowers.

The Dwarf type, sometimes listed as Gem, also is fairly distinct. For the most part this type makes moundlike plants of a foot or so in height and is extremely free-flowering, producing enormous numbers of moderate-sized flowers. These are desirable for border edgings, low masses of color, and especially for pot plants.

The All-Doubles are F-1 Hybrids and comparatively newcomers, some rampant growers forming plants up to three feet across and others quite dwarf. In this group we have found Allegro, deep salmon; Mrs. Dwight D. Eisenhower, light salmon; and Burpee Orchid, particularly attractive. These are best grown in porch or terrace boxes or in large pots with some support such as birch twigs. If grown on level ground, they should be well mulched to keep the heavy flowers from trailing in the dirt. They are very effective as cut blooms. Single F-1 Hybrids include the two All America winners: Ballerina, a lovely salmon, and the brand-new Prima Donna, deep, pure rose color. Both are strong growers with extra-large flowers of fine stamina.

Of the Giant-flowered sorts, there are two quite distinct types: those with ruffled petals, giving the effect of double flowers, up to six inches across (Fluffy Ruffles is a typical variety); and the Giant Fringed, of which Theodosia is probably the best-known variety. (To us the fringed type has always seemed much more attractive than the ruffled.)

The Bedding type is a sort of catch-all group, some varieties making stems as long as the Balconies, and others—such as Snowstorm and White Cloud, two of the best whites—much more compact plants.

Culture

Any trouble encountered in the growing of Petunias is likely to be in getting the plants started rather than during their later growth. All Petunia seeds are very fine, but while some varieties start readily even when sown out of doors in the open, others, to be perfectly frank, should be placed in the "very difficult" list. These include all the Doubles and the Fancy Large-flowered varieties, the seeds of which are so small as to be almost invisible. Great care should be exercised also with the F-1 Hybrids, not because they are weak growers but because a package usually contains very few seeds, and it is desirable to make every one count. Some catalogues note which varieties need particular care. It is best to start these indoors or in a frame, not only because conditions can be better controlled, but because they require a considerably longer period before coming into bloom. When such varieties must be planted in the open, they may be sown in areas of specially prepared soil in a small circle that can be protected with a plastic tent until the little seedlings are well up. Double varieties and the Fancy Large-flowered ones require about twice as long to germinate as the ordinary bedding sorts—sometimes as much as three weeks.

Starting indoors

As Petunia seeds are extremely fine, take extra pains in preparing the compost in which they are to be started. (See page 94.) They need no covering but should merely be pressed into the soil. A pane of glass or a plastic cap placed over the flat or pot in which they are sown will aid greatly in keeping the surface constantly moist and getting them safely germinated. Seeds should be scattered evenly and not too thickly. Mixing them with fine, dry sand is of considerable help in getting even distribution—though this will hardly be necessary with those high-priced varieties that require the use of a magnifying glass to discover any seed in the packet.

Once up, the little seedlings are easily transplanted; and the sooner this is done, the better. A second transplanting to small pots or dirt bands is desirable, especially if the plants are to be used for setting out among other plants in a mixed border, in the rock garden or window boxes.

Seed sown in the open should be thinned out at an early stage to stand several inches apart each way, and later to twelve inches, which is none too much space for the dwarf types in good soil.

Pinching back when plants have made about six inches of growth

Double Petunias are difficult to germinate. These were started in bulb pan, covered with plastic dome.

Transplanted to flat for a few weeks (like these Forget-me-nots). BELOW: *They made bushy plants like this.*

will result in bushier plants. If this is not done, the gardener can at least cut the first blooms with a few inches of stem.

Where Petunias are grown in any quantity, it is of course not possible—as is frequently advised by writers who do not grow them—to keep all blossoms cut off as they fade. It is possible, however, to go over a planting two or three times during the season and cut back to within a few inches of the base of the plant the old long stems that are flowering only at the tips. Usually this can be done in such a way as to leave some branches that are still flowering freely, so that the result is not a floral crew haircut. Neglected plants that have been allowed to flower out can be cut back severely and will rapidly develop new growth. This procedure, however, leaves a hiatus in the production of bloom.

Supports are not usually required by Petunias, but the more vigorous-growing varieties, especially the Doubles, if grown on a level surface or in pots or boxes, will be greatly benefited so far as the display of blooms is concerned by moderate support with a light trellis or, better, with light, twiggy branches. The latter, if put in place before the plants have begun to "flop," will be pretty much covered from sight by the foliage as they grow. Whatever support is used should be put in place while the plants are still small: it is almost impossible to tie them up after they are grown without getting such a messy effect that it is worse than no support at all.

For winter bloom indoors

Petunias are among the most satisfactory of all annuals for winter bloom. Seed may be sown for new plants (see page 168), old plants may be cut back and potted up to make new growth (see page 173), or cuttings which root readily (see page 171) may be made in August or September to give good-sized flowering plants by midwinter. We have found the latter method most desirable with the Double-flowering and the choice Large-flowered Fringed and Ruffled sorts. These same plants will supply cuttings in February or March to provide plants to be set out again for summer bloom. So you see, even if you pay a buck for an infinitesimal packet of an extra-fine Petunia, you can get your money back many times over.

ZINNIA

From a disregarded, if not an almost despised, position in the world of flowers, the Zinnia has gradually gained in popularity to vie with the Petunia for first place among all annuals. By not a few authorities, indeed, it is considered to be entitled to first place.

The development of the Zinnia, a native of Mexico, from a small-flowered, coarse, and unattractive plant to the many types and numberless varieties of today has taken place within a single long life span. As the development of horticultural varieties of flowers go, this is a remarkable thing in itself.

When first introduced to gardens, the Zinnia was considered a sort of poor relation, tolerated only because it was one of the easiest of all flowers to grow, even under adverse conditions. The blooms were as stiff and about as attractive as the head of a worn-out mop, and the colors were strong and raw or decidedly muddy. But its ease of culture and exceptional resistance to heat and drought kept it from being discarded. Nearly half a century ago, under the skillful hands of Luther Burbank, it had been greatly improved and the groundwork for the modern varieties had been laid. In 1924, Bodgers, world-famous seed growers of California, introduced the Dahlia-flowered type, and the Zinnia was on its way to the top of the list.

The development of the Zinnia is certainly one of the most striking of all examples of improvement in a flower under the hands of the hybridists, as a glance at the color illustration (see page 129) will indicate. Indeed, there are now so many types of Zinnias that the inexperienced gardener finds himself somewhat confused when it comes to sending in his order for seeds. These types vary so greatly that it is well to know something about them so one can make an intelligent selection to suit the various purposes for which they may be used.

As with Petunias, so with Zinnias; there is no standard classification of these types used by the catalogues. Perhaps the easiest way to make a selection is on the basis of height, for the tallest ones make towering plants up to three and a half or even four feet; the medium, eighteen to twenty-four inches; and the dwarf, which are usually under eighteen, with some as low as twelve. In general, the size of the individual flowers is in relation to the height of the plant. Some of the tall varieties have blooms up to six inches

Zinnia linearis, a much-overlooked species, is one of our favorites; flowers are two-toned.

across; those of medium height are usually under three, and some of the dwarfs as little as one. One of the smallest-flowered of all, *Zinnia linearis,* forms a solid mass of foliage and flowers, ten inches tall.

In each of these groups there are several subtypes, differing in flower form and in color combinations.

Tall. In the tall, large-flowered group, there are the Dahlia-flowered, with long, flat, spatula-shaped petals arranged like those of a formal Dahlia; California Giant and Super-Giant with plain petals, slightly reflexed; Burpee's Giant Hybrids, informal and with curled or feathery petals; Cactus-flowered, with very irregular, narrow, twisted petals—a complete joy for the flower arranger; Crown-of-Gold, formal, plain petals, bicolored; and the David Burpee Strain, in a wonderful range of colors and with curled and quilled petals and curled leaves.

Medium. In medium-tall varieties, with two- to three-inch flowers, are the Cut-and-Come-Again *(pumila);* Fantasy, with narrow, twisted, and curled petals; Harmony, crested, with a distinct collar; and the older *pumila* varieties, with plain, reflexed petals.

Dwarf. The dwarf, smaller-flowered group includes Lilliput (Baby or Pompon), extremely free-flowering on dwarf compact plants; Tom Thumb, an even more dwarf form of Lilliput; Cupid, with one-inch cone-shaped flowers on slender stems; Mexicana, with distinct pointed petals in color blends of Indian red, yellow, and cream, of which the new, extremely popular Persin Carpet, eighteen inches, is the best strain; and Z. *linearis,* with single, starry flowers in two tones of yellow and quite distinct from any of the preceding.

Uses

The possibilities of using Zinnias of one type or another in the garden are almost without limit. For eye-stopping brilliance and variety of coloring for a season-long mass of bloom it would be difficult, if not impossible, to find anything superior to the tall-growing, large-flowered varieties. So vigorous are they, indeed, that a double, staggered row with the plants set about eighteen inches apart forms quite a substantial flowering hedge. The medium-tall serve excellently in a mixed border, and these can, in turn, be faced down with the low-growing sorts, smaller varieties of which are unexcelled for edging or, used with discrimination, even in the rock garden. Z. *linearis* is one of the best annuals for the use in connection with rock plantings or as an edging along a drive or walk.

Zinnias of all sizes, from the smallest to the largest, are excellent for cutting and in arrangements by themselves or in combination with other simple garden flowers.

Color

In selecting Zinnias, the important thing, as already pointed out, is to secure a type suited to the purpose for which you intend to use it. After that comes the selection of colors. Here the individual varieties will give you almost anything your heart desires with the exception of blue. The range of lovely pastel tints available in Zinnias is surpassed by that of few other flowers. It is safe, too, to order Zinnias in mixtures, for most of the colors harmonize wonderfully well. Plantings of mixed varieties are often used to provide flowers for cutting, even where individual varieties are used in the planting scheme.

Culture

Here little need be said other than to make a reference to the information provided in Chapter ·8. Zinnia seeds are large and germinate quickly, often in four or five days. In the open they should not be planted until the soil has thoroughly warmed up, about Tomato-planting time. As practically every seed will sprout, they may be planted a half inch to an inch apart with a covering about a quarter of an inch deep. Thin out to three or four inches apart each way as soon as they have made a few inches of growth and then again before they begin to crowd. They transplant readily, so such plants may be used elsewhere or given away. The final thinning should leave a space of twelve inches or so between plants of dwarf sorts, eighteen to twenty inches for those of medium growth, and up to twenty-four inches for the tall, large-flowering ones.

If plants are to be started indoors or in a frame, it is not necessary to allow more than four or five weeks to get good-sized plants for setting out or repotting.

Pinching is not as important with Zinnias as it is with Petunias and many other annuals. When the first center bloom has been cut they will branch freely. It is desirable but not essential to remove the dead flowers.

MARIGOLD

Marigolds—third of the big three among annual flowers—have, like Zinnias, been developed from two or three original species into a galaxy of types which range in height from six inches to four feet and in flower size from one to six inches or more. In this case, however, it has taken the hybridizers a little longer to do the job, as Marigolds were grown in European gardens nearly four centuries ago.

The original garden types were known as African Marigolds and French Marigolds—though the former did not come from Africa nor the latter from France. These names, though they have no justification, still stick. As a matter of fact, the Marigold *(Tagetes)* is an American plant native from New Mexico to Argentina.

Naturally enough, Marigolds like plenty of sun and are fairly resistant to dry weather; a fact that makes them favorites for growing where facilities for watering are limited. Next to Zinnias, they are the most easily grown of all popular annuals.

Types

Until fairly recently the African Marigolds and the French Marigolds remained quite distinct. Such changes as were made consisted of the development of new flower forms, colors, and habits of growth within each of the two separate classes. Finally, however, Mr. Burpee succeeded in crossing them, giving us the now popular Red-and-Gold Hybrids.

The gardener of today has a wide field to choose from when it comes to Marigolds, with flowers covering almost all the conceivable tints and tones of orange and yellow, and a goodly range of reds in many combinations, in plants that vary in height from six inches to four feet. The types line up as follows:

African. Robust-growing plants, eighteen inches to four feet tall, according to variety and with very large flowers:

Chrysanthemum-flowered, with densely double blooms resembling formal Chrysanthemums. Mammoth Mum is one of the largest and best known; Limelight, a pleasing primrose yellow, is one of our favorites in this group.

Carnation-flowered is densely double, with the petals waved and rolled, giving them much the appearance of a very large carnation. Guinea Gold is perhaps the best-known variety of this type. Tetra is similar but with much larger flowers. In this group, Primrose and the new Man-in-the-Moon, lightest in color of all Marigolds, are particularly desirable for cutting. The comparatively new Sunset Giants have the advantage of extreme earliness, two weeks or more ahead of the usual varieties. Spanish Gold, the Hedge Marigold, is Carnation-flowered, plants uniformly twenty inches high and very bushy, the golden-orange flowers three inches across.

French (Tagetes patula). Both flowers and plants of the French Marigolds are quite different from the Africans. The blooms, whether they are single or double, are small, usually not over two inches across, and the plants only ten to eighteen inches tall.

Doubles. Here the typical variety is Harmony, with one-and-a-quarter-inch flowers, golden at the center, surrounded by red-brown outer petals. Spry is almost equally well known. One of our own favorites is Yellow Pygmy, a uniform lemon yellow on very dwarf bushy plants that are ideal for a compact edging.

Singles. These were formerly little grown, but the great improvement achieved in more recently introduced varieties has made them favorites of many gardeners. Most widely grown are the Dwarf Single French, such as Flash and Redhead. We particularly like Sunny with its broad, overlapping petals of the most cheerful yellow imaginable. The taller, Single French type has its place in the mixed border. Reaching eighteen to twenty-four inches, the variety Flaming Fire varies from bright red to yellow. It is excellent for cutting because of its long stems.

African-French hybrids. Any lover of Marigolds should try this strain, even though as yet there are no fixed colors to be had. The Red-and-Gold Hybrids are decidedly unfixed, the colors varying with soil and season, but they are fascinating in a mixed border or for cutting and have the decided advantage of being very early, beginning to bloom within eight or nine weeks from seed. Some seedlings will revert to the straight African type. These can be distinguished by their green stems and should be discarded or transplanted to another location.

Signet (T. signata pumila). These are varieties developed from a dwarf, spreading species. The flowers are tiny, usually less than an inch, but borne so profusely as to make the plants a solid mass of color for many weeks on end. Golden Ring is perhaps the best-known variety; Lulu is canary-yellow, and Ursula, a golden orange, as is also Gnome.

Other dwarfs. Cupids are very dwarf varieties available in golden and orange. The flowers are Chrysanthemum-like, two inches across or more. Lemondrop and Tangerine, the former nine, the latter fifteen inches tall, make moundlike plants and produce masses of very double two-inch flowers.

Signet Marigold (Tagetes signata pumila) *is a dwarf well suited to the rock garden.*

Culture

Marigolds, like Zinnias, have fairly large seeds which can be covered a quarter of an inch deep and which germinate vigorously in four to five days under favorable conditions. They make such strong seedling plants that they may be transplanted directly from the seed bed to the open garden without benefit of intermediate transplanting. If this is to be done, allow not over three to four weeks between dates of sowing and setting out. As they are very tender, they cannot be transferred to garden beds until the soil has thoroughly warmed up. For extra-early flowers out of doors, start seeds five or six weeks before setting-out time and transfer seedlings to flats or pots as soon as true leaves have formed. For winter bloom, sow in August or early September.

When transplanting to the open, set the French, Hybrid, and Signata types twelve to eighteen inches apart, according to the variety, and the Africans eighteen to twenty-four.

The sunnier the position that can be allotted to Marigolds, the better. While good soil is desirable, it is possible to have it too rich. Fertilizers especially high in nitrogen should be avoided, or plants may run to foliage instead of flowers. (See photograph page 86.)

China-aster

China-asters *(Callistephus)* are popular not because they are easy to grow but despite the fact that they are not easy. No more convincing proof of their desirability could be offered.

In the garden Asters make a magnificent show. For cutting they are in a class by themselves, clean and neat, with long stems and attractive foliage, fresh-looking and fresh-smelling, providing a wide range of exceptionally pleasing colors, easily arranged and long-lasting.

Although Asters are subject to injury by several diseases and insect pests and in general are considered on the temperamental side, we have known many gardeners who have succeeded in growing them for years without any trouble and few who have ever been content to give them up, even if they did encounter troubles, once they had grown them. For some years many gardeners abandoned Asters because of the inroads of the disease known as wilt. With the development of wilt-resistant strains, however, this ghost has been laid, and they are now almost universally grown again the country over.

Asters do best in fairly rich soil and in full sunshine or very light broken shade. Good drainage is especially important, and mulching is desirable because they are very shallow-rooted.

Types

In the catalogues one can find lister literally dozens of various types, often with only one or two varieties under each. The classification is badly in need of revision and unification, but no one seems to do anything about it. Any particular variety of Aster blooms for a comparatively short period—five to seven weeks—but Asters may be had in flower from midsummer to frost either by planting early, mid-season, and late varieties, or by making succession plantings.

In each of the time groups may be found several different types of flowers. These range from the simple, Daisy-like blossoms of the Single and California Sunshine Asters, through the tousle-headed Giant Cregos and California Doubles, the Chrysanthemum-like blooms of the Giant Branching and American Beauties, to the tight, pincushion-like heads of the Pompons. "You pays your money and you takes your choice." A list of approximate flowering seasons follows. They vary somewhat with individual varieties, and of course there is considerable overlapping.

Early. These are sufficiently early to escape, in most seasons, both wilt and yellows, as they are through blooming by the time these diseases are likely to appear. Also particularly desirable for northern sections where the growing season is short.

Burpeeana. Extra early, American Beauty type.

Burpee Early. Narrow, twisted petals. We can especially recommend Navy Blue.

Pompon or *Bouquet.* Small dense flowers, very chic.

Mid-season. These include many of the most popular types; flower in general for a longer period than the Earlies but complete bloom before frost except in northern sections.

Queen of the Market. Mid-early, hardy, generally satisfactory.

Peerless

Giant Fluffy. Loose, open flowers.

Improved Crego or *Ostrich Feather.* Giant-branching. (Vicks, Semples, American.)

Princess. Many colors. Exceptionally good for cutting and shipping.

California Giant Sunshine (Single Crested). Single flowers with raised, quilled centers.

Rainbow. Daisy-like. Many-colored in mixture. Nice for cutting.

Early Beauty. American Beauty type.

Late. The Late Asters come into bloom in late summer and continue until cut down by frost. Some of these are of the florists' type but are equally valuable in the home garden for autumn color and cutting.

American Beauty. Standard, large Chrysanthemum-type blooms.

Super Giants. Wilt-resistant strain of California Giant.

Ball Asters. A florist type, very large, fully double, with very long stems. Rust-resistant. Fine for cutting. White, blue, rose, pink, purple, and white.

Culture

As Asters are fairly hardy, withstanding temperatures down to freezing without a setback, seeds may be planted in the open about the time of the last hard frost, as it will take the seeds one to two weeks to germinate. Nevertheless, as they require a longer period than most annuals to come into bloom, it is well to start at least a few indoors or in a coldframe or, lacking that, under plastic tents in the open. In the general latitudes of New York, Chicago, and Kansas City they may be sown indoors in early March and three to four weeks later in frames. Four to six weeks will be required to grow plants of transplanting size. They should not be transferred to the open until well after danger of killing frost. Another advantage of having some started plants is that they can be used for filling in after spring bulbs or in other places where a vacancy occurs.

If possible, Asters should never be planted in the same soil where they have been grown the previous two or three seasons. Find a new spot if you can. Also, it is advisable to keep them some distance from Calendulas.

Tall-growing varieties in an exposed location are best provided some support. The modern branching types, however, are better able to take care of themselves in this respect than were the older tall sorts.

Insect pests likely to trouble Asters include the Aster-beetle, striped cucumber beetle, leafhopper, and aphids. Plants to be grown for extra-fine bloom for exhibition are best placed in an enclosure screened with plant-protecting cloth or fine netting.

SWEET PEA

Here is a flower for which there can be no substitute—any more than there could be for Lilac or Mignonette. Although Sweet Peas are universally loved in the United States, they are not as universally grown as they are, for instance, in the British Isles. In many sections American gardeners have all but given up trying to grow them. If by any chance you happen to be one of these, read on, for good news awaits you!

The one great obstacle to the successful growing of Sweet Peas is a hot, dry climate, particularly one in which really hot weather with drying winds is likely to strike suddenly after a comfortably cool spring. Sweet Peas love cool, moist weather. The old small-flowered varieties such as Grandmother used to grow were more capable of surviving in an unfavorable climate than the much larger-flowered ones which succeeded them. In fact, the more the Sweet Pea was "improved," the more difficult it became to grow.

Uses

One thinks of Sweet Pea primarily as a flower for cutting, and for this purpose it is indeed indispensable, not only for its attractive form and extremely wide range of lovely colors, equaled by those of very few other flowers, but also for its delicious and inimitable fragrance. In sections where Sweet Peas grow well they make an attractive light screen in addition to providing flowers for cutting for weeks on end. The dwarf varieties are charming and unusual as pot plants or in a window box.

Types

The Spencers or "Wave" Sweet Peas were the first of the modern varieties. They were introduced at the beginning of this century, and for a long time thereafter hybridizers devoted their attention to getting bigger and bigger flowers with more and more wavy petals, as in such types as the so-called Giant and Giant Ruffled. Eventually, however, some breeders began working for earliness, which was especially desirable for commercial crops grown under glass, and Mr. Anton Zvolanek produced the Early or Winter-flowering Spencers, which were much better than the Late Flowering Spencers for growing out of doors where climatic conditions were unfavorable or seasons very short.

Cuthbertson. Mr. Frank Cuthbertson of the Ferry-Morse Company succeeded in developing an entirely new type, the Cuthbertson or Spring-flowering. While these have smaller flowers and shorter stems than the Spencers, they are very heat-resistant and made it possible for thousands of gardeners to enjoy Sweet Peas again. With us this type has continued to bloom well into August, even during a hot season.

Multiflora. Still more recently Mr. Zvolanek has introduced another new type, the distinguishing characteristic of which is a greater number of flowers to a stem, making them most desirable for cutting. While the flowers are not so large as the Giant Spencers, the stems are long and wiry, and many of the flowers are attractively waved.

Burpee's Giant Heat Resistant. In this, the newest type to be developed, earliness, unusual resistance to heat, and large individual flowers, moderately ruffled, seem to have been successfully combined. With us they have flowered longer than any other type.

So there's the good news for Sweet Pea lovers! With these new early-flowering types you can grow Sweet Peas even though you may have regretfully decided that they were not for you. Begin by making a small planting of each, and then you can determine which, under your own conditions, gives the most satisfactory results. Perhaps you'll end up by growing more than one type. The usual succession of flowering is as follows: Cuthbertson, Multiflora, Burpee's Heat Resistant, Early Flowering Spencers, Late Flowering Spencers. Of course these differences are not as definite as A, B, C. Flowering periods overlap and also vary under different conditions.

Cupid (Dwarf). While these have nearly normal-size flowers, blooms are produced on small, trailing plants that attain a height of not over eight inches or so. Sweet heart is a new dwarf.

Culture

Requisites in success with Sweet Peas are: an early start, a deep root run, and an abundance of moisture.

No one of these three by itself will assure strong vines, long-stemmed flowers, and a long-continued season of bloom. The *lack* of any one of them, however, may prevent your achieving these much-desired results. Let us consider them in the order in which they must be attended to.

The trench. Most instructions for growing Sweet Peas suggest that they should be planted in a trench. Too often it is left at that. A trench, in this connection, is not merely a V-shaped furrow scraped out with a hoe just before planting. It means digging out a real trench twelve to eighteen inches deep and wide to be especially prepared for the job it has to do. In old English books elaborate directions are given—complete with diagrams—as to how the proverbial old cow manure, alternated with layers of soil, and each placed at an angle of 45 degrees, shall be incorporated in the soil of a trench two feet or more in depth. Such procedure is not practical for the modern American gardener. In the first place, he can't get the manure, and in the second, such preparation is not essential.

What he can do, however, is to open up such a trench, mix the soil fifteen to eighteen inches deep (if it is a good loam) with compost or peatmoss in the proportions of two to one, and then refill the trench about half full.

Next add a complete fertilizer (we prefer, for this use, one from organic sources) at the rate of three to five pounds per hundred feet of row, plus raw ground limestone at two to three times that amount, the latter rate if the soil is at all acid. Mix these thoroughly down through the soil.

Then fill the balance of the trench level-full with the same mixture and repeat the treatment. The object in making two bites of this cherry is to make certain that the fertilizer and lime are well mixed with the soil clear to the bottom, and this cannot be done if the trench is filled to the top before the other materials are added.

Preferably, the trench should be prepared in the fall. There is then more time to do the work, and the fill-in will have a chance to settle during the winter. Furthermore, and of even greater importance, it will be ready for planting at the very first opportunity in the spring, if the seed is not to be sown until then. If the trench cannot be prepared until just before planting, it is well to settle the bottom layer of the refill with a very thorough watering before the second layer is added.

Such thorough preparation is really not so much work as it sounds, and it will supply the foundation for a maximum crop of Sweet Peas, for you will have provided that deep, cool root run.

Sowing

In regions where climatic conditions make fall sowing feasible it is much to be preferred to spring planting. The objective is to plant so late that the seeds will not germinate until spring. If you try both methods side by side, you will find that the fall-sown seed will have sprouted and begun to make vigorous roots before it is possible to start planting in the spring. The time for fall planting varies from mid-September in the North to mid-November or even later in southern latitudes.

Most failures with fall sowing are due to neglect in providing perfect drainage around the seed. This may be done by making a furrow several inches deep, filling it half full of sand, sowing the seed, and then adding another inch of sand and one to two inches of soil over this. Above all, care must be taken that the surface of the trench is not below the general soil level, thus making a depression which will hold winter rains and melting snows. A slight elevation is desirable. After the soil has frozen a couple of inches deep, a mulch of coarse compost or some similar material will prevent alternate freezing and thawing during the winter and early spring. The mulch should be removed as soon as the seed is safely sprouted in early spring. If you are doubtful as to the results of fall sowing in your particular locality, try making part of your planting this way until you see how it is going to work for you.

If Sweet Peas are to be sown in the spring, they should be got into the ground at the earliest possible moment. In southern New England the traditional Sweet Pea planting day is St. Patrick's. Here at Gray Rock, in the vicinity of New York City, we are sometimes able to better that by a month. If sowing is delayed beyond the middle of March, germination may be hastened by soaking the seed in tepid water for two or three days before planting. We have found this much easier and just as effective as notching or chipping the covering of the seeds (removing a tiny portion of the hard outer shell). We also believe in treating the seeds with a legume inoculant such as Legume Aid, especially if they are to be planted in soil where peas have not previously been grown.

Starting plants under glass

Where seed cannot be got into the ground by the middle of March and early hot, dry weather is to be anticipated, it is well worth while to get a running start by growing seedling plants in dirt bands (see page 105) and then setting them out of doors as soon as danger of very hard freezing is past. A moderate-sized flat will hold fifty two-inch dirt bands filled with compost. By planting two or three seeds in each and then thinning to a single plant when they are well up, you may easily have a supply of sturdy seedlings that will begin flowering several weeks earlier than seed sown late outdoors. They may be started indoors and then transferred to a

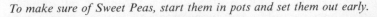

To make sure of Sweet Peas, start them in pots and set them out early.

cold-frame, or started in a frame. Allow four to six weeks to setting-out time. They should of course be thoroughly hardened before being transferred to the open. The plants can be set out twelve inches apart, so a single flat will provide for fifty feet of row.

Whatever method you are going to use, keep in mind that one of the essentials to success is to get an early start.

Watering

After they once get a good start, continued growth will depend largely upon the supply of moisture. Don't wait until they begin to flag before supplying this. An effective and simple method is to open a trench a few inches deep about a foot from each side of the row and occasionally flood this with water; or a length of the porous hose known as Soil Soaker will do the job nicely and be less messy.

Mulching will also help to conserve the moisture in the soil and at the same time eliminate weeding. It has the further advantage, especially important with Sweet Peas, of keeping the soil several degrees cooler than when it is exposed directly to hot sun.

Supports

Whatever type of support is to be used, it should be put in place while the plants are only a few inches high or, better yet, at planting time. Once they have begun to lop over, it is almost impossible to get them to help support themselves. Good pea brush is the best of all for the purpose, but not always available. Wire, frequently used, is one of the least desirable, as it is likely to break the stems in windy weather, and in bright summer sun may become hot enough to injure the stems. The ready-made trellis known as Trainette makes a good support. It is weatherproof, will serve for a number of seasons, and comes in various lengths, five feet wide.

Picking

A common cause of short flowering season with Sweet Peas, even when weather and other conditions are favorable, is neglect to prevent the forming of seed pods. In growing Sweet Peas this is a *very* important point, for once a crop of seed has set, the plant will have accomplished its purpose and have no further interest in continuing to produce flowers. Moreover, stems that are cut as soon as the buds break provide blooms which will last much longer indoors. KEEP YOUR SWEET PEAS CUT!

Under glass

While it is possible to grow Sweet Peas in a sunny window, there is usually too much heat and too little humidity for them to do well. In the greenhouse they are readily grown and are one of the most rewarding of all annuals for this purpose. Select varieties of the Winter-flowering type. Start seeds in dirt bands in August or September in a cool but light place and transplant later to large pots or, better still, to boxes, eight inches wide and deep, filled with rich, humusy soil.

SNAPDRAGON

The Snapdragon *(Antirrhinum)*, with its upright sturdy spikes of flowers in a wide range of colors, produced in succession over a period of several months, is one of the most rewarding of all "annuals." It is really a tender perennial but in cooler sections is almost invariably treated as an annual, although the plants may be carried over in a tight frame, with good protection, where the thermometer occasionally approaches zero. Seedling plants, however, are so readily grown that this is seldom attempted.

The uses to which "Snaps" may be put are many. Neat, clean-growing, and self-supporting upright plants for the middle or the back of the border are few, and for such spots Snapdragons admirably fit the gardener's needs. They are, in addition, quite ideal for cutting. The spikes, on which the florets open gradually from the base to the tip, last for a long time and arrange readily. Moreover, the colors—which include various shades and tints of red, yellow, orange, salmon, orchid, and bronze as well as white and pink—are such that they do not clash with other flowers or among themselves.

Though seldom used in rock walls or rock gardens, the lower-growing varieties of the Semi-tall type, fifteen to eighteen inches,

LEFT: *Spike of old-fashioned "giant" Snapdragon.* RIGHT: *New Tetra Snap-dragon illustrates what science has helped the plant breeders to accomplish in increasing vigor and size of bloom.*

and the Miniatures, only six inches or less, make excellent subjects, particularly because they have such a long season of bloom.

Types

Here again there is marked confusion so far as catalogues and even trial grounds are concerned. It seems to us that we can be of most help to the gardener by discussing them simply in groups according to height—Tall, Intermediate, Dwarf, and Trailing.

Tall. *Skyscraper,* the tallest of all, and with exceptionally long flower heads, grows to three feet or over, with secondary stems reaching nearly the same height. Available as yet only in mixture.

Mostly light shades. *Colossal,* similiar, also in mixed colors. *Tall Giant (A. maximum),* two to two and a half feet. Rust-resistant varieties in many colors. *Double Flowered,* a new type making very massive spikes; two to two and a half feet, many-branched and very effective for color masses in mixed borders.

Semi-tall. Tetra (Giant Ruffled), a distinct break in Snapdragons accomplished through the use of colchicine in breeding, thus changing the chromosome structure. With many flowers, the colchicine treatment has resulted in monstrosities rather than improvements. With Snapdragons, however, the results have been really remarkable. Particularly strong, vigororous plants, 2 feet tall, base branching, extra strong stems. Available in named varieties. *Majestic or Semi-tall Giant Flowered,* sturdy and upright-growing; useful for pot culture. 18 to 24 inches. *Semi-tall Large Flowered* bear long, dense spikes of blooms slightly smaller than those of the Tall Giants. Named varieties and in mixture; fifteen inches

Miniature. Magic Carpet, a compact variety, forms moundlike plants up to six inches high with small flowers. Good for wall.

Trailing. Rock Hybrids are trailing, small-flowered varieties for the rock garden. They are profuse bloomers. *Tom Thumb* is another dwarf type, with named varieties in several colors. Unfortunately the Miniature Snapdragons have been little used in America, and most seed catalogues here do not carry them. They can be obtained from abroad.

Culture

Snapdragons will take a rich soil and prefer it a little on the alkaline side. While they flourish in full sun, they will tolerate light semi-shade. Two or three supplementary feedings during the season will keep them blooming profusely up to frost.

While Snapdragons can be sown in the open—in fact, they frequently self-sow—they require a long period before coming into bloom. As it may take up to three weeks for the seed to germinate, it is highly desirable to sow the seed indoors early (as early as late January or February) even in the North, or a month later in a frame, in order to have strong seedling plants to set out. Only in this way can the gardener get the full benefit of their extremely long flowering season. The tallest-growing giant plants will require a minimum of ten to twelve inches apart to develop fully. Though the plants may be pinched to induce stocky growth, most varieties are branching by nature, and so cutting the first spike for indoor decoration when the bottom florets begin to open will usually provide all the heading back that is needed.

Very-tall-growing varieties may be given some support, particularly if they are in an exposed position or being grown for exhibition. Ordinarily the secondary branches will be self-supporting.

When early bloom begins to peter out, established plants may usually be given a second lease on life by cutting them back to six or eight inches and giving a supplementary feeding.

For winter bloom indoors, plants in the garden which are still in vigorous growth may be cut back to six or eight inches, transferred to pots or bulb pans, and started into new growth. This should be done several weeks prior to killing frost in order that they may get well established in the pots before being brought indoors. If cut back just before hard frost, they should be kept in a frame for three weeks or more to have new growth well under way before being brought in.

As a rule, best results will be had by sowing seed, especially for winter bloom, any time after mid-July. Use varieties of moderate height. Pinching back the seedlings will produce stockier plants, better adapted to indoor culture.

LARKSPUR

In the Larkspur, or annual Delphinium, we have another tall flower which is indispensable for background in any extensive planting of annuals; and few flowers are more prized for cutting. Readily grown from outdoor-sown seed, it well merits a place among the leading ten in popularity.

As the Larkspurs, especially if bought in mixtures, are predominantly of light or pastel colors, they show up to best advantage— either in the garden or in an arrangement—against a darker background. A position against a tall hedge or wall, or to the east or south of evergreens, also affords protection from winds and beating rains. In an exposed position, light support may be desirable.

Types

Until recently the Giant Imperial type, growing to four feet tall and a marked improvement over preceding sorts, was the one most widely planted. Of late, however, a new type, growing a foot or so taller and sturdier, and more heat-resistant, has been developed. In catalogues it is listed as Steeplechase, Regal or Supreme.

While these are unexcelled for garden effects, they are almost too massive for most decorative purposes, and the gardener particularly interested in flower arrangement may wish to have, in addition to these, some of the less vigorous types, such as the older Imperial varieties.

Giant Hyacinth Flowered is non-branching, each spike making one large, tapering column with double flowers.

Another type that is especially good for cutting is Burpee Wonder, three to four feet tall, with large flowers and long-stemmed spikes.

Chinese or Bouquet Larkspur *(D. grandiflorum)* while a perennial, is often grown as an annual. Early-sown seed will begin flowering in June and continue until autumn. (For further description and information see the Catalogue of Annuals, page 215.)

While Larkspurs will grow in full sun, they also are perfectly at home in partial shade. This fact may well be taken advantage of in planning the border.

Culture

As with Sweet Peas, early planting is essential to success. In fact, the sturdiest, most vigorous, and earliest-flowering plants result from seeds sown in the fall. Where this cannot be done, fall preparation of the area in which they are to be grown will make it possible to sow at the first crack o' spring, often a week to two weeks earlier than the soil can be dug.

Still another method is to sow very late—just before hard freezing—in an unheated frame, and in this way have extra-early seedlings which can be transferred to the garden early in spring. While Larkspur is difficult to transplant, it is by no means impossible.

Larkspur germinates very slowly, often taking up to two weeks. On a freshly raked surface it need merely be scattered on top of the soil and pressed in. Our own practice is to cover with a very light sprinkling—not over one eighth inch—of vermiculite, as this not only helps to keep the surface moist but also definitely marks the area that is planted. When seedlings are well started, thin to six or seven inches apart for a mass-color effect, a couple of inches more for the best individual plants.

Under glass Larkspurs do excellently, but one must keep in mind the fact that they will require a good deal of room, also a very cool temperature. For winter bloom, they are greenhouse rather than house subjects.

SWEET ALYSSUM

Modest flower though it is, Sweet Alyssum is one of the indispensables for all gardens—a handy-man type of flower that serves innumerable purposes. And while it is not ordinarily thought of as a cut flower, it often works in nicely in moderate-sized, home-type arrangements.

While its principal role, either by itself or in combination with Lobelia or Ageratum, is that of an edging plant, Sweet Alyssum is equally valuable as a small-area ground cover, among other flowers or after bulbs; as single plants or in small groups of three or four in a rock wall or the rock garden; in window or porch boxes; and as an easily grown and fragrant greenhouse or house plant.

Varieties

While the Alyssum family is a large one (comprising some hundred and twenty species, mostly from the Mediterranean area), there are only a few varieties in general cultivation. These have been developed from the species *A. maritimum* (now called *Lobularia maritima* by botanists) or Sweet Alyssum; spreading or trailing in growth, with honey-scented flowers which the bees love madly.

Carpet of Snow is also spreading but much more dwarf than the species.

Little Gem is a compact-growing dwarf, excellent for pot culture.

Tetra Snowdrift is a new variety which, like the Tetra Snapdragon, is extremely vigorous, with large flower heads and attaining a height of ten inches. The best for cutting.

Alyssum maritinum *(Sweet Alyssum) is a plant of a hundred uses, and one of the last to succumb to autumn's icy breath.*

Violet Queen makes low, spreading plants covered with violet flowers, a few in the center of each head being white; five inches.

Royal Carpet is a more vigorous-growing but dwarfer variety, three or four inches tall but ten or more across. The violet-purple blooms are of a more pleasing color than the preceding. It makes an excellent companion for Little Gem.

Culture

As Sweet Alyssum can be sown early (March or April) out of doors, germinates in a few days, and begins to bloom in a few weeks, it usually is sown where it is to grow. For extra-early bloom, sow indoors a month or six weeks earlier. It is exceptionally easy to transplant.

While under ideal conditions Sweet Alyssum will bloom throughout the summer and fall, we usually find it worth while to make a second planting in late May or June so that we may be certain of having plants in bloom until Jack Frost completely takes possession of the garden, for Alyssum is one of the very last flowers to surrender.

Seedling plants should be thinned out to stand five to ten inches apart, according to variety and growing conditions. While a sun lover, it will tolerate considerable shade. After the plants have bloomed out, shear them back, give a supplementary application of fertilizer and plenty of water, and they will come back astonishingly.

For winter bloom indoors, plants from the garden may be trimmed back, potted up, and grown on. It is much more satisfactory, however, to start a few seedlings in late August or September for winter bloom.

PHLOX DRUMMONDI

Phlox Drummondi well deserves its increasing popularity because of its quick growth, long season of bloom, and interesting color range, running from white through buff to pink, rose, crimson, lavender, and purple, usually with a contrasting eye. Because of the long stems, the flower heads, too, are most useful as cut material. A native of the Southwest, *Phlox Drummondi* is locally known as Texas Pride. Among the easiest of all annuals to grow, it flowers early. Under favorable conditions, if the flowers are kept picked, it will continue to bloom through the summer. To be sure of a real show of color in the fall, however, it is advisable to make a second planting (freezing the seed for a short period before sowing) in late July or August.

Uses

The many available varieties are mound-shaped to spreading and range in height from six to fifteen inches. Dwarf sorts are excellent for edging; others in the second row. In addition to their effective-

Phlox Drummondi *is one of many annuals that have been greatly changed by science. The Tetraploid Hybrids (left) have flowers nearly four times as large as the old standard varieties.*

ness in the general garden scheme, they are also pleasing in or along the top of a wall and, used judiciously, in the rock garden. They find a place, too, in window boxes and as pot plants.

Types

In recent years there have been several very marked improvements in the annual Phloxes, and the old classifications of *P. Drummondi grandiflora, gigantea,* and *nana compacta* no longer cover the situation.

Tetra. Most striking of these new Phloxes are the Tetras, the tallest and most vigorous of all. The difference in size of flower and strength of stem as compared with older varieties must be seen to be appreciated. Individual florets are up to an inch and a half across. (See photograph, page 211.) Tetra Red and Tetra Salmon are the two colors now available. Undoubtedly others will be added.

Beauty. An improved strain of dwarf Phlox producing mound-like plants six to eight inches in height, with flowers nearly double the size of ordinary varieties.

Dwarf Compact. Six to eight inches tall but with large flowers in good colors; fine for pot plants.

Tall, Large Flowered, and Giant Flowered form two groups growing up to fifteen inches in many fixed colors, including pastels and "art" shades.

Starred or Fringed. This is a very old type popular in Europe but little known in this country, with deeply lacinated, pointed petals in a wide variety of colors and color combinations. Much prized for flower arrangements; not nearly so well known as it should be.

Globe is a new strain, recently honored by the All America Selections Committee. The dwarf plants are of perfectly rounded habit. Available in mixture only.

Two of our favorite varieties of *Phlox Drummondi* are Isabellina, an unusual soft primrose-buff, and Apricot. You will find them much commented upon if you use them in arrangements.

Culture

Little need be said here, as Phlox does well in almost any well-drained soil and is more drought-resistant than most. Prefers full sun, and the more it is cut, the longer it will keep on flowering freely.

Seed is slow to germinate, usually over two weeks, but it can be sown as early as desired. Not too easy to transplant, but for early bloom, seedlings may be started indoors three or four weeks ahead of outdoor sowing dates.

MORNING-GLORY (IPOMOEA)

Morning-glories are the most popular of the annual flowering vines. This is small wonder, since recent varieties offer very large flowers in pure, lovely colors. Growing to fifteen feet in height, the clean heart-shaped leaves and profusion of great funnel-shaped

Moonflowers, extremely vigorous and beautiful, are seldom grown because of the long season they require. This drawback is easily overcome by starting plants in pots three or four weeks before time to set them out.

flowers make it a real decoration for trellises, porches, or to cover old tree stumps, posts that support birdhouses, etc. There is also a bush type.

Varieties

Tall, Heavenly Blue is justly the most famous of the Ipomoeas, producing masses of four- to five-inch blossoms of true sky blue.

Blue Star is similar, but each flower is more deeply colored along the mid-ribs, giving a star effect.

Pearly Gates is often planted with one of the above varieties. The flowers are similar in size and shape to Heavenly Blue but are pure white.

Darling is a giant wine red with a snow-white throat.

Scarlett O'Hara has smaller flowers (about three and a half inches) of rose-scarlet. Unfortunately it is a poor climber, and an its natural habit is to scramble over the ground rather than to reach upward, it usually looks gone with the wind.

Giant Cornell has giant red blooms bordered in white.

Bush varieties of *Convolvulus tricolor.* These Morning-glories grow but a foot tall; are satisfactory sun-loving annuals for the rock garden or mixed border. Also fine window-box plants; unlike their tall relatives, they remain open all day.

Pink produces many small pink flowers on spreading plants.

Royal Ensign has very deep blue flowers with golden-yellow throats and white halos. Hearts and Honey is red and buff.

Culture

Morning-glories prefer a soil that is not too rich. Overfeeding results in much foliage and few flowers. The seeds germinate in from eight to ten days in warm soil. Early growth may be hastened by covering the seeds with plastic domes until the seedlings are well started.

For early bloom, plant seeds indoors in March, two to a small pot, after first soaking in tepid water for forty-eight hours or until the hard shell has softened and swollen slightly.

As soon as seedlings develop climbing tendrils they should be given support. Cords stretched vertically or Trainettes (described in the section on Sweet Peas) will suit their needs admirably.

After bloom starts in July or August, it continues uninterrupted until frost. During cool autumn days, flowers remain open all day long instead of only through the morning hours.

CHAPTER *17. Catalogue of Annuals:*
A to Z

KEY TO ABBREVIATIONS

A — Annual
B — Biennial
P — Perennial
H — Hardy Annual
HH — Half-hardy Annual
T — Tender Annual
TB — Tender Biennial
TP as A — Tender Perennial grown as an Annual
TS — Tender Shrub
TS as A — Tender Shrub grown as an Annual

GLOSSARY OF BOTANICAL TERMS

AWN: A bristle-like part or appendage
AXIL: Upper angle made by a leaf stalk with the stem that bears it
BRACT: Much-reduced leaf, especially small scale-like leaf in or about flower head
CALYX: The outer series of floral leaves
CORYMB: Short, broad, somewhat flat-topped indeterminate flower cluster
CYME: Broad, flat-topped determinate flower cluster
DENTATE: With sharp, spreading teeth
DETERMINATE: Definite cessation of growth at the apex or in the main axis
LANCEOLATE: Like a lance
LINEAR: Long and narrow
PANICLE: A branching raceme

PETIOLE: Leaf stalk or stem

RACEME: Elongated indeterminate cluster of stalked flowers

SALVERFORM: Slender-tubed and with an abruptly expanding flat edge, as Moonflower

SPIKE: Compact, somewhat indeterminate, mostly elongated cluster of stalkless flowers

SPIKELET: A secondary spike; one part of a compound spike, as in grasses

OVATE: Shaped like an egg cut in two, lengthwise

WHORL: Three or more leaves or flowers at one node

ABRONIA (Sand-verbena) 6"   TP as A

The Sand-verbenas are tender North American perennials usually grown as annuals. *A. umbellata,* the one commonly grown, is a native of the California seacoast. Its prostrate stems bear rose-purple flowers resembling those of the true Verbena. *Grandiflora* is a variety with larger blooms, and *rosea* produces flowers of a lighter color.

Sand-verbenas are used for edging, in walls, and for window boxes and hanging baskets. Bloom continues through midsummer and early autumn.

CULTURE: Plant seeds outdoors in April or, for early bloom, start indoors in March. The seeds are slow to germinate and consequently the husks are often removed before planting to hasten matters along. South of Washington, D.C., seeds may be sown in the autumn.

Abronia prefers full sun and stands summer drought admirably. Set plants 6 inches apart.

ADLUMIA FUNGOSA (Fumitory, Allegheny Vine, Mountain   B
Fringe) 6'

The Allegheny Vine is really a biennial, but one that can easily be grown as an annual. Native of northeastern America, it is attractive enough to be well worth while as a garden subject.

The fernlike leaves are in three parts with clinging petioles, and the attractive flowers, somewhat resembling those of a Bleeding Heart, are borne in drooping panicles throughout the summer and early fall.

Ideal for planting on a fence in part shade or to cloak the bareness of a dead tree, Adlumia is happiest in a moist, sheltered position.

CULTURE: Plant seeds in April in a cool, moist, sheltered location. Usually self-seeds.

ADONIS (Pheasant's Eye) 18″   H

There are several annual species of Adonis which make excellent garden flowers. Belonging to the Ranunculus family, they have Buttercup-like flowers and attractive, finely cut foliage.

A. aestivalis bears deep crimson flowers in June and July Variety *citrina* has yellow blossoms. This species is native to central Europe and has been in cultivation since the seventeenth century.

A. aleppica, found originally in Syria, has 2-inch bright red blossoms, very showy.

A. annua, from western Asia, blooms from June to September, the crimson flowers having centers of deeper red.

A. flammea, also from western Asia, flowers from May to July with bright scarlet blossoms, spotted black in the centers.

The Pheasant's Eyes are excellent subjects for the open border. By planting several, bloom may be had from May to September.

CULTURE: Since all the above-mentioned species are hardy, seed may be sown in early spring in the open ground, or even in autumn if desired.

They flourish in full sun or partial shade and are not fussy about soil. Plants should be set 1 foot apart.

AGERATUM (Floss Flower) 4–24″   T

Ageratum has long been one of the stand-bys of the summer garden and needs no introduction to most gardeners. Though there are dwarf, medium, and tall-growing varieties, the compact-growing dwarfs are most popular nowadays. The lavender-blue, fluffy flowers, like bunches of tiny powder puffs, literally cover the plants during summer and early fall. There are also pink and white varieties.

> Blue Ball Improved—6"
> Blue Bedder—4"
> King of the Blues—6"
> Midget Blue—3"
> Tall Blue—18"
> Fairy Pink—5", pale pink
> Silver Star—6", white

Dwarf varieties are used chiefly for edgings, often in combination with Sweet Alyssum and dwarf Marigold and Petunia. Also useful in window and porch boxes. The tall type produces less compact flower heads and is useful in the mixed border.

CULTURE: As Ageratum is very tender, for early garden bloom seeds should be started indoors or in a coldframe in March. There is often a variation in habit of growth in dwarf plants grown from seed, and consequently it is necessary to weed out straggling or taller-growing specimens which do not conform to the general moundlike form. There may also be some variation in color. For absolutely uniform plants, cuttings may be taken and grown on through the winter, as with Geraniums.

Plant out in May, after all danger of frost is past, in well-drained, medium-rich soil, in full sun. Pinch back young plants to insure compactness of growth and keep dead flowers removed to induce constant bloom.

Set dwarf varieties 9 inches apart; tall growers, 12 inches.

AGROSTIS NEBULOSA (Cloud Grass) 12–18"   HH

This annual, decorative Bent Grass produces very narrow, short leaves and charming panicles, finely branched, with tiny spikelets near the tips. Its airy grace is pleasing in the border and in bouquets, fresh or dried.

Try it as a contrast in front of Gladiolus, Montbretia, or any other flower which tends to grow erect with somewhat bare unattractive lower stems. The delicate, frail beauty of the grass is an excellent foil for solid, heavy spikes of bloom.

CULTURE: Start seeds in a well-prepared seed bed in mid-April.

Transplant to garden in late May, placing plants 1 foot apart, selecting a sunny situation and well-drained, carefully prepared soil.

ALONSOA (Maskflower) 18–36″   T

Alonsoas come to us from tropical America, the garden species mentioned here being natives of Peru. The bushy plants are clothed with oval, toothed leaves and bear red or white two-lipped, tubular flowers in terminal racemes. By keeping the dead bloom cut back, a satisfactory succession of blossoms can be had throughout the season.

A. acutifolia grows to 3 feet in height and produces cinnabar-red blooms with long upper lips. Variety *candida* is a white form.

A. caulialata is desirable because it reaches only a little more than a foot in height and can therefore be placed in the foreground. The flowers are scarlet.

A. Warscewiczi is an extremely bushy species, growing to 3 feet, the blooms cinnabar or scarlet red, with upper lips four to five times the length of the calyx.

Alonsoas are at their best in open beds or borders in full sun. Like Calendulas, however, they dislike extreme humid heat. In sections were summer nights are hot and humid, plan to use the Maskflower for fall bloom. They are also most useful as pot plants under glass or, started indoors, to decorate the cool patio in summer.

CULTURE: Start seeds indoors in early April or in outdoor seed beds in May, after danger of frost is past. Set out 18 to 24 inches apart.

ALTHEA ROSEA (Hollyhock) to 9′   B

The well-known variety of Hollyhock, Indian Spring, is the best selection for those who wish to treat this reliable biennial as an annual. Indian Spring bears semi-double fringed flowers of pale pink, rose, and carmine and can be counted on to flower the first year from seed. Less tall than many other varieties, it grows from 4 to 5 feet in height. With good luck you will have a second year of bloom from the original plants, and in addition to that it will probably self-seed.

Hollyhocks are particularly useful to decorate the blank walls of an outbuilding or to screen a boundary fence or wall. They are especially suited to use with Early American or English architecture.

CULTURE: Plant indoors in March or outdoors in April. Set 18 inches apart.

As Japanese beetles particularly like the leaves of Hollyhocks, do not plant where this pest is rampant.

ALYSSUM LOBULARIA MARITIMUM, see page 208

AMARANTHUS (Love-Lies-Bleeding, Tassel-flower) 48–72″   T

This stately and colorful genus includes many species with colored foliage. Since some are very dark red or bronze, it is best to stick to varieties that can be counted on for brilliance.

A. caudatus, the sort commonly grown, makes a stout, branched 5-foot plant with red leaves and long, rope-like crimson panicles of flowers.

A. hypochondriacus, or Princess Feather, bears slender, graceful panicles of bronze-red bloom and bronzy-red foliage on 2- to 3-foot plants. Excellent for accessory foliage in flower arrangement.

A. tricolor is grown for its foliage. The erect plants grow to 4 feet in height with large oval leaves, variegated in green, yellow, and red. Other varieties of this species produce leaves strangely blotched and marked in rose, red, green, and yellow.

Amaranthus is so large and coarse that it is most useful as a substitute for shrubbery in the back of the large mixed border, or to form a temporary annual hedge. Both flowers and foliage are in demand by flower arrangers.

CULTURE: Sow seeds indoors in April or in an outdoor seed bed in late May. Set out in rather poor soil, in sun, 18 inches apart. Amaranthus endures dry conditions well.

AMBERBOA (Star-of-the-desert) to 30″   T

The Amberboas are native to the Mediterranean region, western Asia, and India. Though not so popular as they should be, they make excellent tender annuals for beds and borders. Leaves are ovate, deeply cut or dentate, and the purple, blue, or white tubular flowers are borne in heads or panicles.

A. maroccana grows to a height of 30 inches and bears small white flowers in long, dense panicles. Leaves are toothed.

A. muricata is 2 feet tall, with lanceolate leaves and heads of purple flowers. Variety *rosea* bears pink blossoms.

Star-of-the-desert does well in full sun and may be used for bedding or for the mixed border. Plant a row, too, in the cutting garden.

CULTURE: Plant seeds outdoors in May after danger of frost is past, and set out 15 inches apart in open, sunny, rather dry location. Stands drought well.

AMMOBIUM ALATUM (Winged Everlasting) to 36"   TP AS A

The Winged Everlasting is so named because of the winged branches. Really a tender perennial, it is commonly grown as an annual for its white, yellow-centered everlasting flowers and white, woolly foliage. The variety *grandiflorum* bears larger flower heads.

Though one of the least attractive of the Everlastings, Ammobium is in demand for use in dried arrangements.

CULTURE: Plant outdoors in seed bed in April and set out in full sun, in sandy soil, 12 inches apart. In mild climates seed may be sown in fall. Cut flowers as soon as the blossoms open, and hang upside down in a shaded, well-ventilated building to dry.

ANAGALLIS (Pimpernel) 2–18"   HH and TP AS A

The Pimpernels are gay plants for rock-garden work and edgings. Their red or blue flowers are bright and colorful and freely borne throughout the summer and early fall on spreading or low-growing plants.

A. arvensis is a tiny, spreading annual with trailing stems and bright scarlet, salmon-red, or white flowers. Ideal for the rock garden.

A. linifolia, a tender perennial, is a species with many varieties in cultivation. Heights vary from 4 inches to 18 inches and colors

are blue, red, or flesh pink. Sometimes listed as *A. grandiflora.*
Varieties are: *carnea* (pink); *coccinea* (scarlet); *caerulea* (large
bright blue); *Monelli,* dwarf (blue).

A. arvensis is at home on the top of a sunny wall in the rock garden or in other warm locations in full sun.

Other varieties may be used as edgers or even in the front of
beds or borders. *A. caerulea* is often grown as a pot plant under
glass or indoors.

CULTURE: Plant seeds of annual species in April or early May
where they are to grow. *A. linifolia* and its varieties should be
started indoors in March and set out in May, 6 inches apart.

ANCHUSA (Bugloss) to 18"   B

The biennial *Anchusa capensis* Blue Bird is easily grown as an
annual. It is desirable for its bright, true-blue blossoms freely
borne on bushy plants with rather coarse, hairy leaves. This is a
color rare among annual flowers and for that reason most valuable
for bedding or borders. Bloom continues throughout the summer
and autumn if dead blossoms are removed.

CULTURE: Plant seeds outdoors in April where they are to grow
or in a seed bed. Transplant to 12 inches apart in full sun. Of easy
culture, but needs plenty of water during the growing season.

ANODA lavateroides (Snowcup) to 36"   T

The Snowcup is a little-grown annual native to Texas, Mexico,
and South America. It has heart-or arrow-shaped leaves and purple, violet, or white solitary flowers to 2 inches across, borne in the
leaf axils.

Because of their height, Anodas are subjects for the back of the
sunny border or to be used as a temporary hedge.

CULTURE: Plant outdoors in May and set out 15 inches apart in
sandy soil in full sun.

ANTIRRHINUM (Snapdragon), see page 203.

ARCTOTIS (African-daisy) 24"   HH

This dainty African is one of the most charming of our garden annuals, with its white-woolly elongated leaves and large single Daisy-like blossoms of pure pearly white, tinted with lavender-blue in reverse, and with blue centers. Though quite tall-growing, the stems are not strong, so that the plants sometimes have a rather untidy appearance, especially if grown in soil that is too heavy for them. Bloom continues over a long period.

Arctotis is striking near the front of the sunny border and makes very fine cut flowers, dainty and long-lasting.

CULTURE: Plant seeds indoors in March or outdoors in a seed bed in April. Set out 12 inches apart in sandy soil in full sun. Withstands drought well.

ARGEMONE, 3–4'   TB

A. grandiflora, or Prickly-poppy, is a Mexican species which grows to 3 feet. The prickly leaves are white-veined and the 2-inch white flowers are borne at the stem tips. Variety *lutea* has yellow blossoms.

A. mexicana has yellow or orange flowers.

A. platyceras or Crested-poppy is even taller, to 4 feet, with white or purple flowers. *Rosea* produces dark, pinkish-purple blooms.

These large, coarse, but showy tender biennials are suitable for the back of the border. Can be used for screening or as a protective, temporary hedge, also for cutting.

CULTURE: Plant outdoors in May in a seed bed. Set out 15 inches apart in a warm, dry, sunny situation. Soil should be sandy and well drained but rich in humus.

ASPERULA AZUREA SETOSA (Blue Woodruff) 12"   HH

Woodruffs are pleasing garden and rock-garden subjects because of their whorled leaves and funnel-shaped flowers borne in cymes. Blue Woodruff is much branched, with 8 leaves in a whorl and very small blue flowers in terminal clusters surrounded by leafy bracts.

Ideal for the rock garden, the shady border, or the brookside.

CULTURE: Though Blue Woodruff thrives in poor soil, it must have plenty of moisture. It prefers shade but can be grown in the mixed border. Plant seeds in a moist seed bed in shade in early May. Set out 6 inches apart.

ASTERS, see page 194.

BEGONIA SEMPERFLORENS (Wax Begonia) 12–18″   TS as A

Wax Begonias have for many years been among the most reliable of bedding plants. The cheerful little white, pink, or red flowers are borne almost continuously throughout the year, while the glossy green, bronze, or deep red foliage is almost equally decorative.

Because of the constant bloom these bright little plants are also much in demand for window gardens indoors in winter and for porch or window boxes in summer. The dwarf varieties make excellent edging plants for summer, while taller-growing varieties are much used for massed bedding work.

CULTURE: Plants may be purchased from a florist and increased at will by cuttings, or they may be raised from seed planted indoors in February. Do not set plants out until all danger of frost is past. They do equally well in full sun or partial shade. The soil should be thoroughly worked with plenty of humus and well drained.

BELLIS PERENNIS (English Daisy) 6″   B

The English Daisy is one of the loveliest of the very early spring flowers. Though a biennial, it may be grown as an annual by planting seed early indoors.

The white, pink, or rose, very double composite flowers are large and showy, rising a few inches above a pretty rosette of glossy green leaves.

Ideal for edging in the border, they are often planted with Pansies for very early bloom.

CULTURE: Plant seeds late in summer in a partly shaded seed bed or frame. Thin or transplant as needed and leave in frame over win-

Indian Summer, a Holly-hock flowering readily the first year from seed, is an ideal tall accent plant for rear of the border.

Coleus — ordinarily grown as a house plant —provides color in shady garden spots. These are typical of the Rainbow strain, grown from seed.

In this long border at GrayRock, flanking steps to the Rose garden, annuals carry on after the Tulips are gone. BELOW *A single plant of Ageratum Blue Perfection.*

ter. Set plants out in the garden as soon as the ground can be worked. They are perfectly hardy and should give bloom the second year without further attention.

BRACHYCOME IBERIDIFOLIA (Swan River Daisy) 12"   T

The Swan River Daisy is a pleasing tender annual which produces single blue, white, or pink Daisy-like flowers over a short period. The foliage is finely cut and attractive.

Brachycome is excellent for edging or massing near the front of the border or in the rock garden. It also makes a satisfactory cut flower.

CULTURE: Plant seeds indoors in April or outdoors in mid-May. This annual is not fussy about soil or moisture but prefers full sun. For a long period of bloom plant seeds in succession and replace exhausted plants with younger ones just ready to bloom.

BRIZA (Quaking Grass) 12–18"   T

There are two annual species of Briza: B. maxima, which reaches a height of 1½ to 2 feet and produces decorative panicles of bronzy spikelets; and B. minor, only a foot tall with panicles of triangular spikelets.

Grasses make most attractive edging plants for large borders and are particularly useful in dried-flower arrangements.

CULTURE: Plant seeds outdoors about mid-May where they are to grow. Transplant or thin to 12 inches apart. Full sun.

BROMUS BRIZAEFORMIS (Quake Grass) 2'   H

This decorative grass is a hardy annual which reaches 2 feet in height and bears long, oval spikelets in 8-inch, branching panicles.

Like other grasses, this may be used in the border, in the cutting garden, for dried bouquets, or in a mass planting to cover some difficult spot where a decorative effect is needed.

CULTURE: Plant in the open ground in early spring and thin to 1 foot apart.

BROWALLIA 12–24″　　　　　　　　　　　　　　　　　　　T

There are few tender annuals more satisfactory than the Browallias. In the first place, they are a deep and beautiful blue, and in the second, the plants bloom profusely over a long period.

B. americana, a native of tropical America, makes a bushy plant to 2 feet in height with glossy leaves and blue, violet, or white flowers, tubular in form. Sapphire is a dwarf variety to 10 inches with deep blue, white-eyed blossoms.

B. speciosa is the species usually grown for greenhouse and pot plants. The plants grow much taller, are bushy, and produce much larger, dark blue flowers to 2 inches in diameter.

B. americana is easy to grow and a most pleasing border plant. It can also be brought indoors for winter bloom.

B. speciosa, being larger and showier, is ideal for indoor winter blossoms or as a potted plant in the patio or on the terrace.

CULTURE: Plant *B. americana* indoors in April or outdoors in a seed bed in May for summer and fall bloom. Transplant to 9 inches apart.

B. speciosa should be started indoors in early February to produce plants for summer and fall bloom. Summer-planted seeds will give plants for winter bloom indoors.

CALANDRINIA 12–24″　　　　　　　　　　　　HH and TP as A

Calandrinias are members of the Portulaca family, with narrow, fleshy leaves and purple, red, rose, or white fleeting flowers.

C. ciliata is an annual, native to western North America. It grows to 18 inches in height and bears purple or white flowers in the axils of the narrow leaves. Variety *Menziesi* grows to 2 feet, with crimson or rose-red blooms.

C. grandiflora is a South American perennial which may be grown as an annual. It grows to 3 feet in height, with 8-inch leaves and light purple-rose flowers.

C. umbellata is a tender perennial 6 inches tall bearing bright violet-crimson flowers in clusters. The trailing stems make it an ideal subject for the sunny rock garden.

Calandrinias are suitable subjects for the open border and for other warm, sunny situations.

CULTURE: Plant seeds indoors in March for early bloom. Transplant in late May to warm, sandy, open ground in full sun. Or plant seeds in May in a similar situation where they are to grow.

CALCEOLARIA 12–36"   TP as A and T

The hybrid Calceolarias, known to all gardeners as showy greenhouse subjects, are not the only members of this genus satisfactory for use in the annual garden. There are, in addition, a number of colorful annual species.

C. chelidonioides is an annual native to South America and grows from 1 to 3 feet in height. The toothed leaves are to 8 inches long and the pouch-shaped flowers are yellow.

C. mexicana is a 1-foot annual with small pale yellow flowers.

C. profusa is a garden form to 3 feet, with many dainty golden-yellow blossoms.

C. scabiosaefolia, also annual, has hairy foliage, grows to 2 feet, and bears pale yellow flowers.

The annual species are excellent for gardens. The hybrids are grown as greenhouse pot plants and for decoration indoors and in the conservatory and patio.

CULTURE, ANNUALS: Sow indoors in February or March and set out in the open garden late in May.

CALENDULA OFFICINALIS (Pot-marigold) 12–24"   HH

The Calendulas, or Pot-marigolds, have been popular garden annuals for many years, but during the last two decades their usefulness has been greatly increased by many fine new improved varieties. Their buff, cream, primrose, lemon, gold, or orange single- or dobule-ray flowers grow to 4 inches in diameter, some with dark brown centers, and are freely borne over a long period through midsummer and autumn. Named varieties of outstanding merit are listed by leading seed houses. We particularly like Art Shades, running from buff through cream to apricot and orange.

Celendulas are excellent cool-weather annuals for sunny or lightly shaded borders. They also make fine pot plants for the patio or for winter bloom under glass. By all means plant some in the cutting garden, for they make long-lasting and colorful blooms for arrangements.

CULTURE: Sow seeds in April and set out in May in a well-drained bed. Where midsummer days and nights are very hot, plant in June in a partly shaded, cool seed bed and keep moist through the very hot weather. Plant out in the open garden for autumn bloom.

CALLIRHOE (Poppy-mallow) 12–36″   T and TP as A

The Poppy-mallows are showy North American annuals and perennials which should be more widely grown in American gardens.

C. digitata grows to 1½ feet, with deeply parted linear leaves and 2-inch rosy-purple or violet flowers.

C. involucrata is a trailing species only a foot in height with hairy, deeply parted leaves and 2½-inch red-purple or lavender blossoms.

C. Papaver grows also to 1 foot with 3-parted leaves and 2-inch rose or violet flowers. This and the two species described above are tender perennials.

C. pedata is an annual to 3 feet, also with rose-purple or lilac flowers an inch in diameter.

Callirhoes are subjects for warm, sunny positions in sandy soil.

CULTURE: Sow seeds in May where they are to grow, in light, sandy soil in open, sunny ground.

CALLISTEPHUS CHINENSIS, see page 194.

CALONYYCTION ACULEATUM (Moonflower) to 20′   TP as A

Moonflowers, sometimes incorrectly identified as *Ipomoea Bonanox,* are lovely night-blooming tender perennial vines that can be grown as annuals in the garden. Pink varieties are available, but the pure-white sort, with its long-tubed, 6-inch, delightfully fragrant flowers, is the one we have always found most satisfactory. The blossoms open at dusk, unfurling before your eyes like fairy parasols. Once the flowers open, their elusive fragrance is delightful. Unfurling buds may be cut and brought in to decorate the dinner table. They will open and remain fresh until morning. When cool weather comes, the blooms remain open all night and through the morning. On hot days they wither as soon as the sun is up.

Planted with Heavenly Blue Morning-glories, Moonflowers are lovely on a trellis or arbor. The double planting gives flowers both day and night.

CULTURE: Plant seeds indoors in March, two to a small pot, first soaking, or notching the hard covering of each seed, to hasten germination. Set out in late May or after the ground warms up. In the South, seeds may be planted where they are to grow. Select a sunny, sheltered location and not too rich, sandy soil.

CAMPANULA (Bellflower) 6–48" HH, B and TP AS A

The large genus of Campanula includes several species that are either annual or may be grown as annuals. Heights range from a few inches to several feet; blooms are from ½-inch to several inches in diameter. The genus includes many fine blue species, a color always in demand in the flower garden.

C. drabifolia is a hairy annual, only 6 inches tall, bearing handsome violet-blue flowers. It is a natural for the rock garden and rock wall.

C. medium is the well-known and loved Canterbury Bell, a biennial from which a satisfactory annual form has been developed. Though the biennial form reaches to 3 or 4 feet in height, the annual type is only 2 or 2½ feet tall but bears the same white, lavender, blue, rose, or pink bell-shaped flowers in long, showy spikes.

C. propinqua grandiflora is a 1-foot annual with 1½-inch mauve-violet bell-shaped blooms.

C. ramosissima, also an annual, is 1 foot tall with dark violet-blue bells 1 inch across. *Alba* is a white form.

CARDIOSPERUM HALICACABABUM (Balloon-vine) to 10' T

Balloon-vine is a tender annual, biennial, or perennial native to Bermuda and our own South. The white flowers are inconspicuous, but the fruit is borne in inflated, almost globular 3-angled capsules which are most decorative. The pinnate leaves are coarsely toothed. Climbs by tendrils.

Useful as a climber because it is not of too rank growth, Balloon-vine may be used to cover a fence, trellis, or porch, either to provide shade or as a screen.

CULTURE: Plant seeds in May where they are to grow. Of easy culture.

CATANANCHE (Cupid's-dart) 24" P as A

Catananche is an attractive blue perennial which may be successfully grown as an annual. *C. caerulea,* the best-known species, attains 18 inches in height, with narrow, woolly leaves and 2-inch ray flowers of clear blue. *C. bicolor* bears blue-centered white blooms.

Catananches do well in the mixed border and make satisfactory everlastings when dried.

CULTURE: Sow seeds indoors in March and transplant to the open garden in late May, setting 9 inches apart.

CELOSIA (Cockscomb) 12–48" T

The Cockscombs are among the most useful and colorful annuals for the American garden. Because of their varying heights they can be used in the back and middle border as well as for edgings.

Garden forms are varieties of *C. argentea.* The *cristata* varieties or crested Celosias bear velvety, heavy, crested or plumy feathered heads in deep crimson, purple-red, yellow, and gold. The Maple Gold strain introduced a few years ago produces heavy crested heads in soft pastel salmons, chartreuse, cream, and golden bronze. Tall feathered and crested varieties reach 3 feet in height, while dwarfs are available less than a foot tall. *Toreador* is a new prize winner, 20 inches tall, producing uniform bright red, scarlet-edged combs.

Since Celosias may now be purchased as named varieties in separate colors, it is possible to use this dependable flower in planned landscape effects. The soft-toned Maple Golds and the yellow varieties are especially pleasing in mixed-border work and for massed edgings. Dwarfs are useful in window boxes. All are used as dried plant material for winter decoration.

CULTURE: Sow seeds indoors or in a hotbed in March and keep at a temperature between 70 and 75 until seedlings are well advanced. Transplant as needed to give them room and a richer soil mixture. Set out in late May in a rich, humusy soil, well-drained but provided with ample moisture. Full sun or light part shade.

CENTAUREA 24–48″   H, HH and T

This large genus of garden annuals and perennials includes many species widely grown in the average garden. The heads of tubular flowers are blue, pink, white, or rose-purple.

C. americana, or Basket Flower, is a half-hardy annual growing to 4 feet or more, with 5-inch leaves and solitary heads of rose-lavender or lavender-purple flowers to 5 inches in diameter. *Alba* is a white form. This species is a native of Missouri, Louisiana, and Mexico.

C. cyanus, Cornflower or Bachelor's Button, is probably the most universally grown of any member of this genus. It is a hardy annual to 30 inches in height, with grayish, finely cut, or entire but narrow foliage and pink, blue, white, or rose-colored very double flowers to 2 inches across. There are dwarf forms only a foot tall. Bloom can be had all through the season if dead blossoms are removed.

C. moschata, or Sweet Sultan, is a half-hardy annual to 2 feet, with toothed leaves and thistle-like, fragrant white, yellow, or purple very double blooms. *Imperialis* is a giant-flowered form. Colors are yellow, white, lavender, and purple.

There are few positions in the annual garden where Centaureas do not fit. They may be used in the sunny or partly shaded bed or border, being placed according to their respective heights. Valuable for cutting.

CULTURE: Seeds of hardy annuals may be sown in fall or very early spring where they are to grow or in a seed bed, to be transplanted later to the open garden. Half-hardy species may be planted in mid-April in the open or in a seed bed. Full sun or part shade.

CENTRANTHUS *(Spur-valerian)* to 24" HH

The annual species of Centranthus come from the Mediterranian region and produce red or white flowers in heavy terminal clusters.

C. calcitrapa is a low-growing species from 6 inches to 1 foot in height, with rose-violet blossoms. Suitable for the rock garden or wall.

C. macrosiphon, to 18 inches, has brilliant rose blossoms, freely borne. *Albus* is a white form. It is suitable for massing in the open border.

CULTURE: Sow seeds indoors in March or in an outdoor seed bed in April and transfer to the open garden in May, setting plants 6 to 12 inches apart, in the sun.

CHEIRANTHUS *(Wallflower)* to 18" B or TP as A

The Wallflowers are English favorites which do better in the cool, moist British climate than in most parts of the United States. In the Pacific Northwest, however, and along our eastern seacoast, they make a valuable addition to the garden. Siberian-wallflower is adaptable to almost any climatic condition.

C. Allioni (correctly *Erysimum asperum* but listed in catalogues as Cheiranthus), the Siberian-wallflower, is a biennial which produces bright orange flowers on 12-inch plants in spring. Seeds may be started in a seed bed in midsummer and set out in the garden the following spring, or sown indoors in January or February. Thrives anywhere. Edger.

C. cheiri, which grows from 12 to 18 inches in height, has annual forms which bloom the first year from seed sown indoors in February or March. This is the common English Wallflower which produces buff, yellow, gold, deep red, or mahogany blossoms, delightfully fragrant. In England it is perennial in most gardens, but here it should be grown as an annual or biennial.

CULTURE: As a race, the Wallflowers require cool, humid weather to perform well. Even the Siberian-wallflower, which is truly an Erysimum, not a Cheiranthus, is soon killed down by dry heat. As it blooms early, the gardener may have the benefit of its bright blossoms for edging. *C. cheiri* in this country should be given a cool, moist spot in the lee of a sheltering wall.

CHRYSANTHEMUM to 36"   HH

Though Chrysanthemums are usually thought of as perennials, there are annual forms which well reward the gardener for the trouble of growing them.

C. carinatum (C. tricolor) grows from 2 to 3 feet in height and produces large heads of 2½-inch white ray flowers banded with red, purple, or yellow. A purple disk at the base of the rays enhances their brilliance. These may be had in mixtures or separate named varieties. Double forms are also available.

C. coronarium, the Crown Daisy or Garland Chrysanthemum, reaches 1½ to 3 feet in height and is a bushy, branching annual bearing many heads of light yellow, gold, or white flowers, often semi-double. There are dwarf varieties, such as Tom Thumb, which are only 12 inches tall.

C. segetum, or Corn-marigold, is an English native which grows to about 1½ feet and produces 2½-inch yellow flowers on much-branched plants. There are many garden forms in seperate named varieties, such as Eastern Star, light yellow with a dark disk; Evening Star, golden yellow, large; Morning Star, pale yellow; and White Star, cream with a yellow disk. Yellowstone is a sulphur-yellow double on 2-foot plants.

CULTURE: Plant seeds indoors in early March or outdoors in late April. Set plants out in May in full sun in rich, sandy loam. Bloom continues from midsummer to frost.

CLEOME SPINOSA (Spider Flower) 48–60"   H

This common South American annual has had a new lease on life because of improved varieties in desirable colors which have been recently introduced.

The tall straight spikes of Cleome, up to 5 feet in height, branch somewhat, the main flowering stem and side branches producing racemes of spidery flowers which are at their best in the cool of the day, shriveling somewhat and losing color in hot sun.

The original purplish-rose color was not attractive, but pure Pink Queen and snowy-white Helen Campbell are varieties which grace the back of any border or can be used as a mass planting to screen compost heap, wire fence, or other unattractive feature at some distance from the house. Because of its height, Cleome cannot be used in the foreground.

CULTURE: Plant seeds where they are to grow, in full sun or very light broken shade, in late April, and thin to 15 inches apart. Cleome self-seeds freely. Some seedlings will revert to the undesirable rose-purple color of their ancestors. These should be weeded out as soon as they show color.

CINERARIA, see Senecio.

CLARKIA to 24" T

Clarkia, with its showy rose or purplish racemes of bloom, is a popular garden plant.

C. concinna, or Red Ribbons grows 2 feet tall and has pink to lavender flowers with 3-lobed, fan-shaped petals. It is a native of California.

C. elegans, also from California, grows from 2 to 2½ feet in height and may be had in lavender, red, rose, salmon, scarlet, purple, and white named varieties. It is ideal for mass plantings.

C. pulchella, 18 inches, has lavender to white flowers.

Clarkias are ideal for bedding, massing, cutting, or growing under glass. They do not flourish, however, under all climatic conditions.

CULTURE: Unless you live in a section where cool nights are the rule, you may be unable to grow Clarkia successfully. Along the West Coast, where they are native, and in the British Isles, they are among the most useful of annuals. Plant seeds in May where they are to grow and thin to 10 inches. In the East start indoors in March and transfer to the open garden in May, after the danger of frost is past.

COBAEA SCANDENS (Cup-and-saucer Vine) to 30' T

The Cup-and-saucer Vine is one of the most decorative of climbing annuals. The compound leaves and climbing tendrils are attractive in themselves, while the purplish-blue or white 2-inch bell-shaped flowers in saucer-like bracts are freely borne on long stems in late summer and until hard frost. When the blossoms drop, the chartreuse bracts remain and a seed pod forms in the heart of each. These are almost as attractive as the flowers themselves. As cool nights arrive, the foliage turns a rich purplish-green.

The strong tendrils of Cobaea make it possible for the vine to climb on stone or stucco without any support, though strings or other support should be given at first until the plants get a start. Not only are they pleasing against a house wall or climbing up a dead stump or post, but the flowers, with foliage and tendrils, make excellent cut material for line arrangements. Individual flowers may be added to mass bouquets. Can be grown in the window garden.

CULTURE: Start seeds indoors in March, 2 to a small pot or plant band. Set out in sun or light part shade in May after all danger of frost is past. Give support until tendrils take a firm hold.

COIX LACRYMA-JOBI (Job's Tears) to 36"   P AS A

This old-fashioned favorite was grown in our grandmothers' gardens for the beadlike "seeds," to 1½ inches long but more commonly about ½ inch. These whitish or gray beads are hard and glossy and are formed on the pistillate spikelets of this most unusual and interesting grass. The leaves are long and narrow and quite decorative. *Aurea zebrina* is a variety with striped leaves.

Sprays of Job's Tears can be cut, dried, and used in winter bouquets; or the beads can be removed, the soft centers drawn out, and the beads strung. Strings of these were commonly used for teething babies in years gone by, and children strung and wore long necklaces of them.

CULTURE: Start seeds in seed bed in April and transplant to back of border or to cutting garden, 12 inches apart, in late May.

COLEUS BLUMEI to 36"   TP AS A

Our common garden Coleus is a perennial which can be grown as an annual. Most seed houses offer seeds of several varieties or mixtures. After the gardener gets a satisfactory stand, plants may be increased by cuttings.

Grown for their brilliant variegated foliage, the Coleuses are showy garden plants. *Verschaffelti* has crimson leaves. Trailing Queen is a prostrate variety, and there are many fine mixtures offering a number of variegations from yellow to rose and dark red. Rainbow Mixture is new and brilliant (facing page 160).

Coleus is ideal for edging, bedding, and massing as well as for window boxes, pots for patios and terraces, and as indoor window-garden plants.

CULTURE: Start seeds indoors in February or March. Set out in sun or part shade when danger of frost is past. Cuttings are readily rooted in water or damp sand.

COLLINSIA to 24"   H

Collinsias are hardy annuals native to our own West Coast; but, unlike others of the same habitat, they adapt themselves well to varying conditions.

The leaves, in whorls, make an excellent ground cover, while the bright rose, blue, or purple flowers are most attractive. These are bell-shaped and appear in the leaf axils, either alone or in clusters.

C. bartsiaefolia, or the Seaside Collinsia, produces white flowers marked with purple on 1-foot plants.

C. bicolor grows to 2 feet, with white and purple blooms. *Candidissima* is a white variety; *multicolor* produces flowers variegated white, lavender, violet, and rose; *purpurea* is purple, and Salmon Beauty a delicate salmon.

C. grandiflora, or Blue-lips, has large blossoms, the lower lip rose-purple, the upper lip white. One foot.

C. verna, or Blue-eyed Mary, grows 2 feet tall and has flowers with a bright blue lower lip and whitish upper lip.

Collinsias are among the few annuals that thrive in shade. Plant them on a shady bank, as a shady ground cover in gravelly soil or as specimens in the rock garden.

CULTURE: As they are perfectly hardy, seeds may be planted in fall or early spring where they are to grow. Thin to 12 inches. Bloom occurs in midsummer.

COLLOMIA to 24″   HH

Collomias are Gilia-like flowers of which there are two pleasing annual species.

C. biflora is an annual 2 feet tall, native to South America, and bears scarlet flowers, buff in reverse.

C. grandiflora, also 2 feet, produces clusters of buff-salmon blooms.

C. linearis grows to 16 inches; flowers are rose-purple to pink.

Collomias are attractive garden plants for the open border or as specimens in the rock garden.

CULTURE: Sow seeds where they are to grow in April and thin to 12 inches apart. Or they may be started indoors in March and later set out in the open garden.

COREOPSIS (Calliopsis) to 36″   H

The annual species of Coreopsis are usually listed in catalogues as Calliopsis. They vary in height from 1 to 36 inches, are iron-hardy, bloom freely, and self-seed.

C. Atkinsoniana grows to 3 feet and produces heads of 1½-inch ray flowers on long stalks. Rays are purplish at the base with a brown or purple disk. Native to Northwest.

C. calliopsidea, 2 feet, has a basal tuft of leaves and yellow blossoms. Virginia to Florida.

C. Drummondi, to 1½ feet; orange-yellow to crimson flowers with reddish-brown ring around the center.

C. tinctoria, 2 feet; yellow blooms with dark zone at base. *Atropurpurea* is a variety which is dark crimson or garnet. *Florepleno* is double. Dwarf varieties are but 12 inches tall.

Calliopsis can be used for massing in sunny beds, for mixed borders, or to cover waste places. Makes a satisfactory cut flower.

CULTURE: Sow outdoors in fall or early spring where they are to grow, or start in a seed bed and transplant to open garden as soon as plants are large enough. Self-seeds freely.

COSMOS 36–72″ HH

Cosmos is perhaps a less popular flower today than it was in our mothers' gardens, but it still deserves a place in every mixed border and cutting garden. This is especially true because improved varieties offer larger and more strikingly colored flowers with earlier bloom.

C. bipinnatus is the species from which come all the modern varieties of red, rose, and white single, giant, or crested varieties. These may be had in separate colors as named varieties, and most of them are in flower 2 months from seed planting.

C. sulphureus is the original species which has produced such famous yellow and orange varieties as Fiesta, Yellow Ruffles, Orange Ruffles, and Orange Flare. The plants grow to about 3 feet and produce masses of blossoms on long, graceful stems.

Cosmos may be used in the back of the border, against a fence or wall in sun, and should by all means have a place in the cutting garden, as both species and their varieties make fine cut-flower material.

CULTURE: Sow seeds indoors in early April or outdoors in May. Set out in open garden in late May, when all danger of frost is past.

CUCURBITA PEPO OVIFERA; LAGENARIA; SICERARIA, ETC. (Ornamental Gourds) to 20′ T

The growing of Ornamental Gourds is a fascinating hobby, especially for those who live in the warmer parts of the country, where long periods of hot, sunny weather make it easy to bring the fruit to perfect maturity.

Gourds are inedible members of the Pumpkin and Squash family, with hairy, lobed leaves, yellow flowers, and a great variety of interestingly shaped hard-shelled fruits, some very small, others several feet long. Colors are cream, yellow, green, and orange.

Not only are Ornamental Gourds most decorative growing on a trellis, fence, or pergola, but the fruits, when permitted to mature and then dried and shellacked, are much prized for Gourd strings and for use in arrangements of dried material. A number variously shaped and heaped in a bowl make an attractive table decoration.

Formerly the larger fruits were used by Indians and early settlers as dippers, water containers, etc. Medium-sized specimens, properly cured, make excellent birdhouses.

CULTURE: Plant outdoors in May after danger of frost is past. They must have full sun and preferably a sandy loam. The longer the period of hot, sunny weather, the better the chances of gourds maturing completely before frost. They are very tender. When mature—and it is important not to pick them until they have reached maximum growth—the Gourds are harvested and dried gradually in an airy place. When completely dried they may be shellacked or sprayed with clear plastic. This preserves them and enhances the brilliant colors. To make birdhouses, dippers, etc., the hard shell must be carefully cut with a knife or keyhole saw, after which seeds and pith are removed.

CUPHEA (Cigar flower) 12–48"   A and TS

Cupheas are natives of Mexico and Guatamala, grown generally in the North as greenhouse subjects and used as bedding plants in the open garden.

C. platycentra, the species most generally grown, is the Cigar-flower of commerce. The low, bushy plants produce lance-shaped leaves and an abundance of long, tubular scarlet flowers. Firefly is one of a number of improved varieties.

Hybrids of the above species have also been created, like the Avalon Hybrids which are compact-growing, with vermilion, scarlet, crimson, purple, lavender, rose, and pure-pink flowers opening over a long blooming period.

C. lanceolata is entirely different, growing to 4 feet in height and with bicolored flowers, the upper 2 petals dark maroon, veined black, and the lower 4 petals crimson.

C. procumbens, a creeping species, has purple blooms tipped with green.

Massed as bedding plants in the front of the border, Cigar-flowers make a striking display. They are also satisfactory for the window garden in winter and as summer pot plants for terrace or patio. *C. lanceolata* is suitable for the back of the border and *C. procumbens* as an edger.

CULTURE: Start seeds indoors in March in the North and set out in late May after all danger of frost is past. In the South seeds may be sown outdoors in early spring. Easily propagated from cuttings, stock may be carried over from year to year in the greenhouse or window garden.

CYMBALARIA MURALIS (Kenilworth-ivy) to 6'   TP as A

This delicate vine, with its bright green scalloped leaves, dark red hairlike creeping stems, and bright lavender flowers, is one of the daintiest and most satisfactory of vines which can be grown as annuals. Its profuse growth, pleasing appearance, and pretty flowers make it a "must," especially for owners of rock walls and rock gardens.

Once planted in a wall or among rocks, Kenilworth-ivy self-seeds freely, appearing where it will, and always adding a bright touch to its chosen resting place. Indoors it will grace a hanging basket or cover the pot soil of Amaryllis or other bare-stemmed house plants. In window or porch boxes it hangs down in a graceful cascade. It is not fussy about soil or other growing conditions.

CULTURE: As seed is not generally available, get a "start" of Kenilworth-ivy from a friend or from a greenhouse, where it often makes itself at home in or under the benches. Once it is planted in your garden, you can depend on it to self-seed. Plants can then be dug and transplanted to other locations or potted for indoor or window-box decoration. Equally happy in sun or deep shade.

CYNOGLOSSUM AMABILE (Chinese Forget-me-not) 24"   B as A

Cynoglossum is prized for its many tall, graceful sprays of deep or heaven-blue Forget-me-not-like blossoms borne throughout the summer on rather slender plants. Though really a biennial, it can be grown as an annual.

Blanche Burpee, including deep, medium, and light blue as well as pure-white flowers, is one of the outstanding mixtures. Snow Bird is a white, and Firmament a deep blue dwarf, growing but 15 inches tall.

As it withstands heat particularly well, Cynoglossum is of great value in hot, dry, sunny locations. Firmament can be used in front of taller-growing varieties to give a mass effect. It makes an excellent cut flower also.

CULTURE: Plant seeds in a seed bed in early May and transplant 9 inches apart after ground is warm; or start indoors in March and set out in late May.

DAHLIA (Bedding Types) to 24"   TUBER as A

Many people do not realize that the small Dahlias can be grown as annuals and that, in one season from seed, they easily produce masses of brilliantly colored single and double flowers of many forms in a wide color range.

Coltness Hybrids make plants 18 to 24 inches tall with large single flowers to 3 inches in diameter, some with fluted petals.

Mignon Mixed, 2 feet, are also singles, in the full Dahlia color range.

Unwin Dwarf Hybrids are famous for their lovely semi-double blooms in many colors.

Zulu, 2 feet, is a mixture of reds with dark red foliage.

Colors in the mixtures range from lemon-yellow through deep yellow, gold, and orange to scarlet, crimson, and salmon. There are also whites, pink, rose, lavender, and purple-rose. In fact, blue is the only color lacking.

These "Bedding" Dahlias give more showy color than almost any other midsummer or fall flower. Mass them in a bed or use groups in the mixed border. Also satisfactory for cutting.

CULTURE: Start seeds indoors in February or March and set out 18 inches apart after all danger of frost. A rich, well-worked loam in full sun or very light broken shade suits them well. Choice plants can be dug in fall and tubers saved over.

DATURA (Angel's Trumpet) 24–60"   T

The annual Angel's Trumpet is a tropical plant which, though coarse in growth, is cherished for its great trumpet-shaped white, yellow, or purplish blossoms borne in midsummer.

D. Metel is available in a number of varieties: *alba,* with 7-inch white trumpets; *caerulea,* blue; *Huberiana,* with blue, yellow, and red blossoms. All have coarse leaves to 8 inches long and heavy, trunklike stems. Ivory King is a new variety with ivory-yellow triple hose-in-hose blossoms very freely borne.

Daturas make impressive specimen plants in patios, on terraces, or planted near the house, and can also be used as temporary hedge material. Flowers are often used in arrangements.

CULTURE: Start indoors in March and set plants out in May. Daturas often self-seed satisfactorily as far north as New York City.

DELPHINIUM (Larkspur) 12–48″   H and P as A

Annual Delphinium, or Larkspur *(D. Ajacis),* is one of the hardiest of annuals and used almost universally by gardeners who want masses of colorful spike flowers. See Chapter 16 for description and details of culture.

D. grandiflorum, usually listed in catalogues as *Delphinium chinense,* is a perennial which flowers the first year from early-planted seed. It is rather a slender plant, 2 or 3 feet in height, much-branched, and with finely cut decorative foliage. The true blue flowers, unlike the usual perennial type, are not closely set, but rather gracefully scattered along the ends of the flowering branches. It is especially useful as a cut flower, where its good color and graceful curves make it most useful for arrangement.

CULTURE: Start seeds indoors in March or plant outdoors in a seed bed in August or September for bloom the following year. Set out 9 inches apart in rich, sandy loam in a well-drained sunny location.

DIANTHUS (Pink, Carnation) to 24″   B or H

The annual Pinks are biennial or perennial form which flower the first year from seed. Most of them are varieties of the species *D. chinensis.* Their bright colors and large, fragrant single or double flowers make them most desirable border plants.

D. barbatus, or Sweet William, is an old-fashioned biennial Pink which is now available in many improved mixtures and named varieties in separate colors. The most famous of these is the lovely salmon-pink Newport Pink. Homeland is a fine crimson with a white eye; Scarlet Beauty is bright scarlet; Midget, a 4-inch dwarf for edging, of mixed colors.

Sweet Wivelsfield, also biennial, is a low-growing form of Dianthus, with very fragrant flowers, in colors from pink to crimson.

There are endless fine varieties of *D. chinensis. Heddewigi* in its various forms produces large single or double flowers, with plain or lacinated petals in colors and color mixtures from white to crimson.

Dianthus is unexcelled for edging and positions near the front of the sunny border. Dwarf forms may be used to good advantage in the rock garden.

CULTURE: Start annual forms in April in an outdoor seed bed and transplant to the open garden in May. Dianthus prefers a well-limed soil. It does not flourish as a rule where the pH is below neutral.

Biennial forms such as Sweet William and Sweet Wivelsfield should be started in a frame or seed bed in late summer for bloom the following year.

DIASCIA BARBERAE (Twinspur) 12"   HH

Twinspur is a pleasing little annual with rosy flowers, shading to salmon, borne in terminal racemes. Its foot-high growth makes it a useful subject for the open border. Salmon Queen is an improved variety.

Diascia may be grown indoors as well as in the open border.

CULTURE: Start indoors in March or outdoors in a seed bed in April. Transplant in May, 6 inches apart.

DIGITALIS (Foxglove) to 72"   B

Foxgloves are true biennials, but they are so easily grown and so prone to self-seed when once planted that they are included here among plants grown as annuals.

Mixtures produce tall spikes of bell-shaped flowers in colors from white through rose to purple. Throats are mottled or blotched. The Shirley Mixture produces very large flowers in delicate colors from white through pale pink to rose with deep red spots and blotches.

Because they do well in quite heavy part shade, Foxgloves are most useful background material in open woodlands or for the back of the partly shaded border.

CULTURE: Start in late summer in a frame or seed bed in part shade and transplant to the garden the following spring.

DIMORPHOTHECA AURANTIACA
(Cape-marigold) to 18"   TP as A

Cape-marigolds are tender African perennnials which are particularly happy in hot, dry situations. They can be grown without difficulty as annuals. The narrow leaves are toothed to 3 inches long, and the ray flowers are orange, lemon, or white.

Cape-marigolds may be planted in beds in hot, dry situations and give fine masses of colorful bloom.

CULTURE: Start indoors in March or plant in the open garden in May. Thin or transplant to 9 inches apart in full sun, in sandy loam.

DOLICHOS LABLAB *(Hyacinth Bean)* to 10'   TP as A

Hyacinth Bean is an attractive vine with broad, 6-inch leaves and clusters of purple or white flowers. It is used chiefly as a covering for fences, trellises, or other supports, where it makes a satisfactory screen.

CULTURE: Plant in May, after danger of frost is past, where they are to grow, in hills, 6 seeds to a hill. Full sun.

ECHIINOCYSTIS LOBATA *(Wild-cucumber)* to 20'   HH

Wild-cucumber is a coarse, hairy-leaved vine with many clusters of white, lacy flowers borne in July and papery, spiny pods in autumn. As it self-seeds very freely, Wild-cucumber should not be planted in a location where it is difficult to remove unwanted seedlings.

Its uses are chiefly for covering debris or unsightly areas. It thrives in sun or shade.

CULTURE: Sow outdoors in April in any desired location.

ECHIUM (Viper's Bugloss) to 24"   T

Echiums are rather coarse annuals or biennials of the Borage family, with hairy leaves and dense flower spikelets.

E. creticum grows to 2 feet, has lance-shaped, hairy leaves and spikelets of brick-red flowers.

E. plantagineum, its varieties and hybrids, is 3 feet tall, with spikelets of blue and purple, mauve, or white flowers. Foliage hairs are white,

Coarse but colorful, Echiums are useful in the large mixed border. They are particularly happy in the California climate, though natives of southern Europe. Thrive on gravel or cinder banks where drainage is particularly good.

CULTURE: Plant indoors in January or February and set out in the sunny border, 12 to 15 inches apart, in May after danger of frost is over.

EMILIA SAGITTATA (Tassel-flower) to 24"   T

Tassel-flower is a slender annual with toothed, oval leaves and heads of ½-inch red or orange-red flowers borne in loose corymbs. The variety *lutea* has golden-yellow flowers.

Emilias like hot, dry situations and do especially well at the seashore, where many annuals are not happy.

CULTURE: Plant seed indoors in April or outdoors in May. Set 9 inches apart in a sunny location in sandy loam after danger of frost is past.

ERAGROSTIS TENELLA (Love Grass) 1–3'   T

Love Grass is a graceful decorative grass growing to about 3 feet, with long panicles of tiny spikelets comprising half of the entire height. It is decorative as a boundary or hedge annual, and the spikelets, dried, are useful in winter arrangements.

CULTURE: Plant seeds outdoors in full sun when danger of frost is past. Thin to 1 foot apart.

ESCHSCHOLZIA CALIFORNICA (California-poppy) to 24"   H

Even the most inexperienced gardener can succeed with California-poppies—and with very little effort at that. Iron-hardy and of easy germination, they can be planted wherever there is full sun and good drainage and will reward the gardener with masses of yellow, orange, salmon-pink, or white single flowers in early summer.

Eschscholzia makes a colorful flower bed of any gravelly or sandy wasteland or slope in hot sun. Or they can be grouped in beds and borders. There are dwarf and prostrate forms for edgings and banks.

CULTURE: Plant seeds in September or March where the plants are to grow. Choose a sunny spot with sandy soil where the plants will have plenty of warmth. Thin to 6 inches apart.

EUPHORBIA to 36"   H and HH

The annual Euphorbias are natives of North America and grown for their showy, colored leaves on 2- to 3-foot plants.

E. heterophylla, Mexican Fire-plant or Painted Spurge, grows wild from Illinois to Florida and is a half-hardy 3-foot annual with large leaves, the upper ones marked or blotched in red, and somewhat resembling its relative, the Poinsettia *(E. pulcherrima).* It is used for color in the back of the border and for accessory foliage in flower arrangements.

E. marginata, the well-known and loved Snow-on-the-mountain, is a 2-footer, the gray-green leaves margined with white and the flowers with white petal-like appendages. It is native from Minnesota to Texas. In the old-fashioned garden it is massed to give a gray-and-white effect as a foil for brighter flowers, but it may well be utilized for the same purpose in less traditional plantings.

CULTURE: Plant seeds of Mexican Fire-plant in April where they are to grow, in full sun. Snow-on-the-mountain seeds may be planted in March as soon as the ground can be worked, also where they are to grow, in sun.

FELICIA BERGERIANA (Kingfisher-daisy) 8″   T

This is a dainty little annual, especially for the South, where it flourishes. It bears bright blue solitary, Daisy-like flowers with yellow disks. Coming to use from South Africa, it thrives on heat.

Use Kingfisher-daisy in southern gardens as an edging or for rock-garden planting. It may be grown in the greenhouse in the North.

CULTURE: Start indoors in March or outdoors in late May and set out 6 inches apart in full sun, in sandy loam.

GAILLARDIA 24″   HH and T

The annual forms of Gaillardia are well worth a place in the garden picture.

G. amblyodon bears mahogany-red flowers to 2 or more inches across on 2-foot plants with 3-inch hairy leaves.

G. pulchella (G. Drummondi) is about 1½ feet tall with large yellow ray flowers, rosy-purple at the base. There are improved double varieties such as red and yellow Fiesta, yellow Sunshine, and the Gaiety Mixture with ball-shaped blooms of yellow, orange, maroon, and claret.

Gaillardias make good bedding and border plants for positions in full sun. Being natives of our own Southwest, they endure heat and drought admirably. The doubles make most attractive cut flowers.

CULTURE: Plant *G. amblyodon* outdoors in a seed bed in April, and *G. pulchella* in mid-May when danger of frost is past. Set out 9 inches apart.

GAMOLEPIS TAGETES 12″ T

This little South African annual is desirable because of its profuse bloom, the heads of yellow or orange ray flowers making a charming edging.

CULTURE: Start seeds indoor in March or outdoors in a seed bed in May after danger of frost. Set out 6 inches apart in a warm, sunny situation.

GAZANIA SPLENDENS prostrate to 18″ P as A

Gazania splendens is a tender perennial hybrid form of this South African genus. The prostrate stems bear leaves which are silky white on the reverse side and large yellow or orange ray flowers with a black-and-white spot at the base of each.

Gazania is most useful in the sunny rock garden or wall, though it may also be used for edging.

CULTURE: Start indoors in February or March; set out when the ground is well warmed up, 18 inches apart in full sun.

GENTIANA (Gentian) to 12″ A and B

The Gentians form a large and charming family. Most of them are perennial, but there are some lovely little annuals also. Not all of them, unfortunately, are available commercially.

G. campestris grows to but 6 inches, with bright, erect, purple-blue flowers borne in great numbers. Annual. Native to Europe.

G. crinita, the beautiful Fringed Gentian, is a biennial; grows to 2 or 3 feet with bright blue solitary flowers 2 inches long, the edges deeply fringed. A native of North America, it grows freely and self-seeds in locations which suit it, but is difficult to transplant because of its long, slender roots. Moist woods and meadows are its natural habitats.

G. thermalis, growing wild in the West (Colorado to Arizona), is an annual; grows to 1 foot, with deep blue solitary flowers to 2 inches, the blooms streaked with a lighter shade.

G. tubulosa is an annual or biennial; grows to 6 inches, with slender, erect stems, narrow leaves, and 1-inch bluish-lilac flowers, solitary or in 3-flowered cymes. This is a native of Argentina.

With the exception of the Fringed Gentian, these little Gentians are rock-garden subjects. Seeds can be obtained from rock-garden specialists, but inexperienced gardeners may well find them difficult.

CULTURE: In general, the requirements of Gentians are: excellent drainage, plenty of moisture, and generally cool weather. Most of them are mountain species.

GERBERIA JAMESONI HYBRIDA (Transvaal-daisy) to 30″ P as A

Gerberias, as they are commonly called, are greenhouse subjects which can be grown in the open garden in the North if seed is planted indoors early in the year.

The woolly leaves grow in a basal rosette. The large Daisy-like flowers, 4 inches or more across, are white, pink, salmon, orange, deep red, and lavender, the petals having a pearly sheen. Flower stems are long and graceful.

Gerberias make a fine show for bedding and are especially good for cutting.

CULTURE: Plant seeds indoors in January. Transplant to pots and set out in rich, sandy loam in full sun in late May, or when the ground has thoroughly warmed up. In southern gardens Gerberias may be treated as a perennial; farther north they may be over-wintered in a frost-proof frame.

GILIA to 48″   HH and T

There are many species of Gilias, all natives of the New World. Most of them are free-flowering and many low-growing.

G. abrotanifolia, annual, to 2 feet, bears large heads of light blue flowers.

G. achillaefolia, also 2 feet tall, bears dense clusters of blue blossoms.

G. aggregata, or Scarlet Gilia, biennial, to 30 inches, has white to scarlet blossoms.

G. androsacea, to 1½ feet; dense heads of yellow, white, pink, or violet flowers.

G. capitata, to 30 inches, has globular heads of light blue flowers.

G. dianthoides is a dwarf, to 6 inches, which grows in tufts of threadlike leaves. Funnel-form flowers are pink, lilac, or white. All the above are from our own West Coast.

G. laciniata, to 8 inches, has clusters of white, blue, lilac, or rose. South America.

G. liniflora, 1 foot tall, is bushy, with white blooms.

G. lutea, 6 inches tall, has deeply cut leaves and yellow-pink and yellow or white flowers.

G. rubra, commonly called Standing-cypress, is a tall, handsome biennial of the South with scarlet flowers in terminal panicles. The daintily cut foliage is most decorative. There are also pink, yellow, and orange varieties. Plant seeds in late summer and carry over in frame.

C. tricolor, or Bird's-eyes, is 30 inches tall, though there are dwarf strains reaching only 12 inches. The white blossoms have tubes and throats marked with purple and are borne in loose clusters. *Rosea* has rose-colored bloom.

CULTURE: Plant seeds of annual species in mid-April where they are to grow, as they do not like transplanting. They require full sun.

GLAUCIUM to 24″   H and B

The Glauciums are bold, handsome plants with deeply cut gray-green leaves and large, solitary, Poppy-like blossoms.

G. corniculatum, or Sea-poppy, is a low-growing species to 12 inches or more with orange-red flowers, the petals spotted with black at the base. It is an annual.

G. flavum, the Horned-poppy, grows to 24 inches and produces large yellow blooms. Variety *Seuperi* has yellow blooms spotted with violet, while *tricolor* bears 3-inch red-orange flowers, each petal spotted with black and yellow. Though a biennial, it can be grown as an annual.

These large, rather coarse-growing but showy flowers are excellent for bedding or massing in an open, sandy location where more difficult annuals refuse to grow. Flowers and foliage may be used for arrangements.

CULTURE: Plant seeds outdoors in March or, with biennial varieties, in midsummer where the plants are to grow. Choose a spot in full sun and with sandy soil. It need not be too rich, for Glauciums are not fussy.

GODETIA to 36"   HH

Godetias are natives of our West Coast, where they flourish in the California climate. Their lavender-red, red, salmon, coral, pale pink, or white flowers are much prized for garden color.

G. amoena, or Farewell-to-spring, is a 3-foot native of the West Coast, of slender, graceful growth, with flowers in all the colors mentioned above. Named varieties in seperate colors are available.

G. grandiflora, 1 to 2 feet, is the species from which most of the popular garden varieties have been derived. The species bears rose-red blooms, sometimes white, with a dark splotch at the base of each petal. Carminea is a deep red variety, and there are many others, including pleasing dwarfs.

Where conditions are suitable for Godetias, they make first-class bedding plants and are much used for masses of color in the mixed border as well as for cutting. Also as potted plants indoors.

CULTURE: Sow seeds in April where they are to grow, in light, sandy soil in full sun or part shade. Thin from 6 to 9 inches apart.

GOMPHRENA GLOBOSA (Globe Amaranth) 18"   T

Globe Amaranth is one of the everlastings—an annual growing to 1½ feet in height, with 4-inch leaves and flower heads of white, purple, rose, and orange. There are many varieties in seperate colors, and a dwarf, nana, growing but 8 inches tall.

Gomphrena may be used for bedding, for cutting, and, when dried, for winter bouquets.

CULTURE: Plant seeds indoors in March or outdoors in a seed bed after danger of frost is past. Transplant to a position in full sun, 12 inches apart.

GYPSOPHILA ELEGANS (Babys-breath) 30"   HH

The annual form of Babys-breath, an old-fashioned favorite garden flower, grows to 18 inches high, with upright, branching stems, lance-shaped leaves, and many small, airy white, blush, or rose-pink flowers. *Muralis,* only a foot tall, is a species much planted in rock walls.

Gypsophila has a place in the mixed border to lighten heavy masses of color; is used frequently as a cut flower, especially in old-fashioned bouquets; can be dried for winter arrangements; and is sometimes planted as background material in the rock garden.

CULTURE: Plant in a seed bed outdoors in the middle of April and set plants 12 inches apart in the garden late in May.

HELENIUM TENUIFOLIUM (Sneezeweed) 24–30"   T

Helenium is a coarse, weedy plant native to our own East Coast. The annual form grows wild from Virginia to Florida and Texas in rich moist soil. Despite its unattractive common name, it makes rather a handsome garden plant with its narrow, whorled leaves and heads of clustered yellow flowers borne during summer and autumn.

This Helenium is useful for massed plantings in wild gardens, in sun, or for the back of the border.

CULTURE: Plant seeds indoors in March and set out in rich soil in a sunny location after danger of frost is past.

HELIANTHUS (Sunflower) 4–12'   T

The Sunflowers, which are native to the Western Hemisphere, most of them to North America, have a well-established place in our gardens despite their coarseness and great height. By selecting several species and varieties, colors from yellow to copper-red and rose-pink can be had, with heights from 4 to 12 feet.

H. annuus, the 12-foot native which grows on the West Coast from Washington to California, produces its plate-like yellow blooms to a foot or more across, with yellow petals and brownish-purple disk. Useful in background plantings, as annual screening, and as bird seed.

H. argophyllus, or Silverleaf Sunflower, grows to 6 feet, with 3-inch, brown-disked flower heads and large (to 10 inches) silvery leaves cherished by flower arrangers as dried material.

H. debilis, native from Florida to Texas, is more easily handled since it grows but 4 feet tall, with flowers to 3 inches across. *Cupreatus* bears copper-red blossoms; *pureus,* pink or purplish-pink; and *roseus,* rose-pink flowers.

CULTURE: There is nothing difficult about growing Sunflowers. Plant the seeds where the plants are to grow, in any soil, but in full sun, after all danger of frost is past. Thin tall varieties to 3 feet apart, smaller ones to 2 feet. If in an exposed position, some plants may need support. If seeds are to be saved for winter bird food, the heads should be removed and dried as soon as seeds have matured. Otherwise the seed may all be taken before harvest.

HELICHRYSUM BRACTEATUM (Strawflower) to 36"   T

This well-known annual everlasting produces solitary 2½-inch heads of white, yellow, orange, or white straw-like flowers. There are a number of varieties in separate colors, and *nanum,* which is dwarf.

Though attractive in the border, Strawflowers are grown chiefly to be dried for winter bouquets.

CULTURE: Start seeds indoors in March or plant outdoors in May where they are to grow. Set out 12 to 18 inches apart in full sun. Harvest flowers for drying just as they open, and hang upside down to dry in a shady, well-aired place.

HELIOPHILA (Cape-stock) to 12"   T

Heliophilas are charming little South Africans bearing long racemes of blue and yellow flowers. *H. leptophylla,* growing but 9 inches tall, has blue-green foliage and blue flowers, yellow at the base. *H. linearifolia,* 12 inches, makes a shrubby plant and bears blue flowers with yellow claws.

Heliophilas are suitable for edging in the front of the border or for the sunny rock garden.

CULTURE: Plant seeds indoors in March and set out, 6 inches apart, in a sunny location in sandy loam when all danger of frost is past.

HELIOTROPIUM (Heliotrope) to 24"   TP

Heliotrope, though not an annual but a tender perennial, is one of the most valuable of our summer bedding plants and one which can easily be grown from seed. The bushy plants resemble small shrubs and bear many heads or racemes of deliciously fragrant lavender or violet flowers.

Heliotrope is a bedding plant *par excellence* and is especially lovely combined with one of the newer salmon-pink Petunias. It also blends well with white annuals. For cutting, especially in old-fashioned bouquets, it is valuable for both color and scent.

CULTURE: Plant seeds indoors in March and set out in late May or after the ground has thoroughly warmed up, 12 inches apart in light, rich soil in a sunny bed. Stock may be easily increased by cuttings or by layering side branches—pegging side stems to the ground and covering the bare portion with soil. When rooted, the stems are cut from main plant and set out.

HELIPTERUM (Everlasting) to 18"   T

The Helipterums are popular annuals for use as everlastings. *H. Humboldtianum* produces yellowish-green or yellow disk flowers and has attractive gray-white foliage. *H. Manglesi,* the Swan River Everlasting, is a slender 1½-foot plant with 1½-inch flower heads surrounded by white to bright pink bracts. *H. roseum* is 2 feet tall with 2-inch heads of flowers surrounded by rose or white bracts.

Plant Helipterums in the cutting garden and harvest the flowers as soon as opened for use in winter bouquets.

CULTURE: Plant seeds outdoors where they are to grow, in May after danger of frost is past. Thin to 9 inches apart. They need full sun.

HIBISCUS (Rose-mallow) 24" to 10'   TP

The Hibiscus genus gives us many of our best garden plants, such as Rose-of-Sharon or Shrub-althea and the Rose-of-China or Chinese Hibiscus. The species mentioned here are either annual or can be grown as annuals. Like the handsomer members of the clan, they are erect-growing plants with divided leaves and showy Holly-hock-like flowers.

H. abelmoschus, or Musk-mallow, is an annual, to 6 feet, with lobed leaves and crimson-centered yellow flowers to 4 inches in diameter. Heavily fragrant.

H. manihot an Asian species, reaches 9 feet in height, and produces 9-inch pale yellow flowers with dark centers. *Grandiflorus* has even larger flowers.

H. trionum, or Flower-of-an-hour, is a low-growing species, to 2 feet, with deeply lobed leaves and sulphur-yellow, dark-centered blooms. *Grandiflorus* has larger flowers.

Mallows are suitable for background plantings, as the huge flowers make a show of color even when viewed from a distance.

CULTURE: Plant seeds in May where they are to grow, or start indoors in February and transplant to open ground after the soil has warmed up.

HORDEUM JUBATUM (Squirrel-tail Grass) to 30"   B

Squirrel-tail Grass is an ornamental species bearing 4-inch nodding spikes with awns or beards 3 inches long. It is a member of the Barley family and much grown for the ornamental feathery plumes of spikelets, which are attractive in the border or dried for winter bouquets.

CULTURE: Sow seeds in April where they are to grow and thin to 12 inches.

HUMULUS JAPONICUS (Japanese Hop) to 25'   HH

Japanese Hop is a very-fast-growing annual vine which literally takes over any area where it gets a good start. Self-seeding freely, its use is to be avoided except where a heavy deciduous cover is needed for a pile of debris, slash, or other unsightly object.

The hairy, much-lobed leaves are marked with white in the variety *variegatus,* the one usually found in gardens, while the fruit resembles that of its relative, the Common Hop.

CULTURE: Plant seeds outdoors where they are to grow. Destroy unwanted seedlings each spring to prevent undue spreading.

HUNNEMANNIA FUMARIAEFOLIA
(Mexican Tulip-poppy, Golden Cup) to 24″   P as A

This Tulip-like flower is of the most brilliant singing canary-yellow imaginable. The variety Sunlite, an All-American Annual silver medal winner, is semi-double.

Excellent for bedding and makes a fine cut flower if taken in bud.

CULTURE: Plant seeds outdoors in early May where they are to grow and thin to 9 inches. They flourish best in a warm, sunny bed which has been well limed.

IBERIS (Candytuft) to 16″   HH

The Candytufts are members of a most useful genus of garden plants, the annual forms being half-hardy and blooming for rather a brief period.

I. affinis, an erect annual, to 16 inches, produces many heads of fragrant white blooms tinged with violet.

I. amara, to 12 inches, is called Rocket Candytuft and bears racemes of large white fragrant blooms. There are many named varieties and dwarf forms. Native of Europe.

I. umbellata, or Globe Candytuft, 16 inches, bears pale blush, pink, red, violet, and purple flowers but is not fragrant. Named varieties are available.

Candytufts are used chiefly for edgings or near the front of the border and in the rock garden. Fragrant forms are also desirable as cut flowers.

CULTURE: As Candytuft does not bear transplanting well, scatter seeds in April where they are to grow and thin to from 12 to 18

Many annuals lend themselves to easily made "quickie" arrangements to cheer up summertime rooms. Here are Zinnias.

The busy gardener finds little time to make elaborate arrangements for everyday use. Such one-flower bouquets as these take but a few moments. ABOVE *Petunia Peach Red*. BELOW *Single Nasturtiums*.

inches apart. Plant seeds in succession, 4 to 8 weeks apart, for un-interrupted bloom throughout the season.

IMPATIENS (Patience Plant, Garden Balsam) to 30″   HH and T

There are two members of this succulent genus which are valuable for the annual garden.

I. Balsamina, Garden Balsam or Ladyslipper, is an old-fashioned, half-hardy annual with light green juicy stems, lance-shaped leaves, and many single or double showy flowers borne close to the main stem along the top third of its length. Colors are white, blush, rose, rose-purple. Improved modern varieties are usually double, the best strain being the Camellia-flowered, with individual blossoms like small Camellias or Tuberous Begonias. Valuable for bedding in sun or shade.

CULTURE: Plant seeds indoors in April or outdoors in early May where the plants are to grow. Sandy loam suits them best. Set out or thin to 18 inches apart and pinch back the young seedlings to produce bushy, branched plants. Balsam self-seeds freely, but self-sown seedlings should be watched carefully so that plants of un-pleasant or poor color may be weeded out as soon as they begin to bloom.

I. Sultani, (Patience Plant), is a tender perennial which may be grown as an annual. This, too, has juicy stems with glossy, pale green leaves and large white, pink, rose, brick-red, or salmon single flowers borne profusely on the bushy, much-branched plants.

Patience Plant is grown under glass, in the winter window garden, in outdoor window or porch boxes, and used as a bedding plant. It blooms almost continuously the year round in sun or part shade.

CULTURE: Start seeds indoors in February or outdoors in early May and pinch back seedlings to produce bushy plants. Set 24 inches apart in beds or boxes, or pot up to be used for decorating a shady patio or terrace. They prefer a rich sandy loam. May be propagated by cuttings placed in pure sand kept moderately moist until rooting occurs.

KOCHIA SCOPARIA (Summer-cypress) to 60″   HH

Summer-cypress is the showiest and neatest of the annual hedge plants. The 3- to 5-foot plants are shrublike, with narrow leaves almost resembling evergreen needles, and a columnar, pyramidal, or globular habit of growth. In the autumn, as soon as cool nights arrive, the foliage turns a burning red, which gives it one of its common names, Burning Bush.

The new home owner who needs a temporary hedge in a sunny location can hardly do better than to plant Summer-cypress. All summer it resembles a neat, formal evergreen shrub, with the added dividend of brilliant color in fall.

CULTURE: Plant seeds indoors in March or outdoors in early May and transplant to 24 inches apart, in sun. If possible, keep a few extra plants in the frame in case any of those set out to form the hedge fail to grow on satisfactorily. If this occurs, replacements are ready when needed from the extra supply.

LAGURUS OVATUS (Hare's Tail Grass) 12″   HH

Hare's Tail is another of the decorative grasses which may be grown easily in the annual garden. The woolly spikelets are very dense, 2 inches long and with ½-inch beardlike awns. It is especially pretty as a border plant or dried for winter bouquets.

CULTURE: Plant seeds outdoors where they are to grow, in sandy soil in full sun. Thin to 12 inches between plants.

LANTANA to 30″, North; to 4′, South   TS AS A

Though Lantana is sometimes a troublesome weed in frost-free regions, in the North it grows more slowly and, when kept within bounds by pruning, makes a splendid bedding plant outdoors or gives winter bloom in the window garden. The rough but handsome dark green leaves set off the many flat-topped heads of yellow, orange, or lavender flowers which are produced in profusion.

L. camara is a bushy shrub which, in the northern garden, seldom reaches more than 2½ feet. The cream, yellow, orange, or red-orange flower heads make it a most attractive plant for beds, borders, terrace plantings, or as specimens in pots or small beds to decorate patio or paved terrace.

L. montevidensis, the Trailing Lantana, is a native of South America and is a plant with vinelike stems to 3 feet, with smaller leaves than *L. camara* and flowers of similar form but lilac in color, often with creamy hearts. This species is excellent for a trailer in window boxes or hanging baskets and to plant along the top of a low wall about a terrace. Used as a ground cover in the South.

CULTURE: Since Lantana is really a tender shrub, seeds must be planted indoors in January and transplanted at least twice, the second time into individual pots, before it is set out after danger of frost is past. It likes sun or very light broken shade and rich loam. Faded flowers should be removed to induce more flowers. After you have a stock started from seed, it may be increased by cuttings.

LARKSPUR (Delphinium), see pages 206 and 242.

LATHYRUS ODORATUS (Sweet Pea), see page 197.

LAVATERA (Tree-mallow) 6–10'   TB

The Tree-mallows are majestic plants from the tropics with Maplelike leaves and large, single flowers similar to those of Hollyhock in general appearance.

L. trimestris is the Tree-mallow usually seen in gardens. It is an annual reaching 6 feet in height, with toothed leaves and rose or red flowers 4 inches in diameter. *Alba* is a white variety, *grandiflora* has even larger rose-colored flowers, and *splendens* is a desirable newer strain.

Tree-mallows are used chiefly for screening, temporary hedges, at the back of a very large border, or in some remote wild part of the garden where color is needed.

CULTURE: Plant seeds outdoors in the middle of May or after danger of frost is past. They may be planted where they are to grow or started in a seed bed. Set plants 18 to 24 inches apart. They are not particular about soil but need full sun.

LAYIA ELEGANS (Tidy Tips) 12–24"   HH

Layias are natives of western North America but, unlike some other western natives, are adaptable to other climatic conditions. Tidy Tips grow to 2 feet in height. The plants are branching, the leaves narrow, and the ray flowers yellow with white tips. *Alba* produces white blossoms tipped with pink. Bloom occurs early in the season.

Useful when placed in groups in the mixed border.

CULTURE: Plant seeds indoors in March or outdoors in April where they are to grow. Give the plants a sunny location in well-drained soil and set 12 inches apart.

LIMNANTHES (Meadow-foam) 6"   H

This dainty little flower, *Limnanthes Douglasi,* is a native of our own West Coast, where it blooms profusely in spring. The yellow, pink, or white blossoms, 1 inch in diameter, are delightfully fragrant. The finely cut leaves are yellowish-green. *Grandiflora* has larger flowers, and *alba* is a white form.

Meadow-foam makes an ideal early ground cover for a moist position near the pool or other moist spot in the rock garden.

CULTURE: Plant seeds outdoors in very early spring where they are to grow, in a moist location in sun.

LIMONIUM (Statice, Sea-lavender) to 24"   T

The Limoniums are seacoast plants, most of them native to the Mediterranean region and the Canary Isles. In our gardens and seed catalogues we know them as Statice. The panicles or spikes of yellow or lavender-blue flowers are airy and dainty in the border and are often dried.

L. Bonduelli is an annual or biennial growing to 2 feet, with winged flower panicles and yellow blooms. Leaves are lyre-shaped.

L. sinuatum, a biennial, also to 2 feet, has leaves similiar to the species mentioned above and similar winged flower panicles. The species is yellow, but there are white, blue, and red varieties available.

L. Suworowi, an annual, 30 inches tall, has tufts of basal leaves and dense spikes of lavender or white flowers.

Sea-lavenders are valuable in the mixed border to give a light, airy effect and should by all means be planted in seashore gardens, where they are right at home. Blooms make good cut flowers, either fresh or dried for winter bouquets.

CULTURE: Plant seeds indoors in March; when danger of frost is past, set plants out in the open garden in sandy loam, in full sun.

LINARIA (Toadflax) to 18″   HH

Linarias are easily grown, worth-while garden plants, the annual forms of which are: *L. bipartita,* or Cloven-lip Toadflax, to 1 foot, with narrow whorled leaves and purple blossoms with orange throats *(alba* is a white variety and *splendida* deep purple); and *L. maroccana,* 30 inches, with yellow-throated purple blossoms, long-spurred. The variety *Excelsior* produces flowers from pink to deep blue.

Linarias are useful in beds and borders, for edging, and in the rock garden.

CULTURE: Sow seeds outdoors in a seed bed in early April, and set plants in garden beds as soon as they are large enough to be moved.

LINUM GRANDIFLORUM (Flowering Flax) 24″   HH

Flowering Flax is an annual with narrow, pointed leaves and large fleeting flowers to 1½ inches across. Though the species is reddish-purple, there are varieties available with red *(rubrum),* rose-pink *(roseum)*, scarlet *(coccineum)*, and bluish-violet *(caeruleum)* flowers.

Linums are attractive border plants. Despite the fact that each flower lasts but a day, new ones appear each morning to continue the show of color.

CULTURE: Sow seeds where they are to grow, in well-drained soil in full sun. Thin to 6 inches.

LOBELIA 4–18"   T

Lobelias produce just about the brightest, most jewel-like blue flowers imaginable, and a well-grown plant is literally covered with them.

L. erinus, or Edging Lobelia, is considered the best edger available when blue is needed. It may be had in trailing or compact, moundlike varieties, and in colors from ultramarine to powder and sky blue. Crystal Palace is but 4 inches tall with dark blue flowers; Mrs. Clibran, dark blue with a white eye, 4 inches; Blue Stone, powder blue, 4 inches; Cambridge Blue, 6 inches. Sapphire is a trailing variety with deep blue blossoms. A dwarf, mixed strain produces blue, white, crimson, and rose flowers.

L. gracilis is a spreading species, to 12 inches tall, the flowers dark blue with a white eye.

L. tenuior reaches 30 inches in some varieties, with larger flowers 1 inch in length, but is somewhat difficult in the open garden. It makes a fine greenhouse and house plant.

The edging and trailing forms are used for edging in narrow beds, in rock gardens and window boxes, while the taller varieties make splendid bedding plants. All endure part shade but may be grown in full sun.

CULTURE: Since bloom begins in late spring, Lobelia seeds should be started indoors in February, or March at the latest. Set the plants out in late May, 6 inches apart. Pinching after the seedlings get a good start encourages bushy growth.

LUNARIA ANNUA (Honesty) to 36"   H or B

Honesty is an easily grown old-fashioned garden flower, a hardy annual or biennial with coarsely toothed gray-green leaves and purplish-red to white flowers borne in May. It is for the flat, oval, papery seed pods, however, that the plants are chiefly grown. When the coverings of these has dropped away or been stripped off, they are satiny and gleaming like mother-of-pearl and are popular as dried material for winter bouquets.

CULTURE: Sow seeds outdoors in fall or early April. where they are to grow. Plants self-seed freely. Part shade suits them better than full sun, and they are not particular about soil. As soon as the seed pods have dried on the plants, cut the branches, strip off the coverings, and store indoors in a shaded, airy place until needed.

LUPINUS (Lupine) 12–36"   HH and T

The Lupines form a large genus, including many fine garden perennials and annuals. Their handsome Palm-like leaves and spikes of showy flowers in many colors make them important garden subjects. The annual forms include:

L. densiflorus an annual, to 2 feet, with 7 to 9 leaflets and spikes of white, yellow, or rose flowers. It is native to California. Blooms in May.

L. Hartwegi, to 3 feet, comes from Mexico. The flowers are blue and rose and appear in late summer and early autumn. There are white, rose, and red forms.

L. hirsutus, to 2 feet, bears blue flowers touched with white in late summer. There are white and red varieties.

L. nanus, a dwarf, to 1 foot, with blue and white flowers.

L. pubescens is the species to which *L. hybrida* is assigned. The species, native to Mexico and Guatemala, produces white-centered, violet-blue flowers, but the hybrids include a variety of colors.

L. subcarnosus is the famous Texas Bluebonnet, growing a foot tall, with blue flowers spotted with white or yellow. Bloom occurs in May.

Lupines are good bedding plants where soil and other conditions suit them. They prefer poor, sandy soil and can endure drought well. Excellent for cutting.

CULTURE: Plant seeds indoors in March or in an outdoor seed bed in May. Transplant 12 to 18 inches apart, depending on the variety, in full sun in well-drained sandy soil which is neutral or slightly alkaline.

LYCHNIS (Campion) 18–36″   HH

The Lychnis genus includes many fine garden subjects, perennial, biennial, and annual. The white, pink, red, or purple flowers are showy and many are fragrant.

L. Coeli-rosa, or Rose-of-heaven, an annual, reaches 30 inches and bears large rose-red blossoms. Alba is a white, kermesina a red, and oculata a purple-eyed variety.

L. Coronaria, or Rose Campion, is a biennial, to 3 feet, with white woolly leaves and deep red flowers in June and July. Though a native of Europe, it has naturalized itself in some parts of the United States.

L. coronata, a biennial, to 20 inches, bears 2-inch salmon, brick, or red blossoms. Sieboldi is a white variety, nobilis a salmon-pink.

Lychnis is an easily grown and satisfactory border plant.

CULTURE: Plant seeds outdoors in a seed bed in April and transplant in May, or sow seeds where the plants are to grow.

MACHAERANTHERA TANANCETIFOLIA (Tahoka-daisy) 24″ B

The Tahoka-daisy is a western native, growing in the wild from South Dakota and Montana to Mexico. It is a biennial but may be grown as a hardy annual. The 2-foot plants have Fern-like leaves and 2-inch ray flowers, the petals a lovely violet-blue, the disk yellow.

Tahoka-daisies are desirable border and bedding plants and make long-lasting cut flowers.

CULTURE: Plant seeds outdoors in a seed bed in September and treat as a hardy annual. Or, if spring planting is necessary, store the seeds in the refrigerator for two or three weeks before planting in an outdoor seed bed in the middle of March or as soon as the ground can be worked. Set plants 9 inches apart in well-drained soil in full sun.

MALCOMIA MARITIMA (Virginia stock) 4–8″   HH

Virginia-stock is an appealing little annual native to the Mediterranean region and the Near East. Stems are delicate and rather weak, with elliptical leaves and small, gay white, rose, or lilac flowers borne in profusion through the early summer. Varieties in separate colors are sometimes obtainable: Crimson King is rose-red; Fairy Queen, carmine. *Alba grandiflora* is white.

Plant Virginia-stock at the very front of a mixed border as an edging, or use it profusely in the rock garden where the dainty plants with ½-inch flowers make a fine show.

CULTURE: Plant seeds indoors in March or outdoors in a seed bed in mid-April. Set out plants in open garden, in sun or very slight broken shade, 3 inches apart. Seeds can also be planted in April in the border where they are to grow. For continuous bloom throughout the summer and fall, start successive seed plantings in the seed bed late in May and late in June and replace original plants with these as needed.

MALOPE (Mallow-wort) to 36″   HH

Malope is an annual, to 3 feet, native to Spain and North Africa, but long popular as a showy garden flower. Leaves are 3-lobed and toothed, and the single flowers, 3 inches or more across, are rose-purple in the original species. *Alba* produces white blooms; *grandiflora*, large rose-red, dark-veined blossoms; and *rosea*, rose-colored flowers. A very floriferous annual, Malope continues to bloom over a long period during summer and autumn.

Malopes are valuable to give needed long-lasting color in the center and back of the mixed border.

CULTURE: Plant seeds in mid-April where they are to grow, in rich but well-drained soil in sun.

MARIGOLD (Tagetes), see page 190.

MATHIOLA (Stock) to 30″   HH

Stocks are among the oldest and most valuable of garden flowers for color and fragrance outdoors and also for cutting. Two species are commonly grown:

M. bicornis, or Evening Stock, is the low-growing, much-branched sort with narrow leaves and terminal racemes of inconspicuous single lilac to purple flowers opening in the evening and cherished for their delightful fragrance.

M. incana is a biennial species from which were bred the handsome double and single Florists' and Ten Weeks' Stocks well known to all gardeners and flower arrangers. Plants reach 30 inches in height and bear showy single or very double white, yellow, blush, rose, red, or purple to delicate lavender blooms in terminal racemes. Dwarf Ten Weeks' Stocks are 12 to 18 inches tall and come into bloom about ten weeks from seed sowing. All of these may be had in named varieties in separate colors or in mixtures. Fragrant.

M. bicornis may be used for edging or massing, especially for gardens featuring night bloom and scent. Combine them with Nicotiana, Petunia, and Moonflower for a delightful effect. *M. incana* varieties are showy bed and border plants and should also be grown in the cutting garden by all flower arrangers.

CULTURE: *M. bicornis:* Sow seeds outdoors in mid-April in the open garden where they are to grow.

M. incana and varieties: Plant seeds indoors in early March. Set plants 15 inches apart in sun when danger of frost is past. Early indoor planting is essential because low temperatures (below 65 degrees) are necessary for flower-bud formation in this species. Seedlings should be transplanted to pots sometime before setting out in late May or early June.

In mild climates the class known as Brompton Stocks, the old-fashioned biennial form, may be planted in a frame in late summer and carried over there to be planted out the following spring.

MATRICARIA 8-24"   HH

Matricarias are members of the Chamomile family, native to South Africa, the Mediterranean, and the Orient. They are old-fashioned garden favorites, pungently scented and with yellow or white ray flowers.

M. aurea, or Feverfew, makes an 8- to 10-inch plant with finely cut, decorative leaves and globular heads of yellow, daisy-like flowers.

M. chamomilla, or Sweet False Chamomile, grows to 24 inches, is much branched, with deeply cut leaves and 1-inch heads of white ray flowers with yellow centers.

The Matricarias resemble small single Chrysanthemums, to which they are closely allied. Valuable for bedding, especially in positions of semi-shade, which they endure well.

CULTURE: Sow seeds in an outdoor seed bed in mid-April; transplant to the open garden in late May in semi-shade.

MAURANDIA ERUBESCENS to 6'   TP as A

Maurandias are tender perennial vines which can be grown as annuals by starting the seeds early indoors. *M. erubescens* is a native of Mexico and is sometimes offered commercially as *M. scandens.* The triangular leaves are toothed and the flowers rose-red to purple, trumpet-shaped, to 3 inches long.

Maurandias are often grown as cool greenhouse plants for hanging baskets but are useful for summer decoration of the porch or terrace and as urn plants.

CULTURE: Plant seeds indoors in January or February in a mixture of 4 parts loam, 2 parts leafmold, and 1 part sand. Keep at 60 degrees. Transplant to pots, urns, or baskets and set out after danger of frost is past.

MENTZELIA (Bartonia) 36-48"   B and T

Mentzelias produce white or yellow fragrant flowers, some species being night bloomers. Biennial and annual forms include:

M. decapetala, a native of the United States, found from South Dakota to Texas. It is a biennial, to 4 feet, with lobed leaves and 5-inch white or cream flowers. Night-blooming.

M. laevicaulis, or Blazing Star, is a familiar garden flower; a western native, biennial, to 3½ feet, with 4-inch pale yellow blooms.

M. Lindleyi, an annual, 4 feet tall, has cut and toothed leaves and 2½-inch bright yellow blossoms. Night-blooming.

Mentzelias are valuable for the back of the border and as background material in the fragrant, night-blooming garden.

CULTURE: Plant seeds outdoors where they are to grow; annual species in May, biennials in late summer for bloom the following year. They require a gravelly soil and plenty of heat. Often found growing in the West in and around abandoned mines.

MESEMBRYANTHEMUM (Ice Plant) procumbent   TP and A

Mesembryanthemums form a large group of plants notable for their bright ray flowers and handsome succulent foliage. Some members have been identified as species belonging rightly to other families yet are sold in commerce as Mesembryanthemums.

M. criniflorum, or more correctly *Dorotheanthus bellidiformis,* is very low and spreading, with 1 to 1½-inch white, pink, red, buff, yellow, salmon, or apricot blooms.

M. crystallinum, the common Ice Plant, is really *Cryophytum crystallinum.* It is an annual, producing prostrate stems, the leaves dotted with glistening spots which give it its common name. The small flowers are white or pink. It is grown more for its handsome foliage than for the rather inconspicuous flowers.

M. pyropeum, or *Dorotheanthus gramineus,* is but a few inches tall, producing rose, pink, or white blooms, sometimes with two to three colors in one flower.

Mesembryanthemums and their close relatives love sunshine, heat, and poor sandy soil. They grow beautifully in California during the dry summer season but are not always easy to handle in the Northeast. They are useful for edging, in the sunny rock garden or window box, and at the seashore.

CULTURE: Plant seeds indoors in February or March for early

bloom outdoors. Transplant to a warm, sunny location in gravelly soil with excellent drainage. For best results, water from below.

MIMULUS (Monkey Flower) 18"   HH

The Monkey Flowers, natives of the Western Hemisphere, flourish in moist shade. Garden varieties are *M. tigrinus*—hybrids between *M. guttatus,* native from Alaska to Mexico, and *M. luteus,* a South American species. In these hybrids the very large yellow two-lipped flowers are spotted red at the throats. They are borne in the axils of the opposite leaves.

Mimulus is a good subject for moist, shaded locations near a pool or stream, in the shady rock garden or wet, open woodland, where *M. guttatus* can be readily naturalized.

CULTURE: Plant seeds indoors from January to March (keep at 60 degrees) or outdoors in April. Transplant to moist, partly shaded situation in humusy soil with plenty of leafmold or peatmoss incorporated.

MIRABILIS JALAPA (Four-o'clock) to 36"   TP AS A

The Four-o'clock is a native of tropical America, not a tremendously valuable garden plant because the flowers open so late in the day, but in cultivation for centuries. Though a perennial in its native habitat, the Four-o'clock is grown as a satisfactory annual in the North. The red, yellow, or white flowers are tubular, striped, and mottled. They open on cloudy days or late in the afternoon in clear weather.

Use Four-o'clocks near the back of the large border as a filler.

CULTURE: Plant seeds outdoors in May in sun. Thin to 18 inches apart. The heavy tuberous roots may be dug in autumn before frost and stored over winter like Dahlias.

MOLUCELLA LAEVIS (Bells-of-Ireland) 24"   T

Though this interesting annual has been advertised in catalogues for some years, it has only recently come into its own, largely because of its great value to flower arrangers. The stems, rising from ground level, are gracefully curved and set along their length with round leaves on inch stems. The whitish flowers, set in the axils of the leaves, are surrounded by enlarged, bell-shaped chartreuse calyxes which give the plant its common name.

Arrangers groom off the leaves and use the tapering stems, set with bells, for line arrangements, especially to give the double or S curve.

CULTURE: Plant seeds in a seed bed outdoors after danger of frost is past and set plants in open, sunny cutting bed 18 inches apart.

MOMORDICA 20–30′   T

The Momordicas are slender annual vines which climb by tendrils and make pleasing trellis plants.

M. balsamina, the Balsam-apple, grows to 20 feet, has shiny, sharp-lobed, toothed leaves, yellow flowers, and ovoid orange fruit 3 inches long.

M. charantia, the Balsam-pear, reaches 30 feet and bears warty, orange-yellow fruit 1 to 8 inches in length.

Mormordicas may be used as decoration on a trellis or as a screen on fence or wall.

CULTURE: Plant seeds outdoors where they are to grow after danger of frost is past. Quick-growing.

MORNING-GLORY (Ipomoea), see page 212.

MYOSOTIS (Forget-me-not) 12–24″   HH and B

Forget-me-nots, with their gay sky-blue, yellow-centered blossoms and pink buds, are what our grandmothers used to call "grateful" plants. They grow easily, flower profusely, and self-seed freely.

M. scorpioides is a perennial species usually sold in the trade as *palustris.* It has glossy, light green leaves, decumbent stems, and bright flowers, true blue with pink buds. *Rosea* is a pink variety.

M. semperflorens, which flowers all summer long, is only 8 inches tall. This is by far the best one to get, and it is worth a little trouble to secure it, as others are all through blooming by June.

M. sylvatica, annual or biennial, grows from 12 to 24 inches but is spreading, the flowers true blue. It is often listed commercially as *M. alpestris* with its several varieties; *alba,* white; *compacta,* low-growing; *Fischeri,* dwarf, bluish-pink; *robusta grandiflora,* tall with large blooms; *rosea,* rose color.

Forget-me-nots love moisture and shade but will grow satisfactorily in almost any shaded or partly shaded garden bed. They make splendid edging, rock-garden, and pool-side or stream-side plants, and will naturalize themselves in moist open woodlands. Valuable for cutting.

CULTURE: Plant seeds indoors in March or outdoors in a partly shaded seed bed in late summer for bloom the following year. Set out in April in part shade where the plants will get plenty of moisture. Once established, Myosotis will self-seed so freely that there is no need to increase stock. Just dig up the seedlings and set them where desired.

NASTURTIUM (Tropaeolum), see page 290.

NEMESIA 12–18″   T

Nemesias are African plants with pretty tubular flowers of white, yellow, orange, pink, rose, scarlet, or crimson borne in terminal racemes. They bloom all summer long where nights are cool but, like Calendulas, resent midsummer heat with heavy humidity.

N. strumosa is an annual, 18 to 24 inches tall, with lance-shaped leaves and white, yellow, or purple flowers with spotted, bearded throats, in 4-inch racemes. *Grandiflora* has larger flowers; *nana compacta* is low-growing; and *Suttoni* is an improved variety with the full color range from white to crimson, including yellow and orange.

N. versicolor, an annual, to 12 inches, has smaller leaves and spurred 2-inch flowers in varied colors. *Compacta* is a dwarf, very floriferous variety.

Where the climate suits them, Nemesias make fine edging, bedding, and border plants because of their bright colors and profuse bloom.

CULTURE: Plant seeds in pots or a seed flat in early April. Place at once in a coldframe, and grow on until late in May when the plants can be set out, 6 inches apart, in sun.

NEMOPHILA MENZIESI (Baby-Blue-Eyes) to 20"   HH

Nemophila is a prostrate edging plant with stems to 20 inches long, lobed 4-inch leaves, and blue, purple, or white solitary wheel-shaped flowers borne in profusion through late spring and summer. Baby-Blue-Eyes in its original form is a native of California, but there are a number of improved varieties: *alba,* white; *atomaria,* pale with dark spots; *grandiflora* with large flowers; *liniflora,* white or blue with dark center; *marginata,* blue with white edges. *N. Menziesi* is sometimes listed an *N. insignis.*

Nemophila is valuable as a border edging or in the sunny rock garden.

CULTURE: Plant seeds outdoors in late April where the plants are to grow. Thin to 9 inches apart. Sun.

NICOTIANA ALATA (Flowering Tobacco) 18–48"   TP AS A

Nicotiana is a plant which should be in every garden. Though really a tender perennial, it is commonly grown in the North as an annual. The tufted leaves form a decorative rosette, while the terminal panicles of flowers on long, graceful stems are salverform, white or delicately colored, and deliciously night-fragrant.

The variety *grandiflora* bears large pure-white blossoms, while the so-called Affinis Hybrids present a palette of lovely colors, including rose, red, crimson, buff-salmon, and cream. There are several dark red varieties, including Crimson Bedder, 15 inches; Crimson King, 30 inches; and Sanderae Sanguinea, very dark red. The Sensation Mixture offers colors from white through pale lavender and chartreuse to deep red and mahogany, 24 inches.

N. sylvestris, to 48 inches, is a species bearing drooping, pure-white typical flowers, which, unlike those of *N. alata* do not close in cloudy weather. Also fragrant.

Daylight has pure-white flowers which remain open during the day, even in sunshine.

Nicotiana is a fine bedding and border plant, especially for shady locations, and is unsurpassed for cutting.

CULTURE: Plant seeds indoors in March or outdoors in mid-April where they are to grow. Set out 9 to 12 inches apart in moist part shade.

NIEREMBERGIA CAERULEA (Cup-flower) 12"   TP as A

Though Nierembergia is really a tender perennial, it can be brought to bloom the first year from seed sown early indoors. The variety Purple Robe, an All-America Medal winner some years ago, produces deep lavender-blue cup-shaped flowers with bright yellow eyes, borne freely at the tips of many slender stems clothed with narrow, simple leaves which give the whole plant a dense, shrublike appearance.

Nierembergia is a splendid plant for porch or window boxes, for edging in the border, around a living terrace, or as specimen plants in the rock garden.

CULTURE: Plant seeds indoors in February, transplant to pots, and set out 12 inches apart in late May in full sun and sandy but well-enriched soil.

NIGELLA DAMASCENA (Love-in-a-mist) 18-24"   HH

Love-in-a-mist is an old-fashioned annual known to most gardeners. Its delicate light blue or white flowers are single or double and surrounded by feathery bracts which add to their attractiveness. The plants are slender and the leaves threadlike. The globular seed pods are pretty too.

Easy to grow from seed planted in the open garden, it makes a fine filler in the mixed bed or border where a touch of true blue is needed.

CULTURE: Plant seeds outdoors about mid-April where they are to grow and thin to 6 inches apart. Choose an open, sunny position for them. As the blooming season is short, plant seeds in succession, about a month apart, for continuous color throughout the season. As a rule Nigella self-sows freely, but since it does not transplant well, many stray seedlings are wasted.

NOLANA 4–12"   TP AS A

Nolanas are prostrate or erect perennials which can be grown as annuals for their colorful tubular blue flowers, shaped rather like those of Convolvulus. The leaves are fleshy and the stems to 12 inches along.

N. atriplicifolia has purplish stems, basal leaves, and 2-inch white-throated blue flowers, yellow within. There is a white variety, *alba;* and a violet, *violacea.*

N. lanceolata is a hairy plant with handsome sky-blue flowers, the throat spotted white and yellow.

N. prostrata has reclining stems to 10 inches and small purple-veined blue flowers with white throats.

Nolanas are good material for covering bare bank or exposed, sunny rocks. They are also attractive hanging-basket and pot plants.

CULTURE: Plant seeds indoors in February or March and set plants out, 12 inches apart, when all danger of frost is past. They require full sun.

OENOTHERA (Evening-primrose and Sun Drops) 20–72"   B and T

The Evening-primroses are a large family, most of them biennial or perennial. Many, however, can be grown and flowered as annuals. Their profuse and brilliant color and wonderful night fragrance make them an important addition in midsummer and early autumn gardens. Though the foliage usually has a rather rough, coarse appearance, the very large, bright, fragrant flowers are most desirable.

O. acaulis is a dwarf Sundrop, a biennial, only 6 inches tall, with white or blush-pink flowers to 4 inches in diameter. Variety *aurea* has yellow blooms.

O. bistorta is an annual Sundrop, to 16 inches, with 1-inch purple-spotted yellow flowers. It is a native of California. Its variety *Veitchiana* is the form usually seen in gardens.

O. caespitosa, a perennial and biennial of our own West, is stemless, with hairy leaves and 3-inch pure-white or pink flowers.

O. odorata is a 4-foot annual with nocturnal yellow flowers fading to reddish. Fragrant.

O. rosea is a biennial, blooming the first year from seed. The 1- to 2-foot slender stems and leaves are softly hairy, the rose-purple flowers small but attractive.

O. trichocalyx, a biennial which can be bloomed as an annual, is but a foot tall, with linear leaves covered with silky hairs and pure-white flowers with nodding buds. This species does not close its blossoms during the day.

Evening-primroses and Sundrops are excellent plants for the hot, sunny border. They endure drought well and give large colorful flowers at a time in late summer when they are most needed. Can be dried, too, for winter bouquets.

CULTURE: Plant seeds indoors in March and transplant to open, dry, sunny ground in May; or start biennial species in a frame or seed bed in late summer for bloom the following year.

OXALIS (Wood-sorrel)   P as A

Oxalis is decorative both for its shamrock-shaped leaves and bright flowers. Though many species are bulbous or tuberous, there are others that can be grown from seed and treated as annuals:

O. rubra has 3 leaflets and pink or rose, red-veined flowers in umbels.

O. valdiviensis is short-stemmed, the flowers yellow, striped brown, in umbels.

Oxalis is used chiefly for edging but also makes a good plant for window box or pots, indoors or on the patio or terrace.

CULTURE: Plant in an outdoor seed bed late in April. Pot up or set plants out 6 inches apart in full sun in sandy but well-fertilized loam.

PAPAVER (Poppy) to 36"   H and B

The annual Poppies are a colorful race, their showy but short-lived flowers graceful on long supple stems. Though each blossom is short-lived, there are so many blooms opening daily that they make very satisfactory bedding plants.

P. caucasicum is a biennial species which can be grown as an annual. The leaves are bluish-gray and the large flowers scarlet, touched with yellow at the base. Two feet.

P. glaucum is commonly called the Tulip Poppy, a 2-foot annual species with deeply cut leaves and scarlet flowers, marked with a dark spot at the base, to 4 inches across.

P. macrostomum is an annual to 1½ feet, with basal leaves and purplish-red blooms 2 inches in diameter, black-spotted at the base and occasionally margined in white.

P. nudicaule, or the Iceland Poppy, is a perennial which blooms the first year from fall-planted seed. One to 2 feet tall; the flowers, to 3 inches across, are white and yellow, yellow and green, orange, pink, rose, and rose-red. There are double forms and varieties available under name in separate colors, such as *album,* Yellow Wonder, and Coonara Pink Improved. *Parkmanni* is double. All have the added charm of fragrance.

P. Rhoeas, Corn Poppy, or Shirley Poppy, is an annual species reaching 3 feet in height, the common red Field Poppy of Europe. All sorts of improved varieties are available, most of them but faintly resembling their progenitor. Single and double forms are to be had in separate and mixed colors: American Legion, for instance, with huge, single red blooms; the Begonia-flowered and Ranunculus-flowered double strains; Celeste, lavender-blue; and Little Gem, a dwarf pink. Double Hybrids include double and semi-double plants, many flowers showing a blend of two colors. Single mixtures include white, pink, salmon, apricot, and oriental red. Some of the massive doubles are excellent for cutting if the tips of stems are burned after picking.

Poppies are unsurpassed for bedding, and the annual species and varieties offer a wider range of soft, pleasing colors than do the Orientals. Some may be used for cutting.

CULTURE: Sow seeds in autumn or very early spring where the plants are to grow, in full sun and in sandy loam.

PELARGONIUM (Geranium) to 36"   TS as A

Geraniums, though not annuals at all, are used as such for bedding purposes. Unless the gardener is a true specialist and collector, he has but two courses open to him: (1) to purchase plants from a grower, selecting the most interesting varieties he can find and afford, and keeping up his stock by taking cuttings; or (2) growing from seed sown indoors in January. The latter method is fun, but results are uncertain, since seeds are in mixture and plants are well grown before the grower can determine color, form, and desirability.

Geraniums are used for bedding, as pot plants indoors in winter, or outdoors on the patio or terrace in summer, and as window-box specimens. The Zonal type is best suited for these purposes. The grower interested in collecting Geraniums will read and search and experiment, finding always new and fascinating facets to the subject, for Pelargoniums are a large family. For use in pots, indoors or out, the Lady Washington or Show Geraniums are handsomer than the Zonals but less easy to keep healthy. In this group the large white, pink, or red flowers have darkly blotched upper petals. They are sometimes called Orchid Geraniums.

CULTURE: Plant seeds indoors in January and grow on until danger of frost is past, when the plants can be set out in not too rich, sandy soil. Keep on the dry side. Or purchase plants and set out as above. Keep plants pruned to the desired shape, using trimings to start new plants from cuttings. (See Chapter 3.) In fall, discard overgrown parent plants which have bloomed themselves out, and take indoors the young plants grown from cuttings. Geraniums will bloom winter *or* summer, but not both. For winter bloom, start young plants in summer and pick off buds until brought indoors.

PENSTEMON (Beard Tongue) to 36"   P as A

Penstemons are perennials, but a few can be flowered as annuals. These include *P. gloxinioides,* a race of hybrids between *P. Hartwegi* and *P. cobaea.* In this strain, the gloxinia-like, tubular flowers are borne in various colors from red to white on long, strong spikes. Leaves are in whorls. To 2 feet. *P. Hartwegi* is taller, to 2½ feet or more, and produces spikes of red, white, and even blue flowers. *P. azureus erectus,* 1½ feet, with blue flowers, is sometimes sold as a variety of *Hartwegi.*

Penstemons are showy plants for the border or rock garden, but they must have full sun and plenty of moisture.

CULTURE: Sow seeds indoors in February or March and transfer to the open garden in late May, selecting a spot in full sun but where there will be ample moisture.

PERILLA FRUTESCENS to 18"   HH

Perilla is grown for its handsome foliage, the cut, wrinkled, or crisped leaves, to 4½ inches long, colored bronze or dark purple. Some varieties are variegated.

Grow Perilla as a foliage plant in the mixed border, as a bedding plant, and in the cutting garden for use as cut material in flower arrangements.

CULTURE: Plant seeds in a seed bed outdoors in mid-April and transplant in late May to a position in full sun or light, broken shade.

PETUNIA, see page 181.

PHACELIA (Harebell Phacelia) 12–24"   HH

There are many Phacelias native to America, most of them growing in the West. Annual sorts include:

P. campanularia, 12 inches tall, with toothed, alternate leaves and blue flowers in crowded clusters. This is a desert plant suitable only for hot, dry locations.

P. ciliata, to 18 inches, is a California wildling with cut leaves and blue flowers.

P. tanacetifolia, to 3 feet, also from California, has blue or lavender flowers.

P. viscida, 2 feet, has Tansy-like leaves, blue or lavender flowers. California.

Phacelias are valuable for use in the border, especially in hot, dry locations in sandy soil.

CULTURE: Plant seeds outdoors in mid-April where they are to grow. Thin to 9 inches.

PHASEOLUS COCCINEUS (Scarlet-runner Bean) to 15'   TP AS A

The Scarlet-runner Bean is a decorative vine, useful for covering the fence to the vegetable garden or for other similar locations. Though a tender perennial, it can be grown as an annual. Like other Beans, it climbs by twining. The leaflets are broad and the flowers brilliant scarlet, very showy. *Albus* is a white variety.

CULTURE: Plant seeds outdoors where they are to grow, near a fence or trellis, in May after danger of frost is past. Thin to 8 inches apart. Full sun.

PHLOX, see page 210.

PLATYSTEMON CALIFORNICUS (Cream Cup) 6–9"   HH

The Cream Cup is a dainty California annual with linear leaves and cream-yellow, Poppy-like flowers an inch in diameter. *Crinitus* is a hairy variety with flowers tinged pink or green. It covers great portions of the country in spring in its native habitat and makes a pleasing garden annual. Especially useful for edging.

CULTURE: Plant seeds outdoors in mid-April where they are to grow. Give full sun and sandy loam.

POLYGONUM ORIENTALE (Prince's-feather) to 6'   H

The Polygonums, or Knotweeds, are useful plants for covering waste places and for background material. Their strong roots help to hold banks and their bright flowers give a mass of color in late summer and autumn.

The annual form, Prince's-feather, has broad ovate leaves, to 3 inches long on 6-foot plants, and dense spikes of bright rose or pink flowers in autumn. Though a native of Asia and Australia, Prince's-feather has become naturalized in some parts of the United States. It is perfectly hardy. The variety *variegatum* has the added advantage of variegated foliage.

Use Prince's-feather as a background planting for very large borders; to make a tall ground cover and give colorful bloom in out-of-the-way parts of the garden which might otherwise grow up to weeds; and to hold the soil on moist hillsides.

CULTURE: Plant seeds in autumn or very early spring in a seed bed or where they are to grow. Thin or transplant 24 inches apart. Flourishes best in moist situations but is a toughie and can take most average conditions in sun or shade.

PORTULACA (Purslane, Sun-rose, Rose-moss) 8"   HH

Portulaca is one of the most pleasing and satisfactory of flowering ground covers and edging plants for hot, dry areas in full sun.

P. grandiflora is the species from which our garden varieties are derived. The prostrate stems are clothed with fleshy, narrow leaves and form a handsome mat, while the large single or double flowers, an inch or more across, are white, yellow, salmon, pink, bright rose, or rose-red. The doubles, which look like little roses, may be had in mixture or separate colors. Most of the singles come in mixtures. Single Jewel, a brilliant rose, is especially large and fine. Bloom starts early and continues throughout the season.

Portulaca is good for edging, to plant among rocks in full sun, and as a colorful ground cover for dry banks and hot, sandy areas.

CULTURE: Plant seeds about mid-April where they are to grow, in full sun and sandy soil. Thin to 6 inches. If garden soil is heavy, lighten the planting bed with sand.

QUAMOCLIT 10–20'   T

The Quamoclits are members of the Convolvulus family, with long-tubed, salver-shaped flowers of red or yellow, and handsome leaves.

Q. coccinea, or Star Impomoea, to 10 feet, is a tropical vine naturalized in the United States. Flowers are scarlet with a yellow throat. *Luteola* bears yellow or orange flowers.

Q. pennata, or Cypress Vine, reaches 20 feet, has finely cut leaves and scarlet flowers. *Alba* is a white form, and Hearts and Honey a new variety of pinkish-orange flowers with contrasting centers of honey yellow.

Q. Sloteri, or Cardinal-Climber, is a hybrid between the two above-mentioned species. The handsome leaves are Palm-like, the 2-inch flowers crimson with white throats.

Quamoclits make showy annual vines for trellises, pergolas, fences, and walls, and may also be grown as winter annuals in a large sunny window.

CULTURE: Plant seeds indoors in March or outdoors in late May where they are to grow. Seedlings started indoors should be potted up as soon as possible. Individual plants can then be set out without retarding growth. Full sun.

RESEDA ODORATA (Mignonette) 6-18″   HH

Mignonette is one of the most traditional and romantic of old-fashioned garden annuals. It is a modest plant bearing heavy spikes of small red, whitish, or yellowish flowers which are delightfully fragrant, and it is an all-summer bloomer. Though varieties may be had in separate colors, the flower spikes are not showy. They are more than worth while, however, for their delicious scent. There are dwarf varieties, and grandiflora arborea, which is extra-large.

Plant dwarf varieties as an edging for the fragrant garden; scatter groups of taller-growing sorts in the mixed border, and by all means have a row in the cutting garden for use in mixed bouquets.

CULTURE: Plant seeds where they are to grow, in cool, moderately moist, rich soil, preferably in part shade. Thin plants to 12 inches apart.

RICINUS COMMUNIS
(Castor-bean,Castor-oil Plant) to 6' or more   T

The Castor-bean is one of the handsomest and most useful of very large annuals. In the tropics is is a tree reaching a height of 40 feet but in the North seldom exceeds 6. The palmate leaves are divided into from 5 to 11 lobes and are very large. Flowers, which are inconspicuous in themselves, are borne in fine heads or panicles and are followed by showy, prickly seed pods. There are numerous varieties, the most popular for garden use being *coccineus,* which has dark red foliage and stems, red flowers, and bronzy-red seed pods. *Gibsoni* is a smaller form, also with red, metallic foliage. Each seed catalogue offers one or two good garden varieties.

Castor-bean is valuable to the new home owner who needs temporary tree or shrub-like plant material. It can be planted as an individual specimen or used as a dense background or screen. Flowers, seed heads, and foliage are all prized as material for flower arrangement. The side branches, particularly, take graceful curves which lend themselves well to line arrangement. Seeds are poisonous if eaten.

CULTURE: Plant seeds indoors in April or outdoors in a seed bed in May. Set out in any well-drained soil in sun. Seeds may also be planted where they are to grow and thinned to 4 feet apart.

RUDBECKIA *(Coneflower)* 24–36"   HH

R. bicolor is the annual form of Rudbeckia, a 2–foot plant with rough stems and leaves and yellow ray flowers, often dark at the base and with a black disk. It is native in the Southwest. Starlight is an All America winner producing double, semi-double, and single flowers colored from pale yellow to dark mahogany, each bloom showing a blend of two colors. Other garden varieties offer huge blooms to 5 inches across.

R. hirta, our common wild Black-eyed Susan, is really a very handsome biennial which might well be cultivated as a garden flower for its golden rays and dark brown cones. It blooms freely over a long period. Can be grown as an annual.

Rudbeckias are useful in groups in the mixed border and for cutting.

CULTURE: Plant seeds in an outdoor seed bed in mid-April and set out in the garden, 18 inches apart, in May. They are not particular about soil, location, or other cultural problems, but flourish almost anywhere.

SALPIGLOSSIS SINUATA (Painted-tongue) 24"   T

Salpiglossis is rather a recent comer to our gardens. From the species, which is a native of Chile, many lovely garden varieties have been developed. The plants are slender, with toothed, oblong leaves and large, funnel-shaped, flaring flowers, and netted or veined with a contrasting color. The Emperor Strain, generally considered the best, can be had in mixture or in separate colors. Lavender-blues are netted with silver or dark blue; crimson and rose with gold, and there are now available self-colors for those who do not like the exquisite contrast of the veining.

Salpiglosis makes a superb bedding plant and is most graceful in mixed bouquets. Where it finds conditions to its liking, it blooms throughout the summer and autumn.

CULTURE: Plant seeds indoors in March and transfer seedlings to pots as soon as possible. Set out in late May in well-enriched soil in full sun. Or prepare a garden bed carefully, pulverize the surface, and plant seeds in mid-April where they are to grow. Thin or transplant to 12 inches apart. In the North, Salpiglossis sometimes sulks after transplanting and finds difficulty in recovering from the shock. Potted seedlings can be moved without disturbing the roots. Seeds sown where they are to grow will be much later coming into bloom.

SALVIA 24–36"   TP as A and T

Salvias are charming plants despite the fact that one of them (Scarlet Sage) is in disrepute these days because of its blazing, unsubtle color. A much more delicate member of the clan is:

S. farinacea, a tender perennial often grown in the North as an annual. It grows to 24 inches, has pretty gray-green lanceolate leaves on quite shrubby stems, and long racemes of violet-blue, tubular flowers. The variety Blue Bedder, listed in all catalogues, is Wedgwood blue, but we prefer the paler species itself. It is a fine plant for the mixed border and makes splendid spike material for flower arrangements. In mild climates it may be grown as a perennial and often, even in the North, may be brought through the winter by heeling the plants into a coldframe in autumn and returning them to the open garden in spring.

S. patens is another perennial species which may be treated as an annual. It is sometimes called the Gentian Salvia, is 30 inches tall, with toothed, arrow-shaped leaves and 2-inch flowers of intense Gentian blue. It is a native of the mountainous regions of Mexico.

S. splendens, or Scarlet Sage, is probably the reddest and one of the most floriferous annuals available for the garden. It grows to 3 feet and is still widely used for bedding, especially in formal plantings in public parks. St. John's Fire, recently introduced, is the most compact and even-growing variety we have ever seen. Where the color is derirable, it makes an excellent temporary hedge. There are dwarf varieties too, 10 inches. A recently introduced strain, the Welwyn Hybrids, produces heavy racemes of pink, salmon, or buff flowers which blend well with almost any color in the mixed border.

CULTURE: Tender perennial and annual species may be raised by planting the seeds indoors in February or March and setting out in the open garden in full sun or very light shade in May.

SANVITALIA PROCUMBENS (Creeping-zinnia) 6", trailing   T

Sanvitalia, or Creeping-zinnia (of course not really a Zinnia at all), is a little trailer which should be more widely planted. The stems are well clothed with ovate leaves and bear many bright little flower heads with yellow rays surrounding dark purple disks. A double variety, *S. procumbens flore pleno,* is the one usually offered in catalogues.

Sanvitalia is ideal as an edger for narrow borders or for use at the top of a low wall in the sunny rock garden, or elsewhere in full sun. It blooms throughout the summer and on to hard frost.

CULTURE: Plant seeds indoors in March or in an outdoor seed bed in May and set out in late May or early June, 6 inches apart, in full sun.

SAPONARIA (Soapwort) to 12" T

Saponarias are valuable rock-garden annuals, their white, pink, or red flowers making a fine spring and summer show.

S. calabrica, 9 inches, has sticky and hairy stems and leaves, and pale or deep rose-colored flowers in the axils of the leaves in spring. Alba is a white form, and Scarlet Queen a red variety.

S. vaccaria is a tall species, to 30 inches, with loose cymes of deep pink blossoms. Rosea bears pale pink flowers; Alba is a white.

The first-named species and its varieties are excellent for the rock garden or front of the border.

S. vaccaria is valuable both as a border plant and for cutting.

CULTURE: Plant seeds indoors in March or in an outdoor seed bed in May and transplant to the open garden in late May. Not particular about soil.

SCABIOSA ATROPURPUREA (Mourning-bride) to 36" HH

The annual Scabiosa is an important garden flower for border and cutting. It is rather slender, with lyre-shaped basal leaves, finely cut, lobed stem leaves, and very double cushion-like flower heads of blue, lavender, red, rose, mahogany, or white. Mixtures or separate colors are available, and there are dwarf, medium, and tall-growing strains for various positions in the border.

Scabiosas make fine subjects for massing in beds and should certainly have a place in the cutting garden, where they are invaluable for arrangement material.

CULTURE: Plant seeds indoors in March or outdoors in a seed bed in mid-April. Set out in the open garden in May, 12 inches apart, in a well-enriched bed.

SCHIZANTHUS PINNATUS (Butterfly Flower) 12–36″   T

Schizanthus is primarily a greenhouse subject but is also useful in the open garden in mild climates, as a pot plant indoors and for the terrace or patio. It is also valued for cutting.

The erect plants are clothed with delicate, finely cut foliage and bear many panicles of lavender, rose, pink, or white flowers marked with yellow or orange. The shape of the lipped flowers and their exotic coloring give the plant its common name.

CULTURE: Seeds sown indoors in March may be set out in late May for late garden bloom. If a greenhouse is available, seeds sown in autumn will produce plants to bloom in spring.

SCHIZOPETALON WALKERI 30″   HH

Schizopetalon is a little-known annual sometimes grown for its white, fringed, very fragrant flowers, which fill the evening garden with scent.

Useful chiefly for its delightful fragrance, it is a "must-have" for the white, night-scented garden.

CULTURE: Plant seeds indoors in March or outdoors early in May and set out 12 inches apart.

SENECIO 24–30″   TP as A

The Senecios of the garden are old-fashioned favorites grown for their gray or woolly-white foliage, which helps to pull together the mixed colors of the average border.

S. cineraria, sometimes listed commercially as Cineraria maritima, is also called Dusty Miller. Though a perennial, it may be grown as an annual. The leaves are interestingly cut into blunt segments, the flowers pale yellow, and the whole plant white-woolly. Aureo-marginatus is a variety with yellow-edged leaves.

S. leucostachys, covered with white hairs, also has cut leaves, but narrower than the above species. It is often sold as S. cineraria candidissimus.

Senecios are used for formal bedding and in groups in the mixed border for their attractive white foliage.

CULTURE: Plant seeds indoors in February or March and set plants out in May, 12 inches apart, in full sun.

SIDERITIS 18″   T

Sideritis is a handsome tender, shrubby perennial offered by at least one of the large seed companies to be grown as an annual for its beautiful foliage. It is a lovely thing with velvety, woolly-white leaves and stems. It grows to about 18 inches but can be kept pinched and trimmed to any desired height.

Use it for white-gray relief in mixed borders or as an edging, pruned to height. Good for cutting.

CULTURE: Plant seeds indoors in March and transplant to the open garden after danger of frost is past. We always take cuttings in the fall and carry them through the winter.

SILENE (Catchfly, Campion) to 24″   H

The Silenes (Catchflies or Campions) form a large and valuable group of perennials and annuals for garden and rock garden. Of the annual species, the most useful are:

S. *armeria*, or Sweet William Catchfly, to 2 feet, which bears rose or pink flowers in terminal cymes from midsummer into September. *Alba* is white, and *splendida* a large-flowered form.

S. *pendula* is a decumbent annual clinging to the ground near the roots, the stems rising about 10 inches tall. The blush-pink flowers in racemes hang their heads gracefully. *Rosea* is a rose-pink variety; *compacta*, more dwarf.

Sweet William Catchfly may be used to advantage in the mixed border, while S. *pendula* is ideal for the rock garden and rock walls.

CULTURE: Plant seeds in autumn where they are to grow for early bloom the following season, or plant out in April for late-summer flowering.

SNAPDRAGON (Antirrhinum), see page 203.

SWEET PEA, see page 197.

TAGETES (Marigold), see page 190.

TAHOKA-DAISY, see page 264.

THUNBERGIA ALATA
(Black-eyed Susan, Clock Vine) to 36" in the North   TP AS A

Thunbergia is a charming little vine, not too heavy or pervasive. The twining stems are clothed with pretty triangular, winged leaves and bear striking little flowers of white, buff, orange-yellow, with dark centers. *Bakeri* is a pure-white variety, but as it is the dark marking that makes the blooms so attractive, we prefer *alba,* which has the contrasting zone at the heart. *Aurantiaca* is the orange-yellow variety. Usually, however, seeds come in mixture, the colors blending well with each other.

Thunbergia is a fine ground cover for narrow beds at the head of a low wall, for an edging, or in urns or window boxes. In the South, where it grows much more strongly, it is frequently used to cover arbors, trellises, and to shade porches.

CULTURE: Plant seeds indoors in March or in an outdoor seed bed in May. Transplant to a position in full sun or part shade where plants can be watered during dry spells.

TITHONIA ROTUNDIFOLIA 36–72"   T

The Tithonia, or Mexican Sunflower, is a large, coarse but showy annual. Though the type can and often does peer into one's second-story window, the new variety Torch is but 4 feet in height. The large, coarse, lobed leaves cover the strong stems and branches pretty well, and in late summer and fall a profusion of burning red-orange flowers are produced. These are 3 inches or more in diam-

*A vase of Marigolds
and a mixed bouquet.*

A coldframe like this will aid immensely in starting plants of annuals for earlier bloom and for "fill-in" supply. BELOW *And here's the kind of little plant factory every gardener dreams of possessing. It belongs to Silas Clark of Wellfleet, Mass., and helps him in the making of that glorious hillside display shown in the frontispiece.*

eter, with broad, flat, velvety orange ray flowers surrounding a showy disk.

Use Tithonias where tall backgrounds are needed, as a temporary screen, and especially for cutting. They remind one rather of handsome single Dahlias.

CULTURE: Plant seeds indoors in March in individual small pots or plant bands. Transfer to the open garden in full sun when danger of frost is past.

TOLPIS BARBATA 12"   T

Tolpis is a pleasing little annual similar in appearance to Hawkweed. Leaves are basal, and the yellow, rose, or white flower heads rise on 12-inch stems. *Rubra* is rose-colored. Use Tolpis as an edging.

CULTURE: Plant seeds in full sun early in May where they are to grow. Thin to 6 inches.

TORENIA FOURNIERI (Wishbone Flower) to 12"   T

Torenias are delightful little annuals meriting much wider use. Plants and seeds are, however, becoming more generally available every year. Blooming in late summer and fall until hard frost, they enjoy shade and cool weather, though summer heat does not make them "curl up" and stop blooming.

The two-lipped tubular flowers are pale violet and yellow, with the velvety lower lip of the blossom rich purple marked with yellow. The clean, shiny leaves and stems turn rosy and then plum in the autumn when cold nights threaten frost, but bloom continues uninterruptedly until real frost.

Use Torenias to follow Pansies in partly shaded beds and borders. They are useful in the rock garden, and we have found them excellent for potting up and bringing indoors for winter bloom.

CULTURE: Plant indoors in March or in an outdoor seed bed in May. Outdoors seeds germinate very late, but after they are up, plants develop rapidly. Thin or transplant to 8 inches. After the first year you are very likely to have a crop of self-sown seedlings, and this despite the fact that Torenias are tender. They like plenty of moisture.

TRACHYMENE (DIDISCUS) CAERULEA
(Blue Lace-flower) 24″ HH

The Blue Lace-flower is a pretty annual with lobed, compound leaves and long-stemmed pale blue flowers in showy umbels—a sort of Queen Anne's Lace dipped in blue sky.

Deservedly popular plant for cutting.

CULTURE: Plant seeds outdoors early in May in a row in the cutting garden. Thin to 12 inches apart.

TROPAEOLUM (Nasturtium) 12–48″ HH

Nasturtiums are old-time favorites in the annual garden, and their popularity has been increased during recent years because improved dwarf, double, sweet-scented varieties have become generally available.

T. majus is the tall climbing species, to 48 inches, producing cream, yellow, gold, salmon, scarlet, and crimson single flowers, and with characteristic round, padlike leaves on slender succulent stems. Climbing is accomplished through the coiling leaf stalks. From this species has been developed the modern dwarf and semi-dwarf varieties of compact habit. These include singles and sweet-scented doubles in lovely colors, such as Golden Gleam. Bloom continues until frost.

Dwarf Nasturtiums are useful for edging, for narrow beds at the top of low walls, and the tall-growing ones for fences or to cover tree stumps. Dwarfs may be brought in for winter bloom indoors. All are valuable for cutting. Branched stems with many blooms make graceful line arrangements and last a long time in water. Green seed of single varieties may be used in salads and pickles.

T. peregrinum (Canary-bird-flower) is a dainty climber, to 10 feet, with pretty 5-lobed leaves and canary-yellow, spurred flowers. Good for covering trellises and fences.

CULTURE: Plant the large seeds ¾ inch deep, in mid-April, in rather poor soil in full sun. Do not transplant, but thin to 9 inches apart for dwarf varieties, 12 inches for tall growers. Watch young plants for infestations of black aphids, and if present, spray at once with Black Leaf 40, which should make a 100 per cent kill if used promptly.

URSINIA (Sphenogyne) 12–18″   T

Ursinias are South African plants desirable for their fragrant, Daisy-like flowers in yellow or orange with purplish markings. Annual species are:

U. anthemoides, 12 inches tall, with lobed leaves and solitary flower heads on long graceful stems. Rays are yellow, purplish in reverse.

U. foeniculacea is another 12-inch species with yellow ray flowers.

U. pulchra grows to 24 inches and bears 2-inch flowers of yellow or orange, spotted at the base with deep plum.

Ursinias are useful for bedding, especially in the fragrant garden.

CULTURE: Plant seeds indoors in March or outdoors in a seed bed in May. Transfer to the open garden in full sun in late May or early June.

VENIDIUM FASTUOSUM 18″   T

Venidiums are South Africans bearing attractive composite flowers. *V. fastuosum,* the annual species, grows to 18 inches, with lyre-shaped leaves and showy 4-inch orange ray flowers, purple at the base.

They make interesting bedding plants, where the large flowers give spots of vivid color.

CULTURE: Plant seeds indoors in March or outdoors in May. Set out in full sun in a well-drained bed.

VERBENA 8–18″   P as A

Verbena hortensis is the common garden Verbena known to all gardeners. Innumerable fine varieties have been developed from this form, which is notable for broad flat heads or corymbs of bright white, pink, rose, red, blue-lavender, or purple flowers. The stems are decumbent and spreading, clothed with ovate leaves. Outstanding varieties include Apple Blossom, blush; Lavender Glory, lavender with a white eye; Salmon King; Spectrum Red; Vivid, scarlet; and Floradale Beauty, a fine mixture from rose-pink to rose-red.

V. pulchella, or Moss Verbena, is frequently grown as an annual. The stems rise to 18 inches, with deeply lobed, hairy leaves and dense, terminal heads of lilac flowers.

Verbenas are ideal edging plants for the border, the rock garden, and the rock wall. They bloom freely throughout the summer and fall, right up to hard freezing. Plants can be brought in for winter bloom in the window garden.

CULTURE: Plant seeds of *V. hortensis* and varieties indoors in February or March. Transplant seedlings at least once. Set out in May in full sun in rich but well-drained beds. Cuttings may be rooted readily and carried over winter indoors or under glass. Plant seeds of *V. pulchella* outdoors in April where they are to grow. Full sun.

VINCA (Periwinkle) 18"   TP as A

The hardy Vincas, or Training-myrtles, are glossy-leaved ground covers valuable in any garden. *V. rosea* (Madagascar Periwinkle) is a tender perennial often grown as an annual, and is just the thing for a ground cover in sun. Unlike Trailing-myrtle *(V. minor)*, it will not stand full shade. The flowers are rose color or white *(alba)* and are set off like jewels on the glossy leaved, erect plants.

Try planting *V. rosea* as a ground cover in the Lily bed or elsewhere, in sun, where a solid mass of low or medium-height foliage is needed.

CULTURE: Plant seeds indoors in January or February; transplant seedlings at least once, and set plants out in May in well-enriched soil in sun.

VIOLA 6–12"   B or P

Violas and Pansies are among the brightest and gayest of bedding and edging flowers. Though biennial and perennial, they are commonly grown as annuals in the North.

V. cornuta, or Tufted Pansy, is a perennial which can be grown as an annual. The flowers are smaller than those of the biennial

Pansies, but some quite large-flowered varieties have been developed. They may be had in separate colors in named varieties. Chantryland, apricot; Yellow Perfection; Jersey Gem, purple; and Purple Heart are a few good ones.

V. tricolor hortensis is the Pansy from which all the fine modern named varieties have been derived. Dwarf Super Swiss, Butterfly Hybrids, Floradale Giants, Oregon Giants, and Mastodon Giants are a few of the famous mixtures. Coronation Gold, canary and gold, is an All America Silver Medal winner; Lake of Thun, blue; Alpenglow, wine; Delft Blue, and Pure White are some of the better separate colors.

Pansies and Violas are the bedding and edging plants *par excellence* for early spring and summer. They grace the rock garden, are happy in part 'shade, and the larger-flowering varieties are fine for cutting.

CULTURE: Plant seeds indoors in January and transplant at least twice before setting plants out in April. Home-grown plants bloom for a much longer time than those purchased in baskets in spring. These have usually been forced into early, heavy bloom. For sturdier, hardier plants, start seeds in a partly shaded seed bed or frame in early August. Transplant and grow on in frame or bed through the winter and set out in the garden in early spring. *V. cornuta* may be with you for years. The large Pansies, especially in the North, should be considered as annuals, or at best biennials,

XANTHISMA TEXANUM (Star-of-Texas) 12–36"   T

We are most enthusiastic about this gay, yellow-flowered native of Texas. In the North the plants grow from 15 to 18 inches tall, with gray-green, linear leaves and light, bright, Daisy-like ray flowers in late summer and autumn. Though the seeds are tender, the plants themselves are among the last to go down under hard frost. They and the Verbenas continue to show color to the very last.

Star-of-Texas is a fine bedding plant for hot, dry locations in sandy soil in full sun. Nice for cutting too.

CULTURE: Plant seeds indoors in March and set out in the open garden, 12 inches apart, in late May. Bloom starts in midsummer.

XERANTHEMUM ANNUUM (Immortelle) to 36"   T

The Imortelle is clothed with white hairs on stems and foliage, so that its general effect is gray-white. The papery flower heads are white, rose, lavender, or purple. *Ligulosum* is a semi-double variety, and *perligulosum* fully double.

Xeranthemum is grown in the mixed border and for cutting, the flowers being dried for winter bouquets.

CULTURE: Plant seeds indoors in March or outdoors in a seed bed in May, and transplant to the open garden in full sun.

ZEA JAPONICA VARIEGATA (Rainbow Grass) 24"   T

Rainbow Grass is a decorative member of the Corn genus, the long leaves being striped in yellow, white, pink, or red. The graceful, variegated foliage makes it a striking plant in the garden and valuable for flower arrangers, who are always looking for unusual accessory foliage.

CULTURE: In May or after all danger of frost is past, plant seeds outdoors where they are to grow, in full sun.

ZINNIA, see page 187.

AVERAGE DATE OF LAST

"Tender" vegetables and flowers—those likely to be injured or killed by a light frost—should not be planted out until after danger of a late frost is past. *Seeds* of tender subjects (such as beans or corn) may be planted a few days earlier, as it will take them a week or ten days to germinate.

KILLING FROST IN SPRING

Local conditions—such as elevation above sea level, exposure to or protection from prevailing winds, and proximity to large bodies of water—may advance or delay the dates indicated on maps by a few days to a week or more. (Figures on the map—such as 4-20, 5-10—indicate dates, April 20, May 10, etc.)

AVERAGE DATE OF FIRST

Hardy shrubs, roses, perennials, bulbs, and many fruits are usually planted in autumn about the time of, or just after, the first killing or "hard" frosts have checked growth. Many of these can be planted up until the time the ground begins to freeze, but in most instances earlier planting is advisable.

KILLING FROST
LIABLE ANNUALLY

KILLING FROST LIABLE
IN HALF THE YEARS

NO RECORD OF
KILLING FROST

KILLING FROST IN FALL

If there is a period of a few weeks between planting and the time the ground begins to freeze, the newly set out plants or bulbs have an opportunity to make some root growth, and thus become established in their new positions. As in the case of spring frosts, local conditions will advance or delay the average dates (indicated on map) by a considerable period.

INDEX

Index

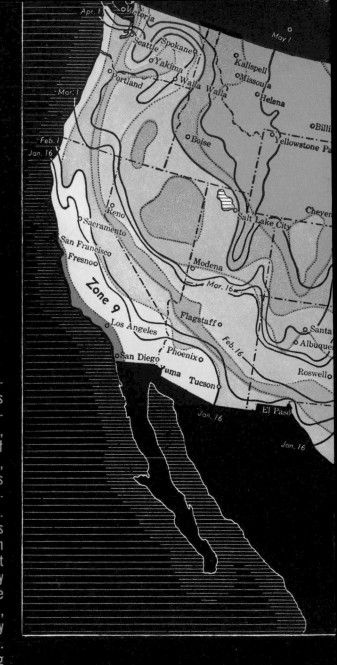

Zoning maps can be approximate only. Local conditions —such as elevation, protection from winds, air flow, proximity to large bodies of water, amount of snowfall, etc. — affect the frost dates and the time at which planting can be begun in spring. Seeds of the hardiest types of annuals may be sown in the open as soon as frost leaves the ground. Half-hardy and tender types may be sown, indoors or in a frame, somewhat earlier, to be ready to transplant to the open. When in doubt about sowing dates, consult gardening neighbors, your local county agent or garden-page editor.

TEMPERATURE